WRITING & GRAMMAR 10 for Christian Schools

second edition

TEACHER'S EDITION

Elizabeth Rose
Kimberly Y. Stegall

Bob Jones University Press, Greenville, South Carolina 29614

NOTE:
The fact that materials produced by other publishers may be referred to in this volume does not constitute an endorsement of the content or theological position of materials produced by such publishers. Any references and ancillary materials are listed as an aid to the student or the teacher and in an attempt to maintain the accepted academic standards of the publishing industry.

WRITING AND GRAMMAR 10 for Christian Schools® Teacher's Edition, Book 2
Second Edition

Coordinating Writers
Elizabeth Rose, M.Ed., M.A.
Kimberly Y. Stegall, M.Ed.

Contributing Writers
Kirsten-Leeann Alexander, M.Ed.
Amy Schwingle Baker, M.Ed., M.A.
Dana Gibby Gage, M.A.
Grace Collins Hargis, Ph.D.
Curtis Hearn
Lesa M. Seibert, S.Ed.
Sarah Abigail Stahl
Danielle J. Sweede

Consultants
Grace Collins Hargis, Ph.D.
 Chairman of the Departments of Linguistics and English Education, Bob Jones University
Coart Ramey, M.A.
Steven N. Skaggs
 Product Development Coordinator, Secondary Level, Bob Jones University Press

Compositor
Kelley Moore

Cover Designers
John Bjerk
Joseph Tyrpak

Designers
Holly Gilbert
US Color

Illustrators
John Bjerk
Matt Bjerk
Jim Brooks
Paula Cheadle
Johanna Ehnis
Cory Godbey
H. Preston Gravely Jr.
Jim Hargis
Jonathan Johnson
Chris Koelle
Mary Ann Lumm
Keith Neely
Kathy Pflug
John Roberts
The Thompson Bros.
Yoo-Kyung Julie Yang

Project Managers
Kathryn E. Martin
Thomas Parr

Photo Acquisition
Brenda Hansen
Joyce Landis
David Palmer
Tara Swaney

Editors
Rebecca S. Moore
Shelby J. Morris

Produced in cooperation with the Bob Jones University Division of English Language and Literature of the College of Arts and Science and the School of Education.

for Christian Schools is a registered trademark of Bob Jones University Press.

ISBN 1-57924-648-6 (set)
ISBN 1-57924-765-2 (Book 2)

15 14 13 12 11 10 9 8 7 6 5 4 3

TABLE OF CONTENTS

TO THE

The reproducible blackline masters in this volume supplement Book 1 of the Teacher's Edition for *WRITING AND GRAMMAR 10 for Christian Schools,* Second Edition. Each blackline master serves a specific purpose. Since every teaching situation is different, these blackline masters are provided to help you adapt your teaching to your students' needs. Refer to Book 1 for more specific instructions about how and when to use these tools.

Pretests

Pretests are diagnostic tools for Chapters 1-12. Evaluating your students' skill levels prior to teaching will allow you to tailor your lessons to the needs of your students.

Teaching Helps

Teaching Helps accompany specific grammar, usage, and reference lessons. Some are designed to be used as overhead transparencies; some are designed to be used as student worksheets.

ESL Helps

ESL Helps accompany specific grammar and usage lessons. These materials give ESL students (those who speak English as a second language) extra help and practice with difficult concepts.

Concept Reinforcements

Concept Reinforcements accompany specific grammar and usage lessons. These worksheets provide students with extra review of certain skills taught in the student worktext. Each set of fifteen questions is divided into three sections, with each group of five questions being more challenging than the one before.

Writing Worksheets

Writing Worksheets accompany specific writing assignments in the student worktext. These worksheets guide students through the steps of the writing process.

Writing Rubrics

Writing Rubrics accompany each specific writing assignment in the student worktext. The rubrics inform the students of your expectations and give you a method for evaluating each student's work fairly yet quickly. The grids allow objective and balanced scoring, and the space at the bottom that begins with the prompt "Overall, this writing . . ." provides room for personalized instruction. Each rubric can be used by students as a revision checklist or by you as an evaluation tool. (See "To the Teacher: Grading Student Writing" on pp. x-xi of Book 1 for further help.)

Chapter 1 Pretest: Parts of Speech

I. Nouns and Pronouns
Underline each noun once and each pronoun twice.

1. *The Four Seasons* is one of my favorite orchestral pieces.

2. Who knows whether it was the Italian composer Antonio Vivaldi who wrote that?

3. Vivaldi himself lived from 1678 to 1741, but the music he wrote lives on today.

4. All of the music Vivaldi composed is in the baroque style.

5. Regular rhythm and elaborate melody complement each other in baroque music.

II. Verbs
Underline each verb and identify it as *action* or *state-of-being*.

_____ 6. Vivaldi did influence Bach.

_____ 7. A progressive musician, Vivaldi developed the concerto.

_____ 8. The concerto is a composition for a small orchestra with a solo lead instrument.

_____ 9. My friend George has heard all 230 Vivaldi violin concertos.

_____ 10. Vivaldi remained a prolific composer for many years.

III. Adjectives
Underline each adjective. Then draw an arrow from each adjective to the word it modifies.

11. Some consider the Italian composer and violinist superb.

12. Vivaldi's baroque compositions are brilliant.

13. His early training was from his father, who was also a competent violinist.

14. Then Vivaldi, talented and dedicated, studied with Giovanni Legrenzi, a violin master.

15. Legrenzi composed several operas, and he is famous for his trio sonatas.

IV. Adverbs
Underline each adverb. Then draw an arrow from each adverb to the word it modifies.

16. Later, in 1703, Vivaldi was ordained as a priest; however, he gave his life wholeheartedly to music.

17. Vivaldi had very red hair, which eventually earned him the nickname "the Red Priest."

18. Vivaldi did not conduct a mass because a chronic illness unfortunately made breathing very difficult.

19. Also in 1703, he was appointed violin master at the Pietà, an orphanage for girls, and there he enthusiastically taught the violin and industriously wrote music.

20. For the rest of his life, Vivaldi constantly remained in contact with the Pietà.

V. Prepositions
Underline the prepositions once and the object of each preposition twice.

21. In 1711 Vivaldi published his first influential concertos for string orchestra.

22. After a few years, the choirmaster of the Pietà left, vacating a position Vivaldi helped to fill.

23. At this time Vivaldi began writing vocal pieces for the choir.

24. These successful sacred works written during this time earned him commissions from several other institutions.

25. His first opera was produced in Vicenza in 1713.

VI. Conjunctions and Interjections
Underline each conjunction once. Then identify each conjunction as *coordinating*, *correlative*, or *subordinating*. Underline each interjection twice.

_____ 26. Well, Vivaldi preferred to work as a freelance composer because he preferred the flexibility it offered.

_____ 27. In the 1720s Vivaldi lived in Venice but frequently traveled throughout Europe to supply music to various customers and patrons.

_____ 28. Wow! Vivaldi wrote not only for the violin but also for woodwind instruments.

_____ 29. While Vivaldi's music declined in popularity before his death, many of his compositions, such as *The Four Seasons,* are very popular today.

_____ 30. Melodic and powerful, *The Four Seasons* is a programmatic piece describing a landscape.

Chapter 2 Pretest: Sentences

I. Finding the Subjects and Predicates

Underline the subject once and the predicate twice. If the subject of the sentence is understood, write the understood *you* to the left of the number.

1. Have you heard John Rutter's *Requiem?*

2. Here is a Rutter recording.

3. Listen to this.

4. Rutter's *Requiem* was composed in 1985 and was first performed in October of that year.

5. The seven sections of the work have an archlike structure.

6. The first and last movements take the form of prayers on the behalf of all humanity.

7. The second and sixth sections are psalms.

8. The third section and the fifth movement are personal prayers to Christ.

9. The very center of the work, the fourth section, affirms the holiness and glory of God.

10. Tell me your opinion of it.

II. Identifying Types of Sentences

Identify each sentence as *declarative, exclamatory, imperative,* or *interrogative.* Insert the appropriate end punctuation for each sentence.

_____ 11. What is a requiem

_____ 12. It is a hymn, composition, or service in memory of the dead

_____ 13. The word *requiem* comes from the Latin word *requiēs,* meaning "rest"

_____ 14. Did you know this musical tradition began around A.D. 1200

_____ 15. In A.D. 998 the abbot of Cluny instituted the Requiem Mass, which became more common when the Catholic Church officially embraced the doctrine of purgatory two hundred years later

_____ 16. What does the Catholic service have to do with the musical compositions

_____ 17. Keep reading

_____ 18. The Requiem Mass, given on All Souls' Day, November 2, is a prayer for Christ to free the deceased from purgatory and to grant them eternal rest in heaven

_____ 19. The Bible does not support the existence of purgatory, by the way

_____ 20. This study of music history is fascinating

III. Analyzing Sentence Patterns

Label the sentence patterns *S-InV, S-TrV-DO, S-TrV-IO-DO, S-LV-PN, S-LV-PA, S-TrV-DO-OC,* or *S-be-Advl.* If the adverbial is a prepositional phrase, underline it.

21. Several other famous composers wrote requiems.

22. Mozart's *Requiem* was not complete at his death in 1791.

23. His pupil Süssmayr gave the unfinished work an ending.

24. Many consider Süssmayr's ending the best.

25. Some works known as requiems differ from true requiems.

26. Brahms's *German Requiem* does not use the Latin text.

27. A commemoration for someone deceased, it is still a requiem.

28. Brahms wrote it for his mother.

29. Brahms's requiem, like Rutter's, contains biblical texts.

30. His recording is on my desk.

Chapter 3 Pretest: Phrases

I. Prepositional Phrases
Underline each prepositional phrase. Draw an arrow from each prepositional phrase to the word it modifies.

1. Africa is the continent with the second largest land area and the third largest population.

2. This vast continent contains an amazing variety of wild animals.

3. In the east, buffalo, antelope, giraffes, and zebras roam the plains.

4. A few large elephant herds live in the east and the southeast.

5. Baboons can be found throughout Africa.

II. Misplaced Prepositional Phrases
Underline each misplaced prepositional phrase. Then rewrite each sentence with the prepositional phrase in its correct location.

6. The photographer pointed his camera at the baboons with the expensive equipment.

   _____

   _____

7. The camera in the tree awakened the baboon.

   _____

   _____

8. Sitting perfectly still, the baboon carefully watched the photographer with his eyes half open.

   _____

   _____

9. The photographer nervously snapped another photo of the baboon with shaking hands.

   _____

   _____

10. In one rapid motion, the baboon grabbed a piece of fruit and hurled it at the intrusive photographer from the tree.

    _____

    _____

III. Appositive Phrases

Underline each appositive or appositive phrase. Then identify the word that each appositive renames.

_____ 11. Baboons, a type of large monkey, have canine teeth and doglike muzzles.

_____ 12. These animals have an interesting diet: eggs, fruit, grass, insects, and roots.

_____ 13. Mandrills, large and colorful monkeys, are very similar to baboons.

_____ 14. The colorful males protect the pack themselves.

_____ 15. Not much is known about the mandrill, a shy and quick creature.

IV. Verbal Phrases

Underline each verbal or verbal phrase. Then identify each verbal or verbal phrase as a gerund (G), a participle (P), or an infinitive (I).

_____ 16. In central and southern Africa, Black and White rhinoceros are endangered species.

_____ 17. Selling rhinoceros' horns brings poachers money on the black market.

_____ 18. Tribes in Yemen use the horns for the making of dagger handles.

_____ 19. African elephants are the largest living land animals.

_____ 20. Hunters kill the African elephants to take their tusks.

_____ 21. The elephants' valuable ivory tusks invite poaching.

_____ 22. The pygmy hippopotamus is an animal to be protected if the species is to last.

_____ 23. The number of pygmy hippopotamuses is starting to decline rapidly.

_____ 24. Selling the hippo meat brings a large profit to the hunters.

_____ 25. Cheetahs are hunted to secure their rare fur.

_____ 26. Considered a magnificent and bizarre creature, the giraffe can be found only in the arid plains of Africa.

_____ 27. Living up to twenty-five years, giraffes may reach eighteen feet tall and may weigh as much as three thousand pounds.

_____ 28. Having never seen giraffes before caused people's assumption that the animals were a cross between a leopard and a camel.

_____ 29. Giraffes like to eat foliage from acacia trees.

_____ 30. A testimony to the creativity of God, the unique and graceful giraffe is a wonderful creature to see.

V. Misplaced and Dangling Participial Phrases
Underline each misplaced or dangling participial phrase. Then rewrite each sentence correctly.

31. Living in a wide variety of habitats, the African mainland contains many leopards.

_____

_____

32. Having highly prized fur, hunters kill leopards.

_____

_____

33. Hunting them as game, the Cape Mountain zebra has become an endangered species.

_____

_____

34. Declining rapidly in number, farmland is taking over the habitat of pygmy chimpanzees.

_____

_____

35. Hunters are the most dangerous predators of African wildlife, seeking material gain.

_____

_____

Chapter 4 Pretest: Clauses

I. Distinguishing Independent and Dependent Clauses
Place parentheses around each dependent clause. Some sentences may not contain a dependent clause.

1. The World Cup is played once every four years.

2. It is the ultimate prize that the world of soccer offers.

3. Each country sends its national team, whose players have been playing together for years.

4. The World Cup has been played every four years since 1930.

5. Each time it is played, the drama of the event is new and different.

II. Kinds of Dependent Clauses
Identify each italicized group of words as an adjective clause *(Adj)*, an adverb clause *(Adv)*, or a noun clause *(Noun)*.

_____ 6. *Because soccer is a popular sport,* many countries submit teams to the event.

_____ 7. Only the countries *that cooperate with FIFA* can play in the World Cup.

_____ 8. FIFA is the international body *that governs the World Cup, as well as soccer in general,* around the globe.

_____ 9. FIFA is an acronym, *since the letters correspond to the first letters of its longer name: the Fédération Internationale de Football Association.*

_____ 10. *That it was established in 1904* is often surprising to people.

III. Adjective Clauses
A. Place parentheses around each adjective clause.
B. Underline each relative pronoun once.
C. Underline each relative adverb twice.
D. In the blank write the word that the adjective clause modifies.

_____ 11. Soccer, which is now played by more nations than any other team sport, is also one of the world's oldest sports.

_____ 12. In A.D. 217, the first recorded soccer game was played in England, where the natives had just won a battle over the invading Romans.

_____ 13. It was part of a victory celebration that they had.

_____ 14. The people apparently enjoyed the game immensely, and this is the reason why it soon became an annual event.

_____ 15. By the late twentieth century, the fans who loved soccer had made it popular enough for the illustrious World Cup and the Olympics.

IV. Adverb Clauses

Place parentheses around each adverb clause. Underline each subordinating conjunction. In the blank write the word that the adverb clause modifies.

_____ 16. Although the sport is popular around the world, soccer teams from Europe and South America are traditionally the best.

_____ 17. Brazil has won the World Cup many times, while the United States has never won it.

_____ 18. The world-renowned Pelé led Brazil to many titles in the 1960s and 1970s because he had amazing ball-handling skills.

_____ 19. Inasmuch as Italy too has sported great teams, one can recognize the great love of the game in that country also.

_____ 20. England's soccer tradition, if it has not been dominant, has certainly been long and rich.

V. Noun Clauses

A. Place parentheses around each noun clause.
B. Identify the function of each noun clause as subject (S), predicate noun (PN), direct object (DO), indirect object (IO), object of the preposition (OP), or appositive (App).
C. Underline each subordinating conjunction once.
D. Underline each indefinite relative pronoun twice.

_____ 21. Some people do not realize that some teams tend to dominate the World Cup more than others.

_____ 22. One reason for the dominance is that the sport is extremely important in the countries with successful teams.

_____ 23. Many fans follow their team to wherever it is playing.

_____ 24. One angry fan assaulted a police officer for a very petty reason, that he was not able to obtain a ticket to see his team play.

_____ 25. Who started the 1969 Soccer War between El Salvador and Honduras is still a mystery.

VI. Using Independent and Dependent Clauses
Identify each sentence as simple *(S)*, compound *(Cd)*, complex *(Cx)*, or compound-complex *(Cd-Cx)*.

_____ 26. France also has produced a dominant European team on occasion, but it could not win the World Cup until 2000.

_____ 27. The English professional league, with its colorful cast of characters, is famous around the world.

_____ 28. In the United States, where American football, a derivative of rugby, dominates, soccer has taken a back seat.

_____ 29. My uncle showed me where to strike the ball when I am shooting, and he demonstrated the kick himself.

_____ 30. He played as a forward in Scotland when he was younger.

VII. Avoiding Errors
Identify each group of words as a sentence *(S)*, a fragment *(F)*, a comma splice *(CS)*, or a fused sentence *(FS)*.

_____ 31. Because my uncle started playing when he was very young, he became a professional soccer player upon graduation from high school.

_____ 32. Although he is very quick with the ball even now.

_____ 33. His shot is still very powerful and accurate, it was even better when he was younger, however.

_____ 34. He twisted his ankle in a match in Scotland then he decided to retire and return to the United States.

_____ 35. Now he coaches Little League soccer at a YMCA, he started doing that about five years ago.

Chapter 5 Pretest: Agreement

I. Subjects and Predicates
Underline the subject(s) in each sentence. Then underline the correct verb from the choices in parentheses.

1. There (*is, are*) many eye disorders resulting in a partial loss of sight.

2. Either an age-related disease or a genetic mutation (*causes, cause*) blindness.

3. Stargardt's disease, a form of macular degeneration, (*occurs, occur*) rarely.

4. What (*is, are*) the cause of Stargardt's disease?

5. This particular type of macular degeneration (*is, are*) genetic.

6. Both teenagers and young children (*develops, develop*) Stargardt's.

7. A mutated gene (*causes, cause*) the transport protein to malfunction.

8. The eye, in processing light, (*produces, produce*) a byproduct called spent retinal.

9. In a pair of healthy eyes, the transport proteins (*is, are*) the removers of the spent retinal, carrying the waste away from the eye.

10. Eyes with Stargardt's (*retains, retain*) the byproduct, a malfunction causing deposits to form on the retina with a high concentration on the macula.

II. Problem Nouns and Pronouns
Underline the subject(s) in each sentence. Then underline the correct verb from the choices in parentheses.

11. Anybody with healthy eyes (*uses, use*) his macula, a small tissue on the retina, for clear, detailed central vision.

12. Someone with Stargardt's (*has, have*) a hard time recognizing people's faces and reading small print.

13. Little (*is, are*) known about Stargardt's.

14. There (*is, are*) no known cures for Stargardt's.

15. Eyeglasses (*is, are*) helpful.

16. One pair of her glasses (*is, are*) for reading.

17. Many (*uses, use*) magnifiers and other low-vision aids to read.

18. *The American Heritage Dictionary* (*defines, define*) blindness as "having a maximal visual acuity of the better eye, after correction by refractive lenses, of one-tenth normal vision or less."

19. Legal blindness (*prohibits, prohibit*) driving.

20. Eleven years (*has, have*) passed since Danielle's diagnosis.

III. Pronoun-Antecedent Agreement
Write the correct pronoun to complete each sentence.

_____ 21. Both Dianna and Deborah have lost some of ? sight because of Stargardt's disease.

_____ 22. Neither Dianna nor Deborah has allowed the loss of sight to limit ? .

_____ 23. God has blessed the sisters, giving each of the girls ? own talents.

_____ 24. Deborah is a track star and the starting center of ? soccer team.

_____ 25. Dianna rides horses, and ? has acted in major roles in several plays.

_____ 26. No matter how imperfect eyes with Stargardt's may seem, God created ? in His absolute sovereignty.

_____ 27. God has lovingly promised to supply ? sufficient grace.

_____ 28. Everybody needs God's strength to overcome ? weaknesses, both spiritual and physical.

_____ 29. No matter what someone struggles with, ? can look to God for help and comfort.

_____ 30. God is glorified when we admit our inadequacy and lean wholly on ? .

Chapter 6 Pretest: Verb Use

I. Auxiliaries and Principal Parts

Underline each complete verb. Then write *Aux* above each auxiliary. Be prepared to identify the principal part of the verb and to tell whether the verb is regular or irregular.

1. What does the word *inventor* mean to you?

2. Many people immediately think of Thomas Edison or Alexander Graham Bell.

3. However, people are inventing new things even today.

4. Professional inventors have often worked for companies to make new or improved products.

5. Some inventors wrote about their research and its results.

II. Simple and Perfect Tenses

Identify each italicized verb as *present, past, future, present perfect, past perfect,* or *future perfect.*

_____ 6. Many famous inventors *began* their careers early.

_____ 7. The NCIIA, an association to help collegiate inventors get their works off the ground, *has awarded* many cash prizes to inventors for high-quality work.

_____ 8. Also, some young minds *work* with companies to create practical products for commercial sale.

_____ 9. Once the inventor *had made* his invention, he was quick to obtain a patent.

_____ 10. The patent *will protect* his invention from being copied by someone else.

III. Progressive Tenses

Identify each italicized verb as *present progressive, past progressive, future progressive, present perfect progressive, past perfect progressive,* or *future perfect progressive.*

_____ 11. Joey's new automatic garage door opener *is developing* into a real improvement.

_____ 12. In his tests, it *has been opening* regularly when the sensor installed on the car approached.

_____ 13. By next month, he *will have been working* on the system for two years.

_____ 14. When the car had moved far enough inside and the engine had been turned off, the door *was closing* just as it should.

_____ 15. Soon, a company *will be manufacturing* his invention.

IV. Voice

Underline the verb in each clause. Then identify the verb as either *active* or *passive*.

_____ 16. Joey promptly obtained a patent for his work.

_____ 17. A patent attorney was called, and all the work was handled for him.

_____ 18. The attorney did charge an expensive fee.

_____ 19. Hopefully, the invention will pay for the patent and the attorney fees.

_____ 20. Now a new glow mechanism for bicycles, capable of covering the entire bike, is being developed by Joey.

V. Mood

Identify the mood of the italicized verb as *indicative*, *imperative*, or *subjunctive*.

_____ 21. If he *had been able* to finish it by December, it would have been in the stores by next summer.

_____ 22. If I buy one, it *will be* the neon green color.

_____ 23. Never *go riding* at night without reflectors!

_____ 24. Now, with reflectors and Joey's new nighttime glow mechanism, the entire bike *will glow* like fire.

_____ 25. Even though he has just started to work on it, *tell* him I will buy one when he's done.

Chapter 7 Pretest: Pronoun Reference

I. Ambiguous and Remote Reference

Underline each pronoun that refers to an ambiguous or remote antecedent. Then rewrite the problem sentence correctly, replacing the unclear pronoun with the intended antecedent.

1. The ancestors of the people living in the Philippines are from Indonesia and Malaysia. They are called Filipinos.

   _____

   _____

   _____

2. Farming, which involves wealthy landowners and laborers, is a major industry in the Philippines. They make up about 40 percent of the Filipino working population.

   _____

   _____

   _____

3. A close relationship with family members is very important in the Philippines, and Filipinos keep in contact with many distant relatives. It includes distant cousins and extended family members.

   _____

   _____

   _____

4. Small rural homes often have wooden walls and thatched roofs, but wealthy city families live in large homes. They are often surrounded by a wall.

   _____

   _____

   _____

5. Gardening is popular in the Philippines, and Filipinos love growing flowers wherever they can. It is done in both rural and urban areas.

   _____

   _____

   _____

II. Reference to an Implied Noun or to a Noun That Is a Modifier
Rewrite each sentence to correct any unclear pronoun reference.

6. If you visit the Philippines, you will probably notice that their food is often highly seasoned.

   _____

   _____

7. In a popular chicken and pork dish called *adobe,* it is cooked in soy sauce and vinegar.

   _____

   _____

8. The abundance of Western clothing worn in the Philippines shows their influence on Filipino culture.

   _____

   _____

9. The Philippine Constitution gives them freedom of worship.

   _____

   _____

10. About 85 percent of Filipinos are Roman Catholic, and it is more widespread in the Philippines than in any other Asian country.

   _____

   _____

III. Indefinite Reference of Personal Pronouns
Rewrite each sentence to correct any unclear pronoun reference.

11. They say that the literacy rate in the Philippines is 90 percent.

   _____

   _____

12. In the Philippines, about 30 percent of them go to college.

   _____

   _____

13. In most schools and universities, they teach English as well as Filipino.

   _____

   _____

14. If you want to learn about Filipino political literature in the 1900s, you should read works by José Rizal.

_____

_____

15. In these works, it talks about the need for national independence.

_____

_____

IV. Reference to a Broad Idea

Rewrite each problem sentence to correct any unclear pronoun reference. If the sentence is already clear, write C in the blank.

16. The well-known Mayon volcano is located in the Philippines. This is a beautiful sight.

_____

_____

17. Mount Mayon's volcanic cone is perfectly shaped, and it is one of the most beautiful volcanic cones in the world.

_____

_____

18. The area surrounding the volcano is mostly flat; this allows the cone to be seen for miles.

_____

_____

19. The volcano has erupted over forty times in the past four hundred years, and it can be devastating.

_____

_____

20. Mount Mayon erupted on July 25, 2001, and this caused about forty-six thousand people to be evacuated.

_____

_____

Chapter 8 Pretest: Pronoun Use

I. Pronoun Case: Personal Pronouns
Underline each personal pronoun and identify it as subjective (S), objective (O), possessive (P), or independent possessive (IP).

_____ 1. Because lions, tigers, and ligers are large cats, they interest many people.

_____ 2. The guide told us that tigers, like other cats, are not extremely sociable animals.

_____ 3. They prefer to hunt and live alone.

_____ 4. Lions travel in their prides, which sometimes contain as many as thirty lions.

_____ 5. Many adult lions have spots that are faded and hard to see; a liger's spots are more visible than theirs.

II. Pronoun Case: Compounds, Appositives, and Comparisons
Underline the correct pronoun from the choices in parentheses.

6. This wildlife preserve has both lions and tigers. Although he is an expert on lions, our guide enjoys the tigers as much as (*they, them*).

7. Our guide told the first-time visitors—Judy and (*I, me*)—that the Gir Forest region of India is the only area of the world where the habitats of lions and tigers overlap.

8. (*We, Us*) students were surprised to see a liger, a hybrid of a lion and a tiger, at the park.

9. Because this liger has a lionlike mane, Judy told Mom and (*I, me*) that it was a lion.

10. Tigers are not known to roar; ligers roar much better than (*they, them*).

III. Pronoun Case: *Who* vs. *Whom*
Underline the correct pronoun from the choices in parentheses.

11. (*Who, Whom*) asked the guide about this liger?

12. The guide (*who, whom*) we met this morning said that nearly all hybrids are sterile.

13. (*Who, Whom*) do you think is the more knowledgeable guide?

14. The visitor (*who, whom*) asked about the name of the exhibit is my neighbor.

15. The contributors for (*who, whom*) the liger exhibit is named have donated money to the wildlife preserve.

IV. Courtesy Order and Correct Use of Reflexive and Intensive Pronouns
Underline the correct pronoun or pronouns from the choices in parentheses.

16. Between (*you and me, me and you*), facing a lion alone in the wild would be a hair-raising experience!

17. Lions (*they, themselves*) can weigh 400 pounds, and tigers often weigh 650 pounds, but the sign says that this liger weighs approximately 800 pounds!

18. You should be careful not to allow (*you, yourself*) to get too close to that wall.

19. Mom took a picture of Judy and (*me, myself*) in front of the liger exhibit.

20. We will take (*you and D'Andre, D'Andre and you*) to the wildlife preserve next month.

Chapter 9 Pretest: Adjective and Adverb Use

I. Comparison with Adjectives
Write the correct form of the adjective in parentheses.

_____ 1. Tom finds his world history class (*interesting*) than his biology class.

_____ 2. His class is studying one of the (*big*) wars of all time.

_____ 3. The teacher gave the (*fascinating*) presentation of the Hundred Years' War that Tom had ever heard.

_____ 4. The war was (*long*), lasting from 1337 to 1453.

_____ 5. There is not a (*long*) war recorded in history.

II. Comparison with Adverbs
Write the correct form of the adverb in parentheses.

_____ 6. For a long time before the war, tension between England and France mounted (*slowly*).

_____ 7. They battled (*constantly*) over English holdings in France.

_____ 8. One valuable territory, Flanders, profited England (*regularly*) than other territories because of its thriving wool trade.

_____ 9. France (*persistently*) tried to gain control of Flanders.

_____ 10. From France's perspective, the English acted (*offensively*) when England's King Edward III claimed the throne of France.

III. Irregular Comparison of Adjectives and Adverbs
Underline the correct adjective or adverb from the choices in parentheses.

11. The English won (*more, most*) battles over the French than the French won over the English.

12. The French fought (*bad, badly*) but still managed to win the war.

13. Unlike the English, the French were supplied (*good, well*).

14. One of the (*worse, worst*) French defeats was at the battle of Crécy.

15. Even though the English were greatly outnumbered, they performed (*good, well*) because they were well organized and had the aid of new weaponry—the cannon and the longbow.

IV. Problems with Modifiers

Rewrite each sentence to make the modifiers clear and correct.

16. After an even more worse French defeat in 1356, a treaty in 1360 ended the first phase of the war.

_____

_____

_____

17. The political scene in England remained unstably after the Peasants' Revolt in 1381.

_____

_____

_____

18. Becoming more weaker from a lack of resources, the English gradually lost much of the land they had in France.

_____

_____

_____

19. King Henry V of England, whose determined spirit could not be stopped by no one, won a decisive victory over France at the battle of Agincourt.

_____

_____

_____

20. Despite Henry V's marriage to Princess Catherine of France, French and English relations remained tenuously.

_____

_____

_____

V. Placement of Modifiers
Rewrite each sentence to make the modifiers clear and correct.

21. Henry V's dying quickly caused war to erupt again.

_____

_____

_____

22. Rallying around the French peasant Joan of Arc, the tides began to turn in favor of the French troops.

_____

_____

_____

23. By 1453 the English only had one holding left in Europe, a territory they later lost in 1458.

_____ _____

_____

_____

24. After the war English kings were able to without distraction focus on building a strong nation.

_____

_____

_____

25. As a result of the war, the nobility began to lose gradually its power as the centralized government gained strength.

_____

_____

_____

Chapter 10 Pretest: Capitalization

I. People and Places
Underline each word containing a capitalization error.

1. There are unique facts about the various states of the united states of america.

2. Arizona is located in the Southwest part of the United States.

3. My neighbor's hometown, tucson, arizona, is famous for its association with astronomy.

4. On kitt peak near tucson is the largest solar telescope in the world.

5. In flagstaff, arizona, in 1930, mr. Clyde W. Tombaugh discovered pluto.

II. Constructions, Organizations, and Businesses
Underline each word containing a capitalization error.

6. The world's first Metal-frame Skyscraper was officially known as the home insurance building; it was constructed in Chicago, Illinois, in 1884 and 1885.

7. In 1942 the first controlled nuclear chain reaction took place at the university of chicago.

8. In Fort Wayne, Indiana, on May 4, 1871, the first professional baseball game was played; the fort wayne kekiongas defeated the cleveland forest citys, 2-0.

9. On May 30, 1911, the first long-distance automobile race in the United States took place in Indiana at the indianapolis motor speedway.

10. The minnesota manufacturing and mining company began producing transparent cellophane tape in 1930; the tape was invented and patented by Richard Gurley Drew of St. Paul.

III. Religious, Cultural, and Historical Terms
Underline each word containing a capitalization error.

11. The first American to win the nobel prize for literature was Sinclair Lewis, who had been born in Sauk Centre, Minnesota, in 1885.

12. In october of 1908, the Gideons first placed Bibles in the Superior Hotel in Iron Mountain, now called Superior, Montana.

13. custer's last stand took place in 1876, when Lt. Col. George A. Custer and about 210 of his troops were killed in Montana in the battle of little bighorn.

14. As the capital of New Mexico, Santa Fe ranks as the oldest seat of government in the United States; Santa Fe was founded as the capital of the spanish province in 1609 or 1610.

15. Independence Hall in Philadelphia, Pennsylvania, is a very famous building because both the declaration of independence and the constitution of the united states were adopted there.

IV. Titles and First Words
Underline each word containing a capitalization error.

16. Published by Andrew Bradford of Philadelphia, Pennsylvania, the first magazine in the American colonies appeared on February 13, 1741; however, the *american magazine: a monthly view of the british colonies* lasted for only three months.

17. One of Connecticut's chief newspapers, known as the *hartford courant,* began publication in 1764 and has been published continuously, a time span longer than any other newspaper in the United States.

18. Published in Hartford, Connecticut, in 1796, the book *american cookery* by Amelia Simmons was the first cookbook written by an American.

19. In September of 1814, during the War of 1812, Francis Scott Key wrote "the star-spangled banner," which became the national anthem of the United States.

20. when he wrote the poem, Key was watching the British bombard Baltimore, Maryland's Fort McHenry.

V. Proper Adjectives and Other Words
Underline each word containing a capitalization error.

21. Log cabins, which were first built in the United States at the mouth of the Delaware River, are actually swedish and finnish in their origin.

22. Delaware's northern boundary with Pennsylvania is a u-shaped boundary, forming the arc of a perfect circle; no other state has such a boundary.

23. Did i tell you that Delaware was the very first state to ratify the United States Constitution on December 7, 1787?

24. The oldest highway in the United States is a european highway called the Royal Highway. Europeans built it in New Mexico in the 1500s.

25. Perhaps this review of United States history will help you earn an a on your next test.

Chapter 11 Pretest: Punctuation

I. End Marks
Insert any missing periods or decimal points, question marks, or exclamation points.

1. The Mongols created the largest empire in world history

2. Did you know that their empire stretched from the East China Sea to the Mediterranean Sea

3. Genghis Khan ruled during the AD 1200s

4. Many Mongol men were shorter than 5 ft 2 in tall

5. Hunting and fighting were the Mongol way of life, for both men and women

II. Commas in a Series and After Introductory Elements
Insert any missing commas. If the sentence is already correct, write C in the blank.

_____ 6. *Yurts ordus* and *Tartars* are all words that come from the Mongol Empire.

_____ 7. Yurts were round felt tents made by the women.

_____ 8. Ordus were camps led by Mongol generals and the word *horde* comes from *ordu*.

_____ 9. Frightened by the approaching invaders Europeans gave them the nickname Tartars.

_____ 10. Originally Mongols were a nomadic group of people but some Mongol empires became more stationary in places such as China and India.

III. Commas to Separate; in Letters; and with Quotations, Dates, and Addresses
Insert any missing commas. If the sentence is already correct, write C in the blank.

_____ 11. Dear Grandson

I wonder if you have ever heard of the ruler Genghis Khan.

_____ 12. Genghis Khan was the founder of the Mongol nation, wasn't he?

_____ 13. He wanted to unite the world into one empire; he conquered most of Asia, beginning near what is Beijing China today.

_____ 14. He united his people to fight under his law code the Great Yasa which required loyalty above all else.

_____ 15. "We must conquer the world" Genghis Khan would tell his people.

IV. Incorrect Commas
Circle any incorrect commas. If the sentence is already correct, write C in the blank.

_____ 16. The Mongols believed that both loyalty, and horses were important.

_____ 17. The Taj Mahal, was built by a ruler of the Mughul dynasty, the Mongol empire in India.

_____ 18. Shamanism was the major religion of the Mongols, while, Nestorianism was also a prominent religion.

_____ 19. "In Xanadu did Kubla Khan / A stately pleasure dome decree" begins Samuel Taylor Coleridge's poem.

_____ 20. In December, 2001 we learned about the Mongols' system of warfare.

V. Semicolons
Insert any missing semicolons.

21. Arrow riders had an important job they had to take messages from one part of the empire to another.

22. Pretend retreat worked well for the Mongols the townspeople would be attacked as they came out to loot the apparently abandoned camp.

23. Siege warfare was used to starve out townspeople of walled cities however, this method was sometimes not as effective as an all-out attack.

24. Silk, made from silkworms and unable to be penetrated by arrows felt, made by crushing and bonding fur and threads and leather, made from horsehide for shields and armor, were common fabrics of the Mongol people.

25. The great Mongol empires were as follows: Genghis Khan's original empire Batu Khan's Golden Horde in Russia Kublai Khan's Yuan dynasty in China Tamerlane's empire in the Middle East and Akbar's Mughul empire in India.

VI. Colons
Insert any missing colons. If the sentence is already correct, write C in the blank.

_____ 26. Although Mongol warriors relied on their horses, Proverbs 21 31 says, "The horse is prepared against the day of battle: but safety is of the Lord."

_____ 27. O Great Khan
We are writing to you to inquire of the state of your empire.

_____ 28. Today central Asia is made up of the following countries Tibet, Qinghai, Xinjiang Uygur, Kazakhstan, Kyrgyzstan, Mongolia, Tajikistan, Turkmenistan, and Uzbekistan.

_____ 29. Next, we will hear what the Great Khan said: "The punishment for horse stealing will be death."

_____ 30. _Genghis Khan Universal Ruler_ is the title of the next book I will read about the Mongols.

Chapter 12 Pretest: More Punctuation

I. Quotation Marks

Insert any missing quotation marks. Circle any unnecessary quotation marks. If the sentence is already correct, write C in the blank.

_____ 1. "Have you read any of the Narnia series?" my teacher asked.

_____ 2. "They were written by C. S. Lewis, right? was my reply."

_____ 3. "What, demanded Rochelle, do the initials C. S. stand for?"

_____ 4. "_Clive Staples:_ at least that's what the essay C. S. Lewis: A Modest Literary Biography by Dr. Bruce Edwards says."

_____ 5. "I wonder why his mother named him Clive Staples," I said. "What do you think?"

II. Ellipses

Read the paragraph and determine whether the quotations following it are correct. Write the letter of the quotation that is properly punctuated.

C. S. Lewis was born in Belfast, Ireland (now Northern Ireland), on November 29, 1898. He fought during World War I in France and was wounded in battle. Later he attended University College, Oxford, and eventually became a professor of medieval and Renaissance literature. Overall, he wrote about forty works of literature. These include works of science fiction, autobiography, children's literature, Christian apologetics, satire, and allegory. His science fiction trilogy, considered by some to be one of the best trilogies in this genre, was a new phenomenon in literature when he wrote it. He wrote the last novel in his science fiction series in 1945.

_____ 6. A. "C. S. Lewis was born in Belfast . . . on November 29, 1898."
       B. "C. S. Lewis was born in Belfast, . . . on November 29, 1898."
       C. "C. S. Lewis was born in Belfast...on November 29, 1898."

_____ 7. A. "He fought during World War I in France and was wounded in battle".
       B. "He fought during World War I in France and was wounded in battle"
       C. "He fought during World War I in France and was wounded in battle."

_____ 8. A. "Later he attended University College, Oxford, and. . .he wrote about forty works of literature."
       B. "Later he attended University College, Oxford, and . . . he wrote about forty works of literature."
       C. "Later he attended University College, Oxford, and...he wrote about forty works of literature."

_____ 9. A. "Overall, he wrote about forty works of literature. . . . He wrote the last novel in his science fiction series in 1945."
       B. "Overall, he wrote about forty works of literature . . . He wrote the last novel in his science fiction series in 1945."
       C. "Overall, he wrote about forty works of literature....He wrote the last novel in his science fiction series in 1945."

_____ 10. A. The passage notes that "many literary writings in many different genres were composed by Lewis."

B. The passage notes that many literary writings in many different genres were composed by Lewis.

C. The passage notes that "many literary writings" in many different genres were composed by Lewis.

III. Underlining for Italics
Underline any words that should be italicized or that are italicized incorrectly. If the sentence is already correct, write C in the blank.

_____ 11. Lewis wrote a poem called *French Nocturne,* which reveals the feelings of a soldier during a quiet night on a battlefield in France.

_____ 12. Lewis wrote the book Mere Christianity, originally a collection of radio talks aired by the *British Broadcasting Company*.

_____ 13. He was also an expert in English literature, and as an expert he was familiar with Spenser's *Faerie Queene* and Milton's epic Paradise Lost.

_____ 14. Upon examining his correspondence, one can easily see that Lewis was a bel esprit.

_____ 15. He had a beautiful writing style that appealed even to children; *The Horse and His Boy* is the name of one his books written for children.

IV. Apostrophe
Insert any missing apostrophes. Underline any words that contain unnecessary apostrophes. If the sentence is already correct, write C in the blank.

_____ 16. During one of the battles of '18, Lewis was wounded and forced to leave the war.

_____ 17. Lewis eventually recuperated and was sent back to the war until its' end in 19.

_____ 18. Lewiss first published work was "Death in Battle."

_____ 19. Someones reading of Lewiss works would be aided by a basic understanding of classical literature.

_____ 20. It was Jack (Lewiss nickname) and his brothers plight to lose their' mother at an early age.

V. Hyphen
Insert any missing hyphens. Underline any words that contain unnecessary hyphens. If the sentence is already correct, write C in the blank.

_____21. Lewis led an extra-ordinary life that included the grief of losing a close friend in World War I.

_____22. Lewis wrote a variety of thought provoking works; and he once feared that others considered him not "a single author . . . [but] a man who impersonates half a dozen authors."

_____23. He always loved to read: from childhood until he died at the age of sixty-five.

_____24. He often read books that would have been too hard for many other children to under stand.

_____25. Since he had few friends to play with, he would often spend from 8:00-to-5:00 in his father's old library.

VI. Dashes and Parentheses
Insert any missing dashes or parentheses.

26. His mother died when he was only ten years old the same year Jack and his brother were sent to Wynyard School in England.

27. The two Lewises always looked forward school life was hard! to vacation time.

28. In his later life after his war experiences, Lewis was considered to be a kind friend of children.

29. He wrote *The Chronicles of Narnia* perhaps his most famous work for young readers.

30. This series though it was written for children contains symbolism that even some adults may not notice.

Teaching Help 1: Commonly Used Prepositions

about	except
above	for
according to	from
across	in
after	in spite of
against	instead of
along	into
along with	like
amid	of
among	off
around	on
as for	on account of
as well as	over
at	past
because of	since
before	through
behind	throughout
below	to
beneath	toward
beside	under
besides	underneath
between	until
beyond	unto
but (when meaning *except*)	up
by	upon
concerning	with
down	within
during	without

Teaching Help 2A: Finding the Subjects and Predicates

Underline the complete subject once and the complete predicate twice. Write the simple subject in the first blank. (If the subject is understood, write _you_ in the blank.) Write the simple predicate in the second blank.

_____ 1. Is the word _treasure_ used in the Bible?

_____

_____ 2. There are at least ninety-seven references to the word _treasure_ (or _treasures_)

_____   in God's Word.

_____ 3. In Job 38:22, God speaks of the treasures contained in the snow and the hail.

_____

_____ 4. Shishak, the Egyptian king, descended upon Jerusalem and seized the

_____   treasure from the king's house as well as from the Lord's house. (I Kings

                             14:25-26)

_____ 5. Some of the leaders in Nehemiah's day contributed much "to the treasure of

_____   the work" of the Lord. (Nehemiah 7:71)

_____ 6. "In the house of the righteous is much treasure." (Proverbs 15:6)

_____

_____ 7. The godly man or woman will diligently search for wisdom.

_____

_____ 8. The most famous reference to _treasure_ in the Bible is, of course, the one

_____   about accumulating treasure in heaven.

_____ 9. Moses considered persecution for God's sake greater treasure than monetary

_____   riches.

_____ 10. Study more for yourself about the use of _treasure_ in God's precious Word.

_____

Teaching Help 2B: Analyzing Sentence Patterns

Label the sentence patterns *S-InV, S-TrV-DO, S-TrV-IO-DO, S-LV-PN, S-LV-PA, S-TrV-DO-OC,* or *S-be-Advl.* If the adverbial is a prepositional phrase, underline it.

1. Members of an Amish community often marry at an early age.

2. An Amish young man gives his fiancée a practical gift instead of a diamond ring.

3. Before the wedding, the couple must "publish" their engagement at a special church service.

4. The wedding ceremony quickly follows this published announcement.

5. These weddings occur in the bride's house.

6. In contrast to a non-Amish wedding, an Amish wedding is long (three or four hours).

7. All Amish weddings are of the same style and length.

8. Instead of wearing a traditional white gown, an Amish bride makes her dress blue or purple.

9. Sometimes, during the rest of the day, the bride and groom will become matchmakers for their unmarried friends.

10. A traditional Amish wedding dinner includes roast chicken, mashed potatoes with gravy, creamed celery, coleslaw, applesauce, and many desserts.

Teaching Help 3: Misplaced and Dangling Participial Phrases

Rewrite each sentence to avoid dangling or misplaced participial phrases.

1. The rookie ran onto the football field grinning nervously.

   _____

   _____

2. Pacing back and forth along the sidelines, orders were shouted to the players.

   _____

   _____

3. Approaching the line of scrimmage, the news media focused on the rookie quarterback.

   _____

   _____

4. Strapping on his helmet, the crowd got almost quiet as the player took his position.

   _____

   _____

5. Passing the ball to the receiver in the end zone, a tough offensive line would be necessary.

   _____

   _____

6. Hurrying onto the field, everyone's eyes were glued to the rookie.

   _____

   _____

7. Crouched behind the center, every fan eyed the young quarterback.

   _____

   _____

8. Ricocheting from player to player, the lineman scrambled for the fumbled football.

   _____

   _____

9. Grabbing wildly, the football was too slippery.

   _____

   _____

10. Running the ball into the end zone, the clock ticked off the closing seconds of the game.

    _____

    _____

Teaching Help 4A: Subordinating Conjunctions

By using different subordinating conjunctions, writers can express several different meanings to show the relationship of an adverb clause to an independent clause.

Meanings	Subordinating Conjunctions	Examples
Time	when, while, as, before, after, since, now that, once, until, till, every time (that), whenever	**When** the Canaanites afflicted Israel, God raised up Deborah to deliver His people.
Place	where, wherever	The Israelites consulted Deborah **where** she dwelt under a tree in Ephraim.
Cause	because, since, as, inasmuch as, whereas *(usually legal language)*	Barak, Israel's captain, led the army of Israel into battle against the Canaanites **because** Deborah had promised to accompany him.
Condition	if, on condition that, provided (that), unless	Barak had said, "**If** thou wilt go with me, then I will go."
Contrast	whereas, while	**Whereas** all of the Canaanite soldiers died, their captain escaped from Barak's troops.
Manner	as, as if, as though	Jael acted **as if** she were a friend of Sisera, the Canaanite captain, but she killed him in his sleep.
Purpose	so that, so *(less formal)*, that, in order that, lest	The Lord delivered Sisera into the hand of a woman **so that** Barak would not receive honor for the victory.

Teaching Help 4B: Avoiding Sentence Errors

Rewrite the paragraph below, paying special attention to errors created by any misplaced commas. In the score box, keep track of how many correct sentences, fragments, comma splices, and fused sentences you find.

Correct Sentence	Fragment	Comma Splice	Fused Sentence

Ancient Egyptian civilization is fascinating, the discovery of the tomb of King Tut was a great archeological find, it deepened appreciation for Egyptian culture. Egypt's kings, called pharaohs. Buried secretly with great amounts of treasure. In the middle of the fourteenth century B.C., a nine-year-old boy became pharaoh Tutankhamen ruled for ten years before he died and was buried in the Valley of the Kings at Thebes. His tomb was soon discovered and robbed. Then rubble from a nearby building project soon covered King Tut's tomb it lay untouched until 1922. British archeologists found the tomb. Soon excavated its many treasures. Though thieves had carried away some of the treasure. An overwhelming amount still remained untouched.

_____

_____

_____

_____

_____

_____

_____

_____

_____

_____

_____

_____

_____

_____

_____

_____

Teaching Help 5: Agreement

Underline each relative pronoun. Then underline the correct verb from the choices in parentheses.

1. Here is the sheet that *(gives, give)* the instructions.

2. Where are the campers who *(has, have)* lost their way?

3. Elise is one of the campers who *(knows, know)* where the picnic shelter is located.

4. Give them the maps, which *(is, are)* necessary for finding the cabin.

5. This is the path that *(confuses, confuse)* many people.

6. It is the only one of the paths that *(was, were)* not marked clearly.

Teaching Help 6A: Principal Parts

bear	bore	borne
beat	beat	beaten (or beat)
begin	began	begun
bite	bit	bitten
blow	blew	blown
break	broke	broken
bring	brought	brought
burst	burst	burst
buy	bought	bought
catch	caught	caught
choose	chose	chosen
climb	climbed	climbed
cling	clung	clung
come	came	come
creep	crept	crept
dig	dug	dug
dive	dived (or dove)	dived
do	did	done
drag	dragged	dragged
draw	drew	drawn
drink	drank	drunk
drive	drove	driven
drown	drowned	drowned
eat	ate	eaten
fall	fell	fallen
fling	flung	flung
fly	flew	flown
forget	forgot	forgotten (or forgot)
freeze	froze	frozen
get	got	gotten (or got)
give	gave	given
go	went	gone
grow	grew	grown
hang (to attach)	hung	hung
hang (to execute)	hanged	hanged
hide	hid	hidden (or hid)
kneel	knelt (or kneeled)	knelt (or kneeled)

know	knew	known
lay (to place)	laid	laid
lead	led	led
lend	lent	lent
lie (to recline)	lay	lain
light	lighted (or lit)	lighted (or lit)
lose (to misplace)	lost	lost
raise (to lift up)	raised	raised
ride	rode	ridden
ring	rang	rung
rise	rose	risen
run	ran	run
say	said	said
see	saw	seen
set	set	set
shake	shook	shaken
shine (to beam or emit light)	shone (or shined)	shone (or shined)
shine (to polish)	shined	shined
show	showed	shown (or showed)
shrink	shrank (or shrunk)	shrunk (or shrunken)
sing	sang	sung
sink	sank (or sunk)	sunk
sit	sat	sat
sneak	sneaked	sneaked
speak	spoke	spoken
spring	sprang (or sprung)	sprung
steal	stole	stolen
swear	swore	sworn
swim	swam	swum
swing	swung	swung
take	took	taken
tear	tore	torn
throw	threw	thrown
wear	wore	worn
weep	wept	wept
wring	wrung	wrung
write	wrote	written

Teaching Help 6B: Troublesome Verbs

Troublesome Verbs

lie/lay

The verb *lie* means "to recline." When *lie* in any of its forms is used, the verb never has a direct object. It is intransitive and used only in the S-InV sentence pattern. The principal parts are *lie, lay, lain;* the progressive form is *lying.*

> After Sunday lunch, I often **lie** down for a nap.
>
> In fact, I **am lying** down now.
>
> Last Sunday, I **lay** down for a short nap, but I slept longer than I had intended to.
>
> I **have lain** down today already, so I should be wide awake for this evening's service.

The verb *lay* means "to put or place." *Lay* must be used as a transitive verb—with a direct object. The principal parts are *lay, laid, laid;* the progressive form is *laying.*

> Every afternoon after school I **lay** my books on my desk.
>
> For years I **have been laying** them there as soon as I walk in the door.
>
> Yesterday, when I **laid** them down, they slid off the desk and onto the floor.
>
> I **had laid** them on a pile of pencils.

The confusion between *lie* and *lay* is probably due to the fact that the past tense of *lie* sounds the same as the present tense of *lay.* Always think carefully about your meaning and the principal parts before choosing which verb to use.

rise/raise

Rise means "to go up." The verb *rise* is intransitive. The principal parts are *rise, rose, risen;* the progressive form is *rising.*

> Both my uncle's and my dad's planes **rise** quickly into the air.
>
> My dad's plane **is rising** above the trees right now.
>
> Yesterday, I watched as it **rose** into the air.
>
> It **had risen** higher than the tallest trees in the field before it reached the end of the runway.

Raise usually means "to make something go up." It must be used as a transitive verb—with a direct object. The principal parts are *raise, raised, raised;* the progressive form is *raising.*

> After a successful round of high jumps, the official **raises** the bar to a higher level.
>
> The official **is raising** the bar for the next round of jump attempts.
>
> He **raised** it only half an inch.
>
> The bar **has been raised** three times today already.

As with *lie* and *lay,* be sure of your meaning and of the principal parts before you decide which form of *rise* or *raise* to use when you are speaking or writing.

sit/set

The verb *sit* means "to be in a seated position." *Sit* is an intransitive verb. The principal parts are *sit, sat, sat*; the progressive form is *sitting*.

Some people **sit** all day at their desk jobs.

Others **are** never **sitting** during the day.

The construction crew actually **sat** and filled out paperwork yesterday.

The day before, they **had** not **sat** until lunchtime.

The verb *set* means "to put or place." It must be used as a transitive verb—with a direct object. The principal parts are *set, set, set*; the progressive form is *setting*.

My brother and I **set** the dirty plates in the sink after every meal.

My dad **is setting** the turkey on the platter before he carves it.

Last year, we **set** the dessert on the table too.

Today we **have set** it in the kitchen until after the main course is finished.

may/can

The auxiliaries *may* and *can* are often used interchangeably; however, *may* usually means "to be allowed or permitted to" and *can* generally means "to have the ability or opportunity to do something."

You **may** now step off the bus and enter the hotel.

With the money we saved on travel costs, we **can** purchase breakfast at the restaurant across the street.

shall/will

Shall and *will* are two more auxiliary verbs that sometimes cause trouble. In older styles of English, *shall* and *will* often had different meanings. Today, *will* usually indicates the future. *Shall* has two main uses (both with the first person pronouns *I* and *we*): it is used to form a question of preference or to make a statement formal.

Shall I take you home?

"We **shall** not be persuaded to change our policy!" the mayor insisted.

Will we be able to see the parade?

Teaching Help 7A: Pronoun Reference I

Answer each question by following the instructions given after each sentence.

1. Jeremiah told Bret that he had a healthy Akita.

   Who owns the healthy Akita?

   Rewrite the sentence, making it clear that the dog belongs to Bret.

   _____

2. Akitas are Japanese hunting dogs that at one time could be owned only by royalty. They were used for hunting bears and other large animals.

   Were the royalty used to hunt bears?

   Rewrite the sentence, making the Akitas the agent used for hunting.

   _____

3. Jeremiah told Bret his dog had the head of a bear.

   Is the scary-looking dog Bret's or Jeremiah's?

   Rewrite the sentence so that Bret owns the dog.

   _____

4. Akitas are still revered by the Japanese people today. They are loved for their loyalty and service as reliable guardians. In the presence of other dogs, they can become aggressive.

   Who becomes aggressive?

   Rewrite the last sentence so that there is no question about the agent of aggression.

   _____

5. Lately, Akitas have been overbred. This has resulted in many overly aggressive, dangerous animals. Sometimes these dangerous animals have to be put to death. Sadly, it has happened to other breeds as well, such as Dalmatians.

   What is the sad thing that has happened?

   Rewrite the sentence so that it is clear what careless action has hurt the breed.

   _____

Teaching Help 7B: Pronoun Reference II

Rewrite the sentences, correcting the pronoun reference problems.

1. Jocelyn arranged a place and time to meet so they could make the trip together to the Dillard House in Dillard, Georgia.

   ⎯⎯⎯⎯⎯⎯⎯⎯⎯⎯⎯⎯⎯⎯⎯⎯⎯⎯⎯⎯⎯⎯⎯⎯⎯⎯⎯⎯⎯⎯⎯⎯⎯⎯⎯⎯⎯⎯⎯

   ⎯⎯⎯⎯⎯⎯⎯⎯⎯⎯⎯⎯⎯⎯⎯⎯⎯⎯⎯⎯⎯⎯⎯⎯⎯⎯⎯⎯⎯⎯⎯⎯⎯⎯⎯⎯⎯⎯⎯

2. Jocelyn's family took her dad's car, who had just taken it in for a tune-up.

   ⎯⎯⎯⎯⎯⎯⎯⎯⎯⎯⎯⎯⎯⎯⎯⎯⎯⎯⎯⎯⎯⎯⎯⎯⎯⎯⎯⎯⎯⎯⎯⎯⎯⎯⎯⎯⎯⎯⎯

   ⎯⎯⎯⎯⎯⎯⎯⎯⎯⎯⎯⎯⎯⎯⎯⎯⎯⎯⎯⎯⎯⎯⎯⎯⎯⎯⎯⎯⎯⎯⎯⎯⎯⎯⎯⎯⎯⎯⎯

3. The Dillard House is located on a plateau in the Little Tennessee River Valley, and it is breath-taking.

   ⎯⎯⎯⎯⎯⎯⎯⎯⎯⎯⎯⎯⎯⎯⎯⎯⎯⎯⎯⎯⎯⎯⎯⎯⎯⎯⎯⎯⎯⎯⎯⎯⎯⎯⎯⎯⎯⎯⎯

   ⎯⎯⎯⎯⎯⎯⎯⎯⎯⎯⎯⎯⎯⎯⎯⎯⎯⎯⎯⎯⎯⎯⎯⎯⎯⎯⎯⎯⎯⎯⎯⎯⎯⎯⎯⎯⎯⎯⎯

4. The Blue Ridge Mountains rise with a serene beauty around the valley, and it creates a peaceful backdrop for the restaurant and resort.

   ⎯⎯⎯⎯⎯⎯⎯⎯⎯⎯⎯⎯⎯⎯⎯⎯⎯⎯⎯⎯⎯⎯⎯⎯⎯⎯⎯⎯⎯⎯⎯⎯⎯⎯⎯⎯⎯⎯⎯

   ⎯⎯⎯⎯⎯⎯⎯⎯⎯⎯⎯⎯⎯⎯⎯⎯⎯⎯⎯⎯⎯⎯⎯⎯⎯⎯⎯⎯⎯⎯⎯⎯⎯⎯⎯⎯⎯⎯⎯

5. At the Dillard House, they serve fantastic meals of authentic Southern cooking.

   ⎯⎯⎯⎯⎯⎯⎯⎯⎯⎯⎯⎯⎯⎯⎯⎯⎯⎯⎯⎯⎯⎯⎯⎯⎯⎯⎯⎯⎯⎯⎯⎯⎯⎯⎯⎯⎯⎯⎯

   ⎯⎯⎯⎯⎯⎯⎯⎯⎯⎯⎯⎯⎯⎯⎯⎯⎯⎯⎯⎯⎯⎯⎯⎯⎯⎯⎯⎯⎯⎯⎯⎯⎯⎯⎯⎯⎯⎯⎯

Teaching Help 8: Compound Constructions

Insert a correct pronoun to complete each sentence.

1. My friend and _____ ran in a 5-K (a five-kilometer race) last week.

2. A T-shirt was given to him and _____.

3. They took his and _____ picture while we were running.

4. My family and _____ came to watch us.

5. When I crossed the finish line, I heard loud cheers from my family and _____.

6. My friend's family and _____ have run several races together.

7. That seasoned runner is training _____ and some of our friends for a half marathon.

8. Here is the training plan for my friend and _____.

9. It was _____ and his friend that got me interested in running races.

10. Now my friend Kim and _____ have joined them in recruiting others to join the world of runners.

Teaching Help 9: Modifiers

Write the correct answer in the blank. Then use your answers to complete the crossword puzzle.

ACROSS

_____ 1. The superlative form of *good* is _?_.

_____ 4. At the _?_ level of comparison, no comparison is made at all.

_____ 5. A _?_ modifier attempts to modify a word that is not actually in the sentence.

_____ 9. The word _?_ is added in front of an adjective or an adverb consisting of two or more syllables in order to make such a modifier comparative.

_____ 10. At the _?_ level of comparison, three or more things or groups are compared.

_____ 12. "You did very (*well, good*) on the test."

DOWN

_____ 2. A _?_ modifier makes a sentence unclear because it stands between two sentence elements and might modify either one.

_____ 3. When a modifier is positioned between *to* and the verb of an infinitive, the error is called a _?_ infinitive.

_____ 6. The comparative form of *great* is _?_.

_____ 7. Your car is very (*well, good*) for long trips.

_____ 8. At the _?_ level of comparison, two things or groups are compared.

_____ 11. The common suffix for superlative modifiers is _?_.

Teaching Help 10A: John 1:1

Old English

On frymthe wæs Word, and thæt Word wæs mid Gode, God wæs thæt Word.

Middle English

In the bygynnynge was the worde (that is goddis sone) and the worde was at god, and god was the worde.

Early Modern English

In the beginning was the Word, and the Word was with God, and the Word was God.

Teaching Help 10B: Works Cited Page

Becker, Carl. *The Declaration of Independence: A Study in the History of Political Ideas.*
New York: Knopf, 1953.

"The Declaration of Independence." *The World Book Encyclopedia.* 1996 ed.

Dumas, Malone. *Jefferson and His Time.* 6 vols. Boston: Little, 1948.

Fisher, Sidney George. "The Twenty-Eight Charges against the King in the Declaration
of Independence." *Pennsylvania Magazine of History and Biography* 31 (1907):
257-303.

Ginsberg, Robert, ed. *A Casebook on the Declaration of Independence.* New York:
Crowell, 1967.

Lucas, Stephen E. "The Stylistic Artistry of the Declaration of Independence." *National
Archives and Records Administration.* 1 September 2001. <http://www.nara.gov/
exhall/charters/declaration/decstyle.html>

Teaching Help 10C: Labeled Works Cited Page

author   **title**

Becker, Carl. *The Declaration of Independence: A Study in the History of Political Ideas.*

New York: Knopf, 1953.

place of   **publisher's**   **year of**
publication   **name**   **publication**

Dumas, Malone. *Jefferson and His Time.* 6 vols. Boston: Little, 1948.

number of volumes in
a multivolume work

"The Declaration of Independence." *The World Book Encyclopedia.* 1996 ed.   **edition**

title of unsigned article in a   **title of familiar**
familiar reference book   **reference work**

title of article in a
scholarly journal

Fisher, Sidney George. "The Twenty-Eight Charges against the King in the Declaration

of Independence." *Pennsylvania Magazine of History and Biography* 31 (1907):

257-303.   **title of journal**   **volume**
                                                    number
inclusive
pages

editor

Ginsberg, Robert, ed. *A Casebook on the Declaration of Independence.* New York:

Crowell, 1967.

title of article accessed
from an online database   **database title**

Lucas, Stephen E. "The Stylistic Artistry of the Declaration of Independence." *National*

Archives and Records Administration. 1 September 2001. <http://www.nara.gov/

exhall/charters/declaration/decstyle.html>

                                          date accessed   **network address**

Teaching Help 11A: Punctuation

Punctuation helps clarify otherwise ambiguous text. Read the following letter and add punctuation to make it understandable. The first words of most sentences have not been capitalized in order to create ambiguity. Correct the capitalization as you add the correct punctuation.

dear Serene

the vacation has been great at first I thought all I would see was the airport in Honolulu after spending hours waiting for our luggage we finally got it and headed for the hotel that night we called my grandparents to let them know that we had arrived in the morning we boarded the plane for the big island

a couple of days later a funny thing happened Jason and I spent the day snorkeling and swimming as we returned home I got a little confused so we decided to stop and ask directions to our street the house we stopped at had a high fence around the yard Jason entered first and I was right behind him a large hedge hid half of the yard as we started down the path we heard a loud low growl come from just beyond the hedge I stepped quickly behind the gate but Jason ran across the lawn towards the street in one smooth motion he jumped the fence and quickly stopped panting we turned to see our predator soon a small Chihuahua ran towards us we laughed pretty hard the owner who saw all this knew Granddad and told us how to get back

I'll tell you all about everything when we get home

your friend

Caleb

_____

_____

_____

_____

_____

_____

_____

_____

_____

_____

_____

_____

_____

Teaching Help 11B: Commas

The numbered sentences below are missing commas. Find the rule that will correct the problem and write its corresponding letter in the blank. Each letter may be used more than once. Insert the missing commas into each sentence.

A. Use commas to separate three or more single words in a series or to separate groups of words of the same type that are joined by a conjunction.

B. Use commas to separate coordinate adjectives.

C. Insert a comma before a coordinating conjunction joining two independent clauses.

D. Place a comma after introductory elements.

E. A noun of direct address should be set off by commas.

F. Use commas to set off parenthetical information.

G. Use commas to set off modifying adjectives after a noun.

H. Use a comma to separate a tag question from the rest of the sentence.

_____ 1. Addison have you ever seen a kangaroo?

_____ 2. Kangaroos are unique animals aren't they?

_____ 3. Kangaroos can be found in Australia Tasmania and New Guinea.

_____ 4. The kangaroo is part of an animal group known as *macropod* a word meaning "large foot."

_____ 5. Built similarly most macropods have large hind legs and feet but small front legs.

_____ 6. The strong powerful legs of the kangaroo can propel it up to thirty miles per hour for a short distance.

_____ 7. Kangaroos usually feed on grass and small plants and they will sometimes gather at feeding sites in large groups called mobs.

_____ 8. After carrying her baby for one month the mother gives birth to a baby kangaroo that is one inch long.

_____ 9. The joey small and undeveloped lives in his mother's pouch for six to eight months.

_____ 10. Hunted for its hide and meat the kangaroo's primary enemy is man.

Teaching Help 11C: Commas, Semicolons, and Colons

Insert any missing commas, semicolons, and colons in the sentences below.

1. Alexander Pope, an English poet living from 1688 to 1744, is known for the following kinds of literary works poetry, essay, satire, and translation.

2. Pope suffered from severe illnesses as a child and his growth was stunted, a misfortune that caused his height to be a mere 4'6" even as an adult.

3. Pope was almost entirely self-educated nevertheless, he was admitted into London literary society when he was only seventeen.

4. Pope made many friends who saw his potential and encouraged him even the satirist Jonathan Swift took an interest in Pope.

5. Pope, self-educated and physically deformed, earned a remarkable title the greatest English critic and verse satirist of the eighteenth century.

Teaching Help 12: More Punctuation

Key punctuation has been left out of the following paragraph. Find the five punctuation omissions and insert the necessary punctuation. (Punctuation marks used in pairs count as one unit.)

In Charles Dickenss famous tale Great Expectations, the protagonist or central character is named Pip. Actually, his real name is Philip Pirrip, but since, as he explains it, my infant tongue could make of both names nothing longer or more explicit than Pip, that is what he was called. His story is told from the point of view of an older Pip looking back on his life and its mistakes. Pip's father and mother had both died, and he was forced to live with his sister and her husband, Joe, the village blacksmith. The story reveals Pip's growing up to disdain his rustic beginnings and to develop into a gentleman. He grows to hate his common roots partly through his infatuation with the beautiful Estella, who treats him badly. In the end, however, he realizes that true gentility actually exemplified by Joe and Pip's childhood friend, Biddy comes not from position, money, and power but from a considerate and compassionate heart.

Teaching Help 13: Revising for Correctness

Rewrite the paragraph, correcting the ten errors in sentence structure, usage, spelling, punctuation, and capitalization.

Lightning produces a sound that we hear as thunder. People in ancient civilizations thought that thunder was the sound of angry Gods, however, scientists today know that thunder is the sound produced by hot air, heated by lightning, colliding with cooler air. The different "parts" of a bolt of lightning causes different sounds of thunder. The main trunk causes the loudest crash; whereas the branches produce the sharp crackling sound. Thunder has different sounds the deep, rumbling roar of thunder is caused by lightning that is furthest away from we observers. We see the lightning before we hear their thunder because light travels faster (186,282 miles per second) than sound does (1,116 feet per second). If we want to calculate how far away lightning is, we count the number of seconds between the lightning and the thunder, and then we divide by five. The resultting distance in miles is the approximate location of the storm. Whenever we see lightning, we know that the sound of thunder is imminent.

Teaching Help 14A: Sentence Variety

Revise the following paragraph to improve sentence variety and emphasis.

Ann Judson kept a journal during the years that the Judsons were in Burma. Her journal records the joys and trials of being a missionary. In the beginning stages of the Judsons' ministry, until prominent men were converted to Christianity, the government of Burma did not pay much attention to the ministry. The unspoken policy of the Burmese government was to allow foreigners to believe what they wished, but the government wanted Burmese people to remain true to the religion of Buddhism. Later in the Judsons' ministry, war with Britain broke out. Adoniram was arrested by the Burmese government as a supposed spy. He was kept in a hot, crowded jail. He had little to eat or drink. He was a prisoner until the end of the war. After Adoniram's release, Ann became ill. She died. Adoniram was away on a trip. Ann had seen some Burmese come to Christ, but only as she followed her Savior in the fellowship of His sufferings.

Teaching Help 14B: Coordination and Subordination

Correctly combine the following sentences according to the instructions in parentheses.

1. Short-term missionaries often go to the field to teach missionary children. The missionaries do not have to send the children away to school. (*Subordinate one sentence to the other.*)

   _____

   _____

   _____

2. The mother may have been teaching the children. The mother is able to participate more fully in other aspects of the mission work. (*Coordinate the sentences.*)

   _____

   _____

   _____

3. A missionary family may have several children. All the children would probably be in different grades. (*Coordinate the sentences.*)

   _____

   _____

   _____

4. The missionary family usually has more than one school-age child. The short-term missionary must teach several children. (*Subordinate one sentence to the other.*)

   _____

   _____

   _____

5. The short-term missionary may have to create several different lesson plans each evening. He may have to grade several different assignments each evening. (*Coordinate the sentences.*)

   _____

   _____

   _____

6. One child may do well at mathematics. Science might be another child's best subject. The easiest subject for another child might be language. (*Coordinate the three sentences into one.*)

   _____

   _____

   _____

7. The missionary children may know multiple languages. The short-term missionary may know only one language. The children could communicate in the language the short-term missionary does not know. *(Coordinate two sentences and then subordinate the two sentences to the remaining sentence.)*

_____

_____

_____

8. Short-term missionaries are usually exposed to a new language. They have the opportunity to learn a new language. *(Subordinate one sentence to another to show cause.)*

_____

_____

_____

9. The short-term missionary teacher must adapt his teaching to each student's needs. The students must adapt to their teacher's teaching style. *(Subordinate one sentence to the other.)*

_____

_____

_____

10. Future short-term teachers might major in education or humanities. An education major gives future teachers experience teaching in the classroom. A humanities major exposes future teachers to a variety of subjects. *(Subordinate two sentences to the other sentence.)*

_____

_____

_____

ESL Help 1A: Positions of Adjectives

Adjectives are usually put in a specific order before a noun, although the order may sometimes vary. The typical order of adjectives as they appear from left to right in a noun phrase can be described as follows:

1. determiner(s)
2. opinion
3. size
4. shape
5. condition
6. age
7. color
8. origin
MAIN NOUN

The following chart illustrates this order.

determiner	opinion	size	shape	condition	age	color	origin	MAIN NOUN
a	pretty	little	round	chipped	old	pink	French	saucer

Exercise in Positions of Adjectives

Rewrite the sentences, placing the adjectives in the correct order to modify the noun that immediately follows the adjectives. Do not forget to capitalize the first word of each sentence.

1. (the, mountain, short) man sat on the back porch of his cabin.

   _____

2. (old, brown, his) porch swing creaked under his weight.

   _____

3. He watched (fluffy, the, white, big) clouds float by.

   _____

4. The clouds cast (huge, gray, their) shadows on the mountains.

   _____

5. (yellow, bright, the) sun reflected off the cabin's tin roof.

   _____

6. (tiny, the, colorful) hummingbird landed on the hummingbird feeder.

   _____

7. (northwestern, a, cool) breeze rattled the chime hanging from the porch.

   _____

8. The hummingbird flew back to (tall, the, strong) oak tree.

   _____

9. (bushy, the, green, tall) trees covered the mountains.

   _____

10. The mountain man's dog buried a bone in (red, the, sandy) dirt.

    _____

ESL Help 1B: Defining and Using Determiners

Determiners, which come before descriptive adjectives, are very important in English. The most common determiners are articles, possessives, and demonstratives. Other determiners are used to indicate counting, numbering, and amount. Determiners come before nouns, not after them or in place of them.

Articles

The English language has one definite article (*the*) and two forms of the indefinite article (*a* and *an*).

Possessives

When possessives modify nouns, possessives are considered determiners. Possessive nouns are made up either of a noun (in its singular or plural form) and *'s* or of a noun (in its plural form already ending in *s*) and an apostrophe.

Singular	Singular Possessive	Plural	Plural Possessive
dog	dog's	dogs	dogs'
woman	woman's	women	women's
Mr. Baker	Mr. Baker's	the Bakers	the Bakers'

EXAMPLES   The *dog's* bowl is brown.
The *woman's* dress looks lovely.
The *Bakers'* bookcase is huge.

English has eight possessive determiners made from pronouns.

Person	Singular	Plural
First	my	our
Second	your	your
Third	his, her, its	their

EXAMPLES   *My* favorite pastime is to watch *their* dog chase *its* tail.
Your sunburn looks painful.

Demonstratives

English has four demonstratives that can be used as determiners before nouns.

Position	Singular	Plural
Near	this	these
Far	that	those

EXAMPLES   *This* coat is for winter, but *that* coat is for summer.
These new shoes hurt my feet more than *those* old ones do.

Some Other Determiners

Words like *one, two, several, many, more, most, some, any, first, second, next,* and *last* can be determiners. Most of these determiners can be used alone before a noun, but sometimes one of them comes after an article, a possessive, or a demonstrative determiner.

EXAMPLES   *Many* people drink spring water.
Most spring water tastes better than tap water does.
I wonder if *more* people drink spring water or tap water.
There are *several* kinds of spring water that you can buy.
The *two* kinds of spring water that I like best are very expensive.
My *first* taste of spring water was very refreshing.

Using Determiners

A singular count noun must have at least one determiner before it.

WRONG | Please bring me chair to sit in.

RIGHT | Please bring me *a* chair to sit in.
Please bring me *one* chair to sit in.
Please bring me *the* chair to sit in.

ESL Help 1C: Article Usage

1. Proper Nouns

1.1   Always use *the* before a plural proper noun.
> ***The*** *Democrats* all voted for the bill to pass.

1.2   Usually, do not use an article before a singular proper noun.
> *Old Glory* is a famous name for the American flag.

1.3   Do not use an article before most geographic names.*
> *New Delhi* is the capital of India.

> *Exceptions include collective names and plurals (***the*** *Philippines* or ***the*** *Adirondack Mountains*), land masses (***the*** *Hawaiian Islands*), bodies of water (***the*** *Pacific Ocean*), and geographic regions (***the*** *North,* ***the*** *Caribbean,* or ***the*** *Far East*).

2. Specific Count and Noncount Nouns

2.1   Use *the* when both you and the hearer know what is referred to.
> ***The*** *pen* is mine.
> ***The*** *milk* is spoiled.

2.2   Use *the* before a noun that has been mentioned before.
> The batter chose *a bat.* ***The*** *bat* broke when he hit the ball.

2.3   Use *the* before a noun modified by a superlative or ordinal adjective.
> ***The*** *brightest* candle burned out.
> ***The*** *first* person in line carries the sign.

3. General Singular Count Nouns

3.1   Use *a* or *an* when representing one member of a class.
> Dwayne owns ***a*** *condor.*

3.2   Use an article unless a possessive or a demonstrative is used with the noun.
> Dwayne owns *this condor.*

3.3   Use *the* in general statements.
> ***The*** *condor* is a type of vulture.

4. General Plural Count Nouns

4.1   Usually, do not use an article with plural count nouns used in a general sense.
> *Books* make nice gifts.

5. General Noncount Nouns

5.1   Usually, do not use an article with noncount nouns used in a general sense (languages, school subjects, etc.).
> Rick knows *Greek.*

5.2   Use *the* if a modifier follows the noun.
> Rick knows ***the*** *Greek of the ancient world.*

ESL Help 1D: Exercise in Article Usage

Choose the correct article *(a, an,* or *the)* **to put in each blank. If no article is needed, put an** *X* **in the blank. Above each answer list the appropriate rule number from the Article Usage sheet.**

_____ Samuel Adams was _____ American patriot and a signer of the Declaration of Independence. _____ history of Samuel Adams's life began when he was born in _____ Boston in 1722. Samuel Adams was a cousin to John Adams, _____ second president of the United States. Samuel Adams grew up and attended _____ Harvard, where he received an undergraduate degree in 1740 and later _____ his master's degree in 1743. He was active in Boston town meetings and served in the Massachusetts legislature from 1765 to 1774. In 1773 the British tried to place _____ monopoly on _____ tea sales in the American colonies. The colonies resisted the British monopoly. _____ climax of the American resistance occurred on December 16, 1773, when a group of _____ Boston's citizens dumped a shipment of tea from _____ Britain into Boston's harbor. Samuel Adams probably led _____ resistance, and his involvement in America's early government shows his dedication to his country. In 1774 Adams served as _____ representative from Massachusetts to the First Continental Congress, and from 1775 to 1781 he served in the Second Continental Congress. Later, Adams served as the governor of Massachusetts from 1793 to 1797.

ESL Help 1E: Adverb Placement

Adverbs of Manner

Adverbs of manner answer the question *How?*

        EXAMPLES   *quietly, well, somehow, cautiously, cheerfully, instantly, prayerfully*

Placement: Adverbs of manner usually come in one of three places:

1. They come directly before the subject when the subject is not preceded by any introductory information (such as a prepositional phrase).

WRONG	*Quickly* through the rain the mouse scampered for shelter. Through the rain, *quickly* the mouse scampered for shelter.
RIGHT	*Quickly* the mouse scampered through the rain for shelter.
WRONG	*Loudly* in the forest the lion roared. In the forest, *loudly* the lion roared.
RIGHT	*Loudly* the lion roared in the forest.

2. They come with the verb.

   - If there are any auxiliaries, place the adverb after the first auxiliary.

     The tennis ball had *carefully* been hit.
     The bird was *effortlessly* gliding across the sky.

   - If there is no auxiliary but there is a *be* verb, place the adverb after the *be* verb.

     The lock was *extremely* rusty.
     Caryn is *always* patient with her little brother.

   - If there is no auxiliary and no *be* verb, place the adverb before the main verb.

     The fountain *aimlessly* splattered water in every direction.
     The bird *effortlessly* glided across the sky.
     Caryn *patiently* taught her dog to heel.

3. They come after the direct object (especially if the direct object is the end of the clause).
   Alan read the book *quickly*.
   Eliza accepted her award *proudly*.

   Note: Adverbs of manner should not be placed between the verb and its direct object.

WRONG	The boy threw *carelessly* the ball.

Adverbs of Place

Adverbs of place answer the question *Where?*

        EXAMPLES   *there, above, inside, somewhere, everywhere, anywhere, down, southward*

Placement: Adverbs of place usually come after the verb or at the end of the clause.
Someone needs to put the bats *somewhere*.
The bats do not belong *here* with the balls.
The bats belong *outside*.

Note: Although these rules will be helpful for placing adverbs correctly in a sentence, they are somewhat variable. Exceptions are possible, especially for emphasis.

Adverbs of Time (Including Frequency)

Adverbs of time answer the questions *When?* and *How often?*

EXAMPLES   *now, later, always, never, often, usually, seldom, daily*

Placement: Adverbs of time usually come in one of three places:

1. They may come before the subject (exception: *never*).

> *Usually* Geoff goes golfing every Saturday.
> *Sometimes* Geoff goes golfing on Tuesdays too.

2. They may come with the verb.

   • They may be placed after the first auxiliary.

   > Joyce will *often* make cookies for dessert.
   > Georgia will *sometimes* make chocolate fudge.

   • They may be placed after a *be* verb.

   > Glenn is *always* ready to play the guitar.
   > Herman is *seldom* sick.

   • They may be placed before any other verb.

   > Robert *never* makes his bed.
   > Gerry *usually* walks five miles a day.

3. They may come at the end of the sentence if not too far removed from the verb (exception: *never*).

RIGHT	Judy walks her dog *often*.
TOO FAR REMOVED	Judy takes her dog to the vet for his shots *usually*.
BETTER	Judy *usually* takes her dog to the vet for his shots.

Qualifiers

A **qualifier** is a special kind of adverb that modifies an adjective or an adverb by either strengthening or weakening the idea of that adjective or adverb. Qualifiers answer the question *To what extent?* about an adjective or an adverb.

EXAMPLES   *very, slightly, rather, even, somewhat, quite, much, extremely, almost, kind of, a great deal* (The last two are somewhat informal.)

Placement: A qualifier is placed directly in front of the adjective or adverb that it modifies.

> The dachshund growled at the *much* larger dog.
> Then it barked *very* loudly.

Note: Unlike adverbs that modify verbs, qualifiers cannot be moved around in a sentence.

ESL Help 1F: Exercise in Adverb Placement

Decide whether the italicized adverbs are placed correctly. If the placement is correct, write *C* in the blank to the left. If the placement is incorrect, write *I* in the blank and then rewrite the sentence correctly.

_____ 1. Adrian balanced *accurately* his checkbook.

_____

_____ 2. Bevan *cheerfully* was cleaning his room.

_____

_____ 3. *Sometimes* Brandon reads books.

_____

_____ 4. Bethany had gone on a walk in the city with her dog *daily*.

_____

_____ 5. *Gratefully* on graduation day Caitlin received a gift from her friend.

_____

_____ 6. Caris *respectfully* refused the free lunch from her supervisor.

_____

_____ 7. *Somewhere* Abbot put his tie.

_____

_____ 8. Cassandra was cheerful *always* at work.

_____

_____ 9. Abner went to the river *down* for the day.

_____

_____ 10. Betsey was obedient *usually*.

_____

ESL Help 1G: Making Sentences Negative Using *Not*

In English, sentences are usually made negative by adding *not*. English has three basic rules for correctly placing *not* in sentences.

1. If there is an auxiliary (such as *will, have, may, do,* or *is*) in the sentence, place *not* after the first auxiliary.

>   Merton *has washed* the dog.
>   Merton *has **not** washed* the dog.

>   Gwendolyn *will need* a new dress for the party.
>   Gwendolyn *will **not** need* a new dress for the party.

2. If there is no auxiliary but there is a *be* verb (*am, is, are, was, were*), place *not* after the *be* verb.

>   The greenhouse *is* grimy.
>   The greenhouse *is **not*** grimy.

>   Waterfalls *are* powerful.
>   Waterfalls *are **not*** powerful.

3. If there is no auxiliary and no *be* verb, add *do, does,* or *did* according to the form of the main verb. Place *not* between the *do* auxiliary and the main verb. The main verb then changes to the first principal part of the verb because the *do* auxiliary will show the number and the tense for the complete verb. The part of the sentence in parentheses may be omitted if it is clearly understood by both the reader and the writer.

>   Evelyn *waters* the garden every Saturday.
>   Evelyn *does **not*** (*water* the garden every Saturday).

>   Ginny *talked* on the phone for three hours.
>   Ginny *did **not*** (*talk* on the phone for three hours).

ESL Help 1H: Exercise in Making Sentences Negative Using *Not*

Rewrite the following sentences to make them negative. Add *not* to each sentence. Change the form of the verb and add an auxiliary if necessary.

EXAMPLE   Charleen will throw the baseball.
Charleen will not throw the baseball.

1. The lake will be calm tonight.

_____

2. I am elated.

_____

3. The bees pollinated the flowers.

_____

4. You may need your umbrella.

_____

5. Cheryl was a librarian.

_____

6. Baxter would like a new hat.

_____

7. Shelly caught the butterfly with her butterfly net.

_____

8. We were watching for the comet.

_____

9. Cherie caught the chicken pox from Sylvia.

_____

10. The strawberries tasted delicious.

_____

ESL Help 1ɪ: Using Prepositions

General Rules

1. Do not leave necessary prepositions out of a sentence.

   WRONG | Shelly and Clara put their books the table.
   RIGHT | Shelly and Clara put their books *on* the table.

2. *During* is a preposition that forms a prepositional phrase (with no verb). *While* is a conjunction that usually introduces a dependent clause; it cannot be followed by a noun phrase. *During* and *while* cannot be used interchangeably.

   OP
   PREPOSITION | No one went outside *during* the earthquake.

   S   InV
   CONJUNCTION | No one went outside *while* the earthquake was occurring.

3. Do not use a preposition when *home* is used with a verb of motion or direction. The same rule applies to *downtown* and *uptown*.

   WRONG | Jay ran *to* home.
   RIGHT | Jay ran home.

   If the verb is not a verb of motion or direction, the preposition is usually necessary.

   Becky's mom works *at* home.
   Rob studied *at* home during his illness.

4. Do not use a preposition when *here* or *there* is used after the verb.

   WRONG | The book belongs *to* here. It does not belong *to* there.
   RIGHT | The book belongs here. It does not belong there.

5. Use *at* for the most specific time or location, *on* for a more general time or location, and *in* for the most general time or location.

   My son was born *at* 7:25 P.M.
   My son was born *on* a Tuesday.
   My son was born *in* the evening.

   I live *at* 381 Maple Street.
   I live *on* Maple Street.
   I live *in* Greenville.

6. Many verbs and adjectives, and even some nouns, must be followed by particular prepositions. Sometimes changing the preposition changes the meaning.

   The players were *rewarded by* their coach.
   (The coach gave the players a reward.)

   He *rewarded* them *for* playing well.
   (Playing well was the action that caused the coach to reward them.)

   The players were *rewarded with* the coach's praise.
   (The coach's praise was the good result.)

ESL Help 1J: Exercise in Using Prepositions

Choose the correct word for each blank from the choices in parentheses. If none of the suggested words is correct or if no preposition is needed, put an X in the blank.

1. Clayton ate popcorn _____ the baseball game. (*during, while*)

2. He was cheering for his favorite team _____ he was eating. (*during, while*)

3. To get to the baseball stadium, he had to walk from his home _____ uptown. (*at, in*)

4. When the game is over, he will have to walk back _____ home. (*at, to*)

5. He often receives a lot of business calls when he is _____ home. (*at, to*)

6. He goes to the baseball game so that he won't be _____ there when people call. (*on, to*)

7. The baseball game ended _____ 10:07 P.M. (*in, on, at*)

8. That is earlier than the baseball games _____ Friday nights usually end. (*in, on, at*)

9. Clayton stayed at the stadium _____ most of the crowd had left. (*through, until*)

10. He had stayed at the game _____ all the innings. (*through, until*)

ESL Help 2A: Inverted Subject and Predicate

English has two basic types of questions: *yes/no* questions and *wh* questions. Some questions use inverted order, and others do not. ("Inverted order" means that the order of the subject and the predicate is reversed.)

Yes/no questions

(questions that require *yes* or *no* for an answer)

- If a sentence contains an auxiliary verb, move the first auxiliary before the subject.

  She *will run* three miles.
  Will she *run* three miles?

  He *has been painting* the house.
  Has he *been painting* the house?

- If a sentence contains no auxiliary but does have a *be* verb, move the *be* verb before the subject.

  Linda *was* a trumpet player.
  Was Linda a trumpet player?

  The bike *is* broken.
  Is the bike broken?

- If there is no auxiliary and no *be* verb, add a form of the auxiliary *do* (*do, does,* or *did*) before the subject. Use the form of *do* that matches the form of the verb and then change the main verb to its first principal part (simple present form).

  It *snowed* today in Florida.
  Did it *snow* today in Florida?

  Keith *mows* lawns in the summer.
  Does Keith *mow* lawns in the summer?

Wh questions

(questions that ask for information using *who/whom/whose, which, what, when, where, why,* or *how*)

- When questioning the subject or something in the subject, do not use inverted order. Replace the word in question with an interrogative pronoun.

  <u>Jordan</u> <u>ate</u> the last grapefruit.⟶ <u>Who</u> <u>ate</u> the last grapefruit? (*Jordan*)

  Their <u>car</u> <u>is</u> old. ⟶ <u>Whose</u> car <u>is</u> old? (*theirs*)

- When questioning something in the complete predicate, use these three steps:
  1. Replace the word(s) in question with an interrogative pronoun or adverb.
  2. Move the interrogative pronoun before the subject.
  3. Follow one of the next three steps.

     - If there is an auxiliary, move the first auxiliary before the subject.

ORIGINAL	The <u>windshield</u> <u>wipers</u> <u>do</u> <u>work</u> sometimes.
STEP 1	The <u>windshield</u> <u>wipers</u> <u>do</u> <u>work</u> *when?*
STEP 2	*When* the <u>windshield</u> <u>wipers</u> <u>do</u> <u>work</u>?
STEP 3	*When* <u>do</u> the <u>windshield</u> <u>wipers</u> <u>work</u>?

ORIGINAL	But <u>we</u> <u>should</u> <u>do</u> it that way for a reason.
STEP 1	But <u>we</u> <u>should</u> <u>do</u> it that way *why?*
STEP 2	But *why* <u>we</u> <u>should</u> <u>do</u> it that way?
STEP 3	But *why* <u>should</u> <u>we</u> <u>do</u> it that way?

- If there is no auxiliary but there is a form of *be (am, is, are, was,* or *were)*, move the form of *be* before the subject.

ORIGINAL	James Madison <u>was</u> the fourth president of the United States.
STEP 1	James Madison <u>was</u> *what?*
STEP 2	*What* James Madison <u>was</u>?
STEP 3	*What* <u>was</u> James Madison?

- If there is no auxiliary or no *be* verb form, insert the correct form of the auxiliary *do (do, does,* or *did)*. Then move the form of *do* before the subject.

ORIGINAL	<u>Albert</u> <u>cleaned</u> the glass window carefully.
STEP 1	<u>Albert</u> <u>cleaned</u> the glass window *how?*
STEP 2	*How* <u>Albert</u> <u>cleaned</u> the glass window?
STEP 3A	*How* <u>Albert</u> <u>did</u> <u>clean</u> the glass window?
STEP 3B	*How* <u>did</u> <u>Albert</u> <u>clean</u> the glass window?

Notice the changes when *do* is added.

clean	do clean	How do <u>you</u> clean it?
cleans	does clean	How does <u>he</u> clean it?
cleaned	*did* clean	How did <u>he</u> clean it?

The main verb *(clean)* has no ending; the auxiliary *do* must show the correct present tense or past tense form.

ESL Help 2B: Exercise in Inverted Subject and Predicate

Change each sentence to a *yes/no* question. Remember to look at the verb tense for each sentence. Then use that same tense for the question.

1. Virginia will sing in the contest.

   _____

2. Virginia has a lovely soprano voice.

   _____

3. Virginia's voice is well trained.

   _____

4. Virginia had been a poor singer at first.

   _____

5. Virginia was successful in learning about music, though.

   _____

Change each sentence to a *wh* question. Use the word in parentheses to form the question. Write the question and its answer in the blank.

6. Virginia will sing in the contest. *(who)*

   _____

7. Virginia has a lovely soprano voice. *(what)*

   _____

8. Virginia's voice is well trained. *(whose)*

   _____

9. Virginia had been a poor singer because of her speech impediment. *(why)*

   _____

10. Due to her many hours of practice, Virginia became successful as a singer. *(how)*

    _____

ESL Help 4A: How to Combine Sentences

There are seven common formulas for combining clauses. These formulas are listed in the right column, and they use the abbreviations given previously for clauses and connecting words. Pay close attention to the punctuation included in each formula. Notice that because the subordinating conjunction introduces the dependent clause, these two elements are enclosed in parentheses as a unit.

EXAMPLE   I washed the car. My sister mopped the kitchen floor.

	Sample Combinations	Formulas
1.	**IC** **, cc** **IC** **.** I washed the car, and my sister mopped the kitchen floor.	IC, cc IC.
2.	**(sc** **DC** **),** **IC** **.** While I washed the car, my sister mopped the kitchen floor.	(sc DC), IC.
3.	**IC** **(sc** **DC** **).** I washed the car while my sister mopped the kitchen floor.	IC (sc DC).
4.	**IC** **. ca ,** **IC** **.** I washed the car. Also, my sister mopped the kitchen floor.	IC. ca, IC.
5.	**IC** **; ca ,** **IC** **.** I washed the car; also, my sister mopped the kitchen floor.	IC; ca, IC.
6.	**IC** **. IC , ca , IC continued** **.** I washed the car. My sister, however, mopped the kitchen floor.	IC. IC, ca, IC continued.
7.	**IC** **. IC , ca .** I washed the car. My sister mopped the kitchen floor, however.	IC. IC, ca.

Notice the correct placement of commas in the sentences above:
- Place the comma after an adverbial clause that comes at the beginning of a sentence.
- Do not use a comma before an adverbial clause that comes at the end of a sentence.

ESL Help 4B: Exercise in How to Combine Sentences

The following chart shows meaning similarities among the three main types of connecting words.

Coordinating Conjunctions	Conjunctive Adverbs	Subordinating Conjunctions
and	besides, likewise, moreover, also	—
or	otherwise	—
so	accordingly, consequently, then, therefore, thus	because, since
but, yet	however, nevertheless, still	while, whereas, although, even though

Combine the following sentences using the formulas indicated. Rewrite each sentence, adding a correct connecting word and the correct punctuation. You may leave the words in parentheses out of the sentence.

> **EXAMPLE**   Joan pulled weeds. (At the same time,) Hadden mowed the lawn.

IC, cc IC. (Formula 1): _Joan pulled weeds, and Hadden mowed the lawn._

IC; ca, IC. (Formula 5): _Joan pulled weeds; also, Hadden mowed the lawn._

IC. ca, IC. (Formula 4): _Joan pulled weeds. Also, Hadden mowed the lawn._

1. Joan likes yellow. (In contrast,) Hadden likes red.

    IC, cc IC. (Formula 1): _____

    _____

    IC. IC, ca, IC continued. (Formula 6): _____

    _____

    IC (sc DC). (Formula 3): _____

    _____

2. Claire's dad owns a blueberry farm. (As a result,) Claire picks blueberries in the summer.

    IC, cc IC. (Formula 1): _____

    _____

    (sc DC), IC. (Formula 2): _____

    _____

    IC; ca, IC. (Formula 5): _____

    _____

ESL Help 5A: Using *Some* Correctly

When a sentence containing the word *some* is made negative using the word *not, some* is replaced with *any.* Replace the words in the left column with the words in the right column when making a sentence negative using the word *not.*

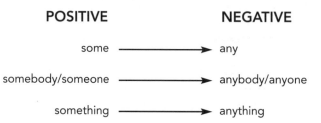

POSITIVE	NEGATIVE
some	any
somebody/someone	anybody/anyone
something	anything

EXAMPLES Mom needed *some* sugar from the grocery store.
Mom did *not* need *any* sugar from the grocery store.

Donna saw *somebody/someone* trying to break into the bank.
Donna did *not* see *anybody/anyone* trying to break into the bank.

The detective was examining *something* on the floor.
The detective was*n't* examining *anything* on the floor.

To make the sentence negative without using the word *not,* add a word that already has a negative meaning.

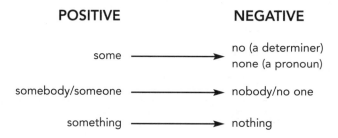

POSITIVE	NEGATIVE
some	no (a determiner) / none (a pronoun)
somebody/someone	nobody/no one
something	nothing

EXAMPLES Mom needed *some* sugar from the grocery store.
Mom needed *no* sugar from the grocery store.

I liked *some* of the flowers.
I liked *none* of the flowers.

Somebody/Someone was trying to break into the bank.
Nobody/No one was trying to break into the bank.

The detective was examining *something* on the floor.
The detective was examining *nothing* on the floor.

ESL Help 5B: Exercise in Using *Some* Correctly

Read the sentences containing the word *some*. Make each sentence negative by using *not* along with *any*, *anybody/anyone*, or *anything*.

1. We saw some snakes during our mountain hike.

    _____

2. We told somebody about the snakes.

    _____

3. My Aunt Beatrice found out about the snakes from someone.

    _____

4. We had something to kill the snakes with.

    _____

5. Snakes scare some people away from hiking.

    _____

Read the sentences containing the word *some*. Make each sentence negative by using *no*, *none*, *nobody/no one*, or *nothing*.

6. Some of the rabbits in the woods eat clover.

    _____

7. Somebody found a rabbit in the woods.

    _____

8. Someone chased the rabbit.

    _____

9. The rabbit found something to hide under.

    _____

10. Some bushes provide good shelter for rabbits.

    _____

ESL Help 6A: Using the Auxiliary *Do* Correctly

Do is generally used in three ways:

1. *Do* is used to add emphasis.

   - Add the correct form of the auxiliary *do* only if the clause does not already have an auxiliary or a *be* verb.

PRESENT TENSE	*does* (third-person singular subjects)
	do (all other subjects)
PAST TENSE	*did* (all subjects)

WRONG	Carl *does will buy* milk at the store.
RIGHT	Carl *will buy* milk at the store.

WRONG	Esther *did was* late to class.
RIGHT	Esther *was* late to class.

   - Place *do* before the main verb. Notice that *do* takes the tense of the verb.

     Alan *fishes* every week.   Cherith *made* dinner for us.
     Alan *does fish* every week.   Cherith *did make* dinner for us.

     In a sentence that repeats information, the part that contains repeated information is often omitted.

     Andy said that Alan did not fish this week, but he *did*. (fish this week)
     Cherith did not want to make dinner for us, but I am glad she *did*. (make dinner for us)

   - Place the stress, or loudness, on *do* for oral emphasis.

     I <u>*did*</u> *practice* the piano.
     Mandy <u>*does*</u> *know* the answer.

2. *Do* is used to help make a sentence negative.

   - Add the correct form of the auxiliary *do* only if the clause does not already have an auxiliary or a *be* verb.

WRONG	You *do* not *may swing* on the hammock.
RIGHT	You *may* not *swing* on the hammock.

WRONG	The apples *do* not *are* ripe.
RIGHT	The apples *are* not ripe.

   - Place *not* between *do* and the main verb. Notice that *do* takes the tense of the verb.

     Ruth *likes* collecting books.   Rick *pulled* weeds for two hours.
     Ruth *does* not *like* collecting stamps.   Rick *did* not *pull* weeds for three hours.

3. *Do* is used to help ask a question.

   Some questions require the use of *do*. Notice again that *do* takes the tense of the verb.

   Rhett *rides* horses.   Rhett *bought* a horse farm.
   What *does* Rhett *ride*?   *Did* Rhett *buy* a horse farm?

ESL Help 6B: Verb Tenses

When speaking or writing about events before or after your current situation, use different tenses based on which tense you are already using for general reference.

- If you are speaking or writing from a present-tense perspective, refer to previous events by using the present perfect and to events that will happen later by using the future.

PRESENT	We *smile* at the camera for every picture.
PRESENT PERFECT	We *have smiled* at the camera several times already.
FUTURE	We *will smile* at the camera until Aunt Hattie takes the picture.

- If you are speaking or writing from a past-tense perspective, refer to previous events by using the past perfect and to events that happen later by using the simple past again.

PAST	We *smiled* until our jaws hurt.
PAST PERFECT	We *had* not *smiled* so much in a long time.
PAST	We *found* someone else to take the next picture.

- If you are speaking or writing from a future-tense perspective, refer to previous events by using the future perfect and to events that happen later by using the future again.

FUTURE	We *will smile* for only two minutes this time.
FUTURE PERFECT	We *will have smiled* for two hours by the time all the pictures are taken.
FUTURE	We *will need* to do jaw relaxation exercises tonight.

ESL Help 6C: Tense Check

Present Perfect

Use the present perfect tense when referring to something completed (finished) during the time period you are in or when referring to something that has continued until the present moment.

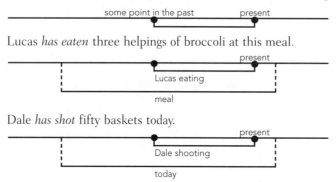

Lucas *has eaten* three helpings of broccoli at this meal.

Dale *has shot* fifty baskets today.

Past Perfect

Use the past perfect tense when referring to X, the first of two points in past time.

When the bakery opened, the baker *had* (already) *made* forty loaves of bread.

Uncle Charlie *had shot* three ducks before the other hunters arrived.

Note: In informal usage, the past tense sometimes substitutes for the past perfect when the time relationships are clear.

Uncle Charlie *shot* three ducks *before* the other hunters arrived.

Before is sufficient to make the time relationship clear.

Future Perfect

Use the future perfect tense when referring to X, the first of two points in future time. In this case the perfect tense emphasizes that something happens *before* another future time or event.

He *will have won* the game by the time we return.

I *will have walked* five miles by 5:00 P.M.

ESL Help 6D: Active and Passive

Active voice is usually the better voice to use, especially in writing. However, as a general rule, writers rely on passive voice when one of the following is true.

1. The doer of the action is redundant or easy to supply.

    Diamonds *are mined* in Africa. *(miners)*

2. The doer of the action is unknown.

    My house *was broken* into last night. *(unidentified thief/thieves)*

3. The doer of the action is very general.

    In the United States, the 1960s *was characterized* by domestic and international turmoil. *(domestic and international turmoil)*

4. The speaker/writer is being tactful.

    Susan *was* not *considered* to be the quietest girl in the school. *(her classmates and teachers)*

5. The speaker is being evasive.

    An error *was made* in the budget. *(the accountant)*

In passive sentences, the doer of the action is often not mentioned at all. However, there are three main instances in which the doer of the action is almost always named.

1. The doer of the action is new information.

    While driving down the road, we passed a tree that *was struck* by lightning. *(lightning)*

2. The doer of the action is nonhuman.

    My grandfather's heartbeat *is regulated* by a pacemaker. *(pacemaker)*

3. The doer of the action is a well-known person.

    Microsoft *is headed* by Bill Gates. *(Bill Gates)*

ESL Help 6E: Exercise in Active and Passive

Change one sentence or part of one sentence in each paragraph so that the new portion uses the passive voice instead of active voice. Use the principle in parentheses as a guide to know which sentence to change. Write the new sentence with passive voice in the blank.

In 1811 Samuel F. B. Morse's parents allowed Morse to go to London to study art. While there, Morse worked with Benjamin West, studied at the Royal Academy of the Arts, and won a gold medal for his first and only piece of sculpture, a piece about the dying Hercules. In 1815 he had used up all his funds for study, so he regretfully returned home.

(The writer wants to be tactful about Morse's finances in order to put Morse in a better light.)

_____

_____

From 1815 to 1837, Morse tried several projects in art that he hoped would bring him financial success. Although he became a successful portrait painter, he still struggled financially. From 1829 to 1832, he returned to Europe in an attempt to perfect his artistic technique. In 1832 someone gave Morse a job as professor of painting and sculpture at what today is New York University.

(The doer of the action is unknown.)

_____

_____

For Samuel F. B. Morse, invention characterized the 1830s. Morse began working on various projects that he hoped would earn him enough money so that he would be financially free to devote himself to his painting. Since his student days at Yale, he had been interested in electricity. About 1832, however, he became interested in the possibilities of transmitting intelligence by electricity. In his diary he mentioned that these transmissions could occur in underground wires; he also improvised possible codes.

(The doer of the action is very general.)

_____

_____

In 1840 Morse sought and gained a patent from the United States government for his new invention—the telegraph. He lacked scientific skills, but he had still been able to invent the telegraph. From 1840 to 1843, Morse proposed that Congress advance funds to construct a telegraph system. Finally, in 1843, Congress granted him thirty thousand dollars to build a test line between Baltimore and Washington, D.C. On May 24, 1844, Morse demonstrated the telegraph system by tapping out the message "What hath God wrought!"

(The doer of the action is redundant or easy to supply.)

_____

_____

Make one sentence or part of one sentence in each group passive, retaining the doer of the action in a *by* phrase. Use the principle in parentheses as a guide to know which sentence to change. Write the new sentence with passive voice in the blank.

Samuel F. B. Morse invented the telegraph, but his career in art was not as successful as he would have liked. His career was hindered by his family's lack of support for him and by his inability to support himself from his paintings. Sometime after 1837, frustrated by not being able to devote himself to painting, Morse stopped painting completely.

(The doer of the action is a well-known person.)

_____

_____

When Samuel F. B. Morse invented the telegraph, he also invented Morse code. Morse code was used to send messages over the telegraph wires. Today it is usually only amateur and maritime radio operators who use Morse code.

(The doer of the action is new information.)

_____

_____

Morse code consists of long and short sounds. The telegraph machine transmits the long and short sounds. A dash represents a long sound, which is called a *dah*. A dot represents a short sound, which is known as a *dit*.

(The doer of the action is nonhuman.)

_____

_____

ESL Help 9: Showing Comparison

In a sense, each of the four major parts of speech can be compared, each one with its own comparative sentence pattern. Here are the patterns along with two sample sentences for each. (Symbols and words in parentheses may be omitted. *LV* stands for linking verb, and *Vb* refers to the same verb as appears in the main clause.)

ADJECTIVE | **Noun**[1] **LV** *more/less* **Adj** *than* **Noun**[2] **(Vb/does)**

This bank looks *more modern* than that restaurant (does).

Jim is *taller* than Bill (is).

As shown in the second adjective example above and the second adverb example below, some adjectives and adverbs are compared with the suffix *er* instead of with the word *more*.

ADVERB | **Noun**[1] **Verb** *more/less* **Adv** *than* **Noun**[2] **(Vb/does)**

Samantha works *more carefully* than Abbie (does).

Rabbits run *faster* than turtles (do).

NOUN | **Noun**[1] **Verb** *more/less* **Noun** *than* **Noun**[2] **(Vb/does)**

Dan has *more lemonade* than I (have/do).

This year I've made *less money* than I did last year.

VERB | **Noun**[1] **Verb** *more/less* *than* **Noun**[2] **(Vb/does)**

Motorcycles *cost less* than cars (do).

Men generally *weigh more* than women (do).

ESL Help 11A: The Most Common Punctuation Marks in English

Mark	Name	Example
.	period	Ted likes to drive.
!	exclamation point	Don't hit that cat!
?	question mark	How did the accident happen?
,	comma	The cat ran into the road, and Ted couldn't swerve to miss it.
'	apostrophe	Ted hit Mimi's cat.
( )	parentheses	Mimi (the cat's owner) cried.
" "	quotation marks	Ted said, "I tried to miss the cat."
;	semicolon	The cat did not die; he was just unconscious.
:	colon	The cat lived for another ten years: he was a very hearty cat.

ESL Help 11B: Cumulative and Coordinate Adjectives

Cumulative Adjectives

Cumulative adjectives build on one another. They come from different meaning categories and are usually placed in a specific order before a noun. (The order in the sentence may sometimes vary, however, especially with words describing shape.) Usually no more than three or four cumulative adjectives are used together.

- **Articles, possessives, cardinal numbers, and most other determiners** (*a/an/the, my/Jenna's, one/two, several/those*)
- **Ordinal (order) determiners** (*first, second, third, last, next*)
- **Evaluative words** (*lovely, charming, considerate, friendly, unskilled*)
- **Words referring to size** (*large, enormous, little, petite*)
- **Shape or length** (*oval, square, oblong, long, short*)
- **Condition** (*clean, dirty, feeble, weary, happy, joyful*)
- **Age** (*young, old, youthful, elderly*)
- **Color** (*orange, blue, brown, magenta, red, yellow*)
- **Nationality** (*Japanese, Spanish, Canadian, French*)
- **Religion** (*Christian, Islamic, Confucian*)
- **Modifying nouns describing material makeup** (*aluminum, plastic, brick, wood*)
- **Other modifying nouns** (*tree* stand, *book* fair)

EXAMPLES I watched *the small dirty* mouse scurry into its hole.
The mouse was carrying *an old yellow* piece of cheese.

Coordinate Adjectives

Sometimes speakers of English may use two adjectives from the same meaning category (e.g., two evaluative words, two condition words, etc.). When two such adjectives from the same category have similar meanings, they are usually separated with a comma.

EXAMPLES The president's wife was a *happy, joyful* hostess.
Her *considerate, friendly* manners impressed everyone.

ESL Help 11C: Exercise in Cumulative and Coordinate Adjectives

Look at the adjectives in italics. If the adjectives are from the same meaning category, write _coordinate_ in the blank and add a comma between the adjectives. If the adjectives are from different meaning categories, write _cumulative_ in the blank.

_____ 1. The _talented black_ Labrador retriever could do many tricks.

_____ 2. His _diligent hard-working_ owner had trained him well.

_____ 3. The owner threw the dog's _bouncy rubber_ ball.

_____ 4. The ball hit the _yellow brick_ wall.

_____ 5. The _swift speedy_ dog ran after the ball.

_____ 6. The dog barked at the ball with a _loud noisy_ bark.

_____ 7. The dog ran around the _big dirty_ puddle

_____ 8. The dog caught the ball in his _large sharp_ teeth.

_____ 9. The ball popped with a _sharp piercing_ sound.

_____ 10. The dog wagged his _long black_ tail.

ESL Help 11D: Spacing of Punctuation

If you speak a language with a non-Roman writing system, you probably need to be especially careful about the spacing of your English punctuation.

- End punctuation (a period, a question mark, or an exclamation point) follows immediately after the last word of the sentence. When using a word processor or a computer, leave one blank space before the next sentence. When typing or writing, leave two blank spaces before the next sentence.

WRONG	He asked me a question .
RIGHT	He asked me a question.

- Most punctuation inside the sentence (a comma, a semicolon, or a colon) has no space before it and one space after it.

WRONG	After he showed me his paper , we discussed spacing.
RIGHT	After he showed me his paper, we discussed spacing.

- Parentheses (like this) "hug" the words they enclose, and so do quotation marks.

- A hyphen comes inside a word, with no spaces (e.g., *open-ended*). A dash—which is longer—comes between words, with no spaces. (A dash can also be typed with two unspaced hyphens--like this.)

A few special uses, such as the unspaced colon between a chapter and verse in Bible references (e.g., I John 1:9), are noted in your student worktext.

ESL Help 12: Direct and Indirect Quotations

Because a direct quotation reports the exact words of the speaker, pronouns and words for time and place are naturally used from the point of view of the speaker. However, an indirect quotation uses pronouns, tense, and time/place words from the point of view of the reporter.

DIRECT QUOTATION | Miss Matsumoto said, "Terry, *you will need to* give *your* report in class *tomorrow.*"

INDIRECT QUOTATION | *Yesterday* Miss Matsumoto told *me* that *I have to* give *my* report in class *today.*

Many questions require inversion of the subject and the first auxiliary. (See p. 151 for a list of auxiliaries.) However, in an indirect *yes/no* question, no question inversion should be used because the sentence is not really a question.

DIRECT QUESTION | She asked, "*Would you like* to give your report at the beginning of class?"

INDIRECT QUESTION | She asked whether *I would like* to give my report at the beginning of class.

Notice that the word *whether* (or, informally, *if*) begins an indirect *yes/no* question. No question mark is used.

Similarly, indirect *wh* questions use normal subject-verb order, not question inversion.

DIRECT QUESTION | She also asked, "What kind of display materials *will you use?*"

INDIRECT QUESTION | She also asked what kind of display materials *I would use.*

Chapter 1: Using Nouns and Pronouns

Practice A

Identify each italicized noun as common (C) or proper (P) and as concrete (Ct) or abstract (Ab). Remember to place two answers in each blank.

_____ 1. My brothers, *Phillip* and Kerry, love to play roller hockey.

_____ 2. Having just moved into town, they asked for *guidance* on where they could play hockey.

_____ 3. They found a great roller hockey rink—of course, it's made of concrete, not *ice*—near our house.

_____ 4. It is nearly always open for the public, and we lace up our in-line skates with *excitement* every afternoon after school.

_____ 5. One afternoon, our principal, *Mr. McClusky*, came out to watch us play.

Practice B

Identify each italicized pronoun as personal (P), demonstrative (Dem), interrogative (Inter), indefinite (Ind), reflexive (Ref), intensive (Int), relative (Rel), or reciprocal (Rec).

_____ 6. Wallace decided to play with *us* today.

_____ 7. *Who* will play for our team when Craig is not here?

_____ 8. It is important in a team sport to assist *one another*.

_____ 9. Perhaps if enough people are interested, we will start a league *that* plays roller hockey in the summer.

_____ 10. Will we have to buy uniforms *ourselves*?

Practice C

Write an appropriate noun or pronoun (following the instructions in parentheses) to complete each sentence.

_____ 11. Kevin told me _?_ he knows a good screen printer. (*relative pronoun*)

_____ 12. Perhaps we could help _?_ by allowing him to advertise his printing services on our uniforms. (*reciprocal pronoun*)

_____ 13. Do we want our _?_ to be the same as those the Pittsburgh Penguins wear? (*plural count noun*)

_____ 14. All of us play roller hockey with a lot of _?_, so we do not often have time to play other sports. (*abstract noun*)

_____ 15. We have decided to call our team the _?_. (*proper noun*)

Chapter 2: *S-TrV-DO-OC* and *S-be-Advl*

Practice A
Label the sentence patterns *S-InV, S-TrV-DO, S-TrV-IO-DO*, or *S-TrV-DO-OC*.

1. The water in the Bay of Fundy fluctuates tremendously between high and low tides.

2. It separates the Canadian province of New Brunswick from its sister province, Nova Scotia.

3. Laura, a member of our mission team, thought the tidal bore amazing.

4. The tidal bore renders the river running into the bay powerless by turning the river back in on itself and filling up the riverbed again.

5. Soon, a wave of water rushes from one end of the river towards the other.

Practice B
Label the sentence patterns *S-InV, S-LV-PN, S-LV-PA*, or *S-be-Advl*. If the adverbial is a prepositional phrase, underline it.

6. Mr. Grove, the bus driver, was clear about the dangers of walking onto the riverbed at low tide.

7. Mr. Grove, a constant joker, is also in the business of protecting students.

8. Notwithstanding, we were not brave enough to venture onto the muddy riverbed before the tidal bore.

9. Owen was the first to see the footprints below the rocks.

10. Mr. Grove was soon into his tale again, trying to scare anyone listening.

Practice C
Rewrite the sentences to make them *S-TrV-DO-OC* or *S-be-Advl*, according to the instructions.

11. This company offers rafting trips on the bore during the summertime. *(S-be-Advl)*

_____

12. The quickly moving water causes the ride to be quite fun. *(S-TrV-DO-OC)*

_____

13. No one in our group had ever rafted the bore before. *(S-be-Advl)*

_____

14. First, we climbed into two large rafts. *(S-TrV-DO-OC)*

_____

15. Soon we found ourselves in life jackets, whirling on a wave from the Bay of Fundy. *(S-be-Advl)*

_____

Chapter 3: Prepositional Phrases

Practice A
Place parentheses around each prepositional phrase. Identify the phrase as either adjectival (Adj) or adverbial (Adv).

_____ 1. Malawi is located on Lake Nyasa's western coast.

_____ 2. Malawi has no access to an ocean.

_____ 3. This African country is beside Lake Nyasa, Tanzania, Zambia, and Mozambique.

_____ 4. Malawi's previous name was Nyasaland, which the British gave it during their domination.

_____ 5. Although it gained independence from Britain, Malawi initially struggled to govern itself.

Practice B
Place parentheses around each prepositional phrase. Underline the word that each prepositional phrase modifies. Then identify the phrase as either adjectival (Adj) or adverbial (Adv).

_____ 6. Malawi, "the warm heart of Africa," is still a largely undeveloped country.

_____ 7. However, it has many scenic vistas, especially along Lake Nyasa's beautiful shore.

_____ 8. Tourists can dive, swim, and snorkel in the beautiful lake.

_____ 9. Malawi does have a border dispute with neighboring Mozambique.

_____ 10. Interestingly, Malawi celebrates Independence Day on July 6.

Practice C
Underline the word the italicized prepositional phrase modifies. Draw a caret (∧) to show where the prepositional phrase should be in order to make it closer to the word it modifies. If the sentence is already correct, write C in the blank.

_____ 11. *By a popular vote,* Malawi's president is elected every five years.

_____ 12. The first presidential elections were won by Dr. Hastings Banda *in the new country.*

_____ 13. Dr. Banda had been the leader *of the independence movement.*

_____ 14. *In rural areas* most of Malawi's citizens live.

_____ 15. *In state-operated game reserves,* Malawi is also a land of exotic wildlife.

Chapter 3: Gerunds

Practice A

Underline the gerunds. Identify the function of each gerund as subject *(S)*, direct object *(DO)*, indirect object *(IO)*, predicate noun *(PN)*, or object of the preposition *(OP)*.

_____ 1.   Hitting was a subject Ted Williams certainly mastered.

_____ 2.   He often greeted pitching rudely.

_____ 3.   One year he joined an elite group by maintaining a great record at bat of over .400.

_____ 4.   His game was also hitting for power, which he did as well as anyone in either league.

_____ 5.   Even from his rookie year, scouts gave his batting tremendous credit.

Practice B

Underline the entire gerund phrase. Underline any gerund complements twice. In the blank identify the function of each gerund as subject *(S)*, direct object *(DO)*, indirect object *(IO)*, predicate noun *(PN)*, object of the preposition *(OP)*, or appositive *(App)*.

_____ 6.   Pitching the baseball was also a desire the young Williams had.

_____ 7.   He dreamed of throwing for the Red Sox as he had done for his high-school team.

_____ 8.   In high school, his best performance was striking out twenty-three batters in one game.

_____ 9.   The task, hitting his pitches, was one he thought that few could do.

_____ 10.   However, Williams soon gave pitching little thought and concentrated again on his strengths as a hitter.

Practice C

Underline the gerunds. In the blank identify the function of each gerund as subject *(S)*, direct object *(DO)*, indirect object *(IO)*, predicate noun *(PN)*, object of the preposition *(OP)*, or appositive *(App)*. If there is no gerund in the sentence, write *none* in the blank. Do not underline participles.

_____ 11.   A blossoming talent named Ted Williams began playing for the San Diego Padres.

_____ 12.   Banking on his continuing success, the Boston Red Sox traded for Williams.

_____ 13.   Building on his solid hitting performances won him two Triple Crowns for Boston.

_____ 14.   The continuing activity of his bat, a graceful, yet powerful swinging for the fences, resulted in 521 towering round-trippers.

_____ 15.   Wanting to be remembered as the greatest hitter that ever lived, he built a living legend for himself by the awe-inspiring exploits of his game.

Chapter 3: Participles

Practice A
Underline the present participles once and the past participles twice. Place parentheses around the entire participial phrase.

1. In 1939 when the Red Sox first obtained Williams, much needed for his tremendous bat, he hit .327 and led the league with an astounding 145 RBIs.

2. Amazing every expert two years later, Ted Williams hit over .400 for the first time.

3. That famed average handed him the batting title for 1941.

4. He once noted that the only pitch he ever had continuing trouble with was the knuckle ball, fluttering and dipping like a butterfly.

5. Also in his storied 1941 season, he hit thirty-seven high-flying home runs.

Practice B
Underline the participles once and the nouns they modify twice. Do not underline passive or progressive verbs.

6. Whenever he was beaten by an opposing pitcher, Williams eagerly anticipated the challenge.

7. Part of the reason he was so successful at the plate was his sharpened eyesight.

8. He could see the spinning stitches on a fastball even at ninety-five miles per hour.

9. Once, when Williams played at another ballpark, he noticed that the closely measured angle at first base was just a few degrees more than it should have been.

10. The officials measured the questioned base and found that it was off by only two inches.

Practice C
Insert a logical participle or participial phrase. Underline each noun modified by a participle.

11. Sadly, Williams's _____ career was interrupted by war.

12. _____, Williams's draft board classified him as 1-A.

13. The Red Sox's _____ manager, Joe Cronin, said that if Uncle Sam wanted him, Williams would make a mighty fine soldier.

14. _____, Uncle Sam did want him, and Williams spent five years out of his baseball career in military service.

15. _____, the marks he left warranted his _____ induction into the Hall of Fame in 1966.

Chapter 3: Infinitives

Practice A
Underline each infinitive phrase and identify it as an adjective (Adj), an adverb (Adv), or a noun (N).

_____ 1. Many biologists wish to see the unclassified wildlife of the Amazon rain forest.

_____ 2. In fact, to classify the unknown wildlife is what brings many to the region.

_____ 3. In the nearby marketplace, fish that are brought to be sold often remain unidentified.

_____ 4. To see piranhas, jaguars, sloths, armadillos, spider monkeys, and river dolphins one would probably travel to the Amazon.

_____ 5. Another fact to know is that over eighteen hundred species of butterflies are there.

Practice B
A. Underline each infinitive phrase once.
B. Underline each complement of an infinitive twice.
C. Circle any words that split an infinitive.
D. Identify each infinitive phrase as an adjective (Adj), an adverb (Adv), or a noun (N).

_____ 6. The city of Manaus is a good starting place to begin a trip to the Amazon.

_____ 7. Manaus is located beside the Rio Negro, which proceeds to promptly join the Solimões River and become the Amazon.

_____ 8. Another biological wonderland to definitely see is the Pantanal.

_____ 9. To find the Pantanal would not take a long time; it is nearly half the size of France.

_____ 10. It is a large marshland, and to see everything in it would be impossible.

Practice C
Underline each infinitive phrase and identify it as passive (P) or active (A).

_____ 11. Because there are no towns to stay in comfortably, trips to the Pantanal are usually not long.

_____ 12. The Pantanal is to be found to the south of the Amazon.

_____ 13. Giant river otters, anacondas, iguanas, jaguars, cougars, deer and anteaters—these are some of the animals to be watched.

_____ 14. However, it would be an altogether different experience to be attacked by them.

_____ 15. The giant river otter has been known to be seven feet long in some cases!

Chapter 4: Adjective and Adverb Clauses

Practice A
Identify each italicized clause as adjectival *(Adj)* or adverbial *(Adv)*.

_____ 1. The giant sloth *that roamed many years ago* is presumed to be extinct today.

_____ 2. Remains of the giant sloth, *when they were found in both North and South America,* revealed that the animal had existed on a very large scale.

_____ 3. *If you want to see a giant sloth,* its remains are on display at the National Museum of History.

_____ 4. *Although many scientists oppose the view,* some scientists believe that the sloth has been extinct for only about five hundred years.

_____ 5. Others *who have seen large, unusual, and unidentified creatures with characteristics of the giant sloth* believe that the animal may still exist today.

Practice B
Place parentheses around each dependent clause and identify it as adjectival *(Adj)* or adverbial *(Adv)*.

_____ 6. It was a large creature that in some instances measured eighteen to twenty feet long.

_____ 7. While it usually walked on four legs, it sometimes walked upright.

_____ 8. Its large tail was used so it could stand and eat from tree branches.

_____ 9. The giant sloth, whose four feet had long claws, was a fierce, frightening opponent.

_____ 10. Though it had long, sharp claws, it was not a carnivorous animal.

Practice C
**A. Underline each relative pronoun once and each relative adverb twice.
 Circle each subordinating conjunction.
B. Place parentheses around each dependent clause.
C. Identify each clause as adjectival *(Adj)* or adverbial *(Adv)*.**

_____ 11. Although the modern tree sloth is relatively small, the giant sloth was similar in size and weight to an elephant.

_____ 12. Some sources that ignore the significant findings in the North American continent call South America the only home of the giant sloth.

_____ 13. The time of the 1890s, when a hunting party sighted a large sloth-like creature in Argentina, generated new interest in finding the creature alive today.

_____ 14. The hunters stopped at the place where they were to try to capture the animal.

_____ 15. Soon scientists who were investigating found skin from a supposed giant sloth.

Chapter 4: Noun Clauses

Practice A

Identify the function of each italicized noun clause as subject (S), predicate noun (PN), direct object (DO), indirect object (IO), object of the preposition (OP), or appositive (App).

_____ 1. Scientists give *what many people call the giant armadillo* a classification closely related to the giant sloth's classification.

_____ 2. One interesting fact is *that the giant armadillo has more teeth than any other mammal.*

_____ 3. It grows to be very large in a few instances, *when it is almost four feet long and weighs over one hundred pounds.*

_____ 4. *That it stands on its hind feet at times* is perhaps what makes the giant armadillo most like the ancient giant sloth.

_____ 5. The giant armadillo, in its armored back, still has *what all armadillos have in common.*

Practice B

Place parentheses around each noun clause and identify its function as subject (S), predicate noun (PN), direct object (DO), indirect object (IO), object of the preposition (OP), or appositive (App).

_____ 6. Many Texans can tell whoever visits their state stories about armadillos.

_____ 7. Armadillos' nine-band armor is what protects the animals from their enemies.

_____ 8. Some can even ball up into whatever position they need to protect themselves.

_____ 9. Although armadillos eat insects, they can also eat whatever plant material they can find.

_____ 10. What dining they do is done nocturnally since they hide in burrows during the day.

Practice C

A. Place parentheses around each noun clause.
B. Underline each subordinating conjunction once and each indefinite relative pronoun twice.
C. Identify the function of each noun clause as subject (S), predicate noun (PN), direct object (DO), indirect object (IO), object of the preposition (OP), or appositive (App).

_____ 11. Scientists consider whether the armadillo is in one category or another by looking at its size, appearance, and habits.

_____ 12. In Texas, armadillos are what homeowners want to avoid to maintain their lawns.

_____ 13. However, armadillos' armored bodies protect them from whoever would hurt them.

_____ 14. Typically slow armadillos can quickly escape whatever predator would harm them.

_____ 15. That armadillos love to burrow into the ground for shelter and to find grubs for food is obvious to most Texas homeowners.

Chapter 4: Using Clauses

Practice A
Identify each italicized clause as an independent clause (IC) or a dependent clause (DC).

_____ 1. Parasailing is an activity *that George did at the beach.*

_____ 2. *He looked like a tiny dot in the sky from the room* where we watched.

_____ 3. Once, we saw him swing nearly upside down, and *we began to worry for his safety.*

_____ 4. *When his feet touched the boat's deck again,* he encouraged everyone else to try it.

_____ 5. *His fifteen-minute ride was well worth the money.*

Practice B
Identify each sentence as simple (S), compound (Cd), complex (Cx), or compound-complex (Cd-Cx).

_____ 6. Wesley decided to parasail also, and he quickly climbed into the harness.

_____ 7. As the boat picked up speed, the large parachute filled up with air.

_____ 8. Slowly, with one hand over the other, the workers let out the parachute with Wesley into the air.

_____ 9. Wesley floated higher and higher into the bright blue sky.

_____ 10. Although he was afraid of falling, he reassured himself that all he would hit was water, and he began to admire the beautiful view of the coastline.

Practice C
Identify each group of words as a sentence (S), a fragment (F), a comma splice (CS), or a fused sentence (FS).

_____ 11. Wesley, the rider of the skies.

_____ 12. Thankfully, the ride ended safely.

_____ 13. After fifteen minutes, the workers pulled the parachute in, Wesley set his feet solidly within the boat.

_____ 14. But since Maryann was only two years old at the time.

_____ 15. Dad refused to let her parasail that year he said that she could when she was older.

Chapter 5: Subject-Verb Agreement

Practice A
Underline the subjects in the following sentences. Then write the correct form of the verb in parentheses.

_____ 1. Both Japan and England (is, are) known for their beautiful golf courses.

_____ 2. Hole one and hole four (is, are) over five hundred yards.

_____ 3. Either your driver or another wood (is, are) acceptable for this par four.

_____ 4. There (is, are) either trees or sandpits or water hazards to avoid on every hole.

_____ 5. Sandpits and lakes always (attracts, attract) even my best golf balls.

Practice B
Underline the subject in the following sentences. Place parentheses around any intervening phrases. Then write the correct form of the verb in parentheses.

_____ 6. Here (is, are) a really wide fairway.

_____ 7. Down the sides of this fairway (is, are) groves of trees.

_____ 8. A shot into those trees invariably (costs, cost) a penalty.

_____ 9. A five iron from here, not from the trees, easily (approaches, approach) the green.

_____ 10. There, from the tee of the ninth hole, (is, are) the most beautiful views of the entire course.

Practice C
Underline the subject in the following sentences. Then write the correct form of an appropriate verb.

_____ 11. The United States also _?_ many beautiful golf courses.

_____ 12. Riches _?_ not required to play on all of them.

_____ 13. Forty dollars _?_ required to play this course.

_____ 14. Nearly every one of my friends _?_ on that public course.

_____ 15. My golfing club _?_ every Tuesday afternoon.

Chapter 5: Pronoun-Antecedent Agreement

Practice A
Underline the correct form of the pronoun from the choices in parentheses.

1. Lamentations follows Jeremiah; like the Psalms, (*it, they*) is a book of Hebrew poetry.

2. Either the Psalms or Lamentations refers to the fall of Jerusalem as (*its, their*) subject.

3. The sins of God's people or the hope of God's grace is a major theme in each chapter, and (*it, they*) can be found in nearly every verse.

4. Even the priests and the prophets were found guilty, and the ugliness of (*his, their*) sins was revealed.

5. The grace of God is emphasized in both verse 22 and in verses 55-57, and (*it, they*) remind the reader that repentance can still bring mercy.

Practice B
Write the correct form of the pronoun in parentheses. If none of the pronouns in parentheses is correct, write NA (no answer) in the blank.

_____ 6. The students in the class read Lamentations chapter 5, but (*it, they*) did not understand the parallelism in the Hebrew verse.

_____ 7. While Jeremiah is traditionally considered the author of Lamentations, either of the views about authorship has (*his, their*) own degree of validity.

_____ 8. After reading Lamentations, nobody could assert (*his, their*) doubt about whether the mercies of God are beyond what man deserves.

_____ 9. Several of the poems speak of the effects of Israel's sins; (*it, they*) lament about the city of Jerusalem or the country of Judah.

_____ 10. One of the chapters tells (*its, their*) story about the effects of the judgment upon the speaker personally.

Practice C
Underline any pronoun that disagrees with its antecedent. Then write the correct pronoun in the blank. If the sentence is already correct, write C in the blank.

_____ 11. The readers of Lamentations have the results of sin impressed upon him.

_____ 12. When they read Lamentations, many see the ugly side of sin hidden by Satan.

_____ 13. All of the church has people who can identify with the devastating effects of Israel's rebellion against God because of an awareness of their own sin.

_____ 14. Each of the books of the Bible, including Lamentations, contains their own version of the theme of God's undying love towards fallen men.

_____ 15. Little of Lamentations or few of the Psalms speak its words of comfort as powerfully as the phrase in Lamentations 3 does: "His compassions fail not."

Concept Reinforcements   **103**

Chapter 6: Auxiliaries and Principal Parts of Verbs

Practice A
Underline each complete verb.

1. Have you ever seen a comet?

2. Comets do travel in a definite pattern throughout the solar system.

3. Some comets can be seen near the sun.

4. By the sun, some comets will develop bright tails.

5. These tails may extend as far as one hundred million miles.

Practice B
Underline each complete verb. Then write *Aux* above each auxiliary.

6. Edmond Halley, an English astronomer, did increase scientific knowledge about comets.

7. He had calculated the orbit of the comet observed in 1682.

8. He could correctly predict the next appearance of the comet.

9. Halley's comet has been recorded as early as 240 B.C.

10. The comet should appear again around the year 2061.

Practice C
Write the correct present, past, or past participle form of the verb in parentheses.

_____ 11. Since ancient times, superstition (*surround*) the sighting of comets.

_____ 12. People once (*believe*) that comets foretold plagues, wars, and death.

_____ 13. Comets (*appear*) to have "hairy" tails.

_____ 14. The name *comet* (*be*) from the Greek word *kometes,* which means "hairy one."

_____ 15. In the seventeenth century, scientists (*begin*) to understand comets better.

Chapter 6: Tense

Practice A

Identify the tense of each italicized verb as *present, past, future, present perfect, past perfect, future perfect, present progressive, past progressive, future progressive, present perfect progressive, past perfect progressive,* or *future perfect progressive.*

_____ 1. Our class *has been studying* comets.

_____ 2. Mr. Littlejohn, our teacher, *had planned* many interesting activities.

_____ 3. We *will be visiting* a planetarium in a few weeks.

_____ 4. A comet *differs* from an asteroid in its orbit and chemical makeup.

_____ 5. Many comets *will* not *develop* tails.

Practice B

Write the progressive form of each italicized verb. Do not change the tense of the verb.

_____ 6. Most comets *move* in elliptical, oval-shaped orbits.

_____ 7. Other comets *may travel* in parabolic or hyperbolic orbits.

_____ 8. The time it *takes* a comet to orbit the sun is called a period.

_____ 9. Some comets *take* less than seven years to complete an orbit.

_____ 10. Other comets *will travel* hundreds of years before completing an orbit.

Practice C

Write an appropriate form of the verb in parentheses.

_____ 11. In the fourth century B.C., Aristotle *(suggest)* that comets were bits of Earth sent out into space.

_____ 12. In the sixteenth century, Tycho Brahe *(prove)* that comets indeed were heavenly bodies.

_____ 13. Sir Isaac Newton *(disprove)* the theory that comets traveled in a straight line, a false theory earlier developed by Kepler.

_____ 14. Halley *(use)* Newton's calculations to discover the orbit of the comet that now bears his name.

_____ 15. Many more comets *(discover)*; each one gives testimony to the magnificence of God's creation.

Chapter 6: Voice and Mood

Practice A
Underline each complete verb. Then identify it as *active* or *passive*.

_____ 1. Planetariums strive to create a realistic picture of space.

_____ 2. Many differently sized projectors are employed by planetariums to simulate space.

_____ 3. Planetariums are used to teach descriptive astronomy and celestial navigation.

_____ 4. The planetariums offer regular demonstrations, or sky shows, to the public.

_____ 5. The first planetarium was opened in Deutsches Museum in Munich in 1923.

Practice B
Identify the mood of each italicized verb as *indicative*, *imperative*, or *subjunctive*.

_____ 6. John T. Desaguliers, a friend of Newton, *invented* the planetarium.

_____ 7. If Desaguliers were alive today, he *would be amazed* at how modern technology has enhanced his invention.

_____ 8. Originally, the term "planetarium" *described* devices used to portray the orbit of the planets.

_____ 9. Now computers *are able* to create realistic, accurate projections of space.

_____ 10. *Visit* a planetarium to see and learn about the heavens.

Practice C
Underline each complete verb. If the sentence is passive, rewrite it to change the verb to active voice.

11. The Hayden Planetarium in New York City uses a high-tech virtual reality system to produce the most realistic star show available today.

_____

_____

12. Visits to local planetariums are used by teachers to inspire students toward a deeper interest in science.

_____

_____

13. See the beauty and splendor of God's creation!

_____

_____

14. The order of the universe is sustained by God.

_____

_____

15. By looking at the heavens, you will be in awe of God's handiwork.

_____

_____

Chapter 7: Pronoun Reference

Practice A

Underline each personal pronoun. Identify the pronoun reference in each sentence as *clear* or *unclear.*

_____ 1. A national cemetery is a burial place for men and women of the armed forces of the United States unless they were dishonorably discharged from the military.

_____ 2. The United States government has 119 national cemeteries in the United States and Puerto Rico, and about 50 of these cemeteries have no more space for additional gravesites. They are maintained by government agencies.

_____ 3. In addition, the Department of Veterans Affairs provides headstones for all graves in national cemeteries without them.

_____ 4. The government cares for the graves and the headstones; it is an enormous job.

_____ 5. In 1862, during the Civil War, Congress established the National Cemetery System by granting to Abraham Lincoln permission to establish them for Union army veterans.

Practice B

Questions 6-10: Rewrite the following paragraph, correcting the five pronoun reference errors.

The Gettysburg National Cemetery was dedicated on the battlefield of Gettysburg on November 19, 1863, by him when he gave the Gettysburg Address. The dedication ceremony set part of it aside to be used as a national cemetery. More than seven thousand men are buried in it. Today, Gettysburg National Military Park contains the battlefield and it as well as numerous monuments to the battle. It was set up in 1895.

_____

_____

_____

_____

_____

_____

_____

_____

Practice C
Rewrite each problem sentence to correct any unclear pronoun reference.

11. The Arlington National Cemetery is one of the largest and most famous of them in the United States.

   _____

   _____

12. The cemetery was created from the estate of Robert E. Lee's wife, Mary Custis Lee; and before 1864, the estate was where he lived.

   _____

   _____

13. Robert E. Lee's wife was the daughter of George Washington Parke Custis; he was the commander of the Confederate army.

   _____

   _____

14. George Washington Parke Custis was the grandson of Martha Washington, not of George Washington. He was related to him only by marriage.

   _____

   _____

15. Before Martha was married to George Washington, she had been married to Daniel Parke Custis. After he died, Martha married him.

   _____

   _____

Chapter 7: Pronoun Reference II

Practice A
Underline each personal pronoun. Identify the pronoun reference in each sentence as *clear* or *unclear*.

_____ 1. George and Martha Washington adopted George Washington Parke Custis after his father died; it was very sad.

_____ 2. Robert E. Lee and Mary Custis Lee lived in Arlington House, which had been built by her father, George Washington Parke Custis. They left the house when the Civil War broke out in 1861.

_____ 3. They say that the Union government claimed the property and the house in 1864.

_____ 4. The Union government set apart part of the property for Arlington National Cemetery in 1864; it was a relatively new idea.

_____ 5. It was eighteen years before the government bought the house and property from the owner.

Practice B
Underline each personal pronoun and write its antecedent in the blank. If the antecedent is unclear, write *unclear* in the blank.

_____ 6. George Washington Custis Lee was declared the owner after the war and received $150,000 from the government for the house and property; he was the son of Robert E. Lee.

_____ 7. They say the Arlington House is also known as the Robert E. Lee Memorial.

_____ 8. They will bury only certain people in the Arlington National Cemetery.

_____ 9. Arlington National Cemetery is a burial place for Americans who served our country; our country honors these men and women by burying them there.

_____ 10. Although the cemetery was originally for Union soldiers, today only members of certain categories within the armed forces and only officials elected to an office of the federal government, given an appointed cabinet-level position, or appointed to the Supreme Court may be buried in it.

Practice C
Correct any unclear pronoun reference by rewriting the unclear sentence. If the sentence is already clear, write *C* in the blank.

11. President John F. Kennedy and President William Howard Taft are buried in Arlington National Cemetery; he was the thirty-fifth president of the United States.

   _____

   _____

   _____

12. The Tomb of the Unknowns is located in Arlington National Cemetery; this has meaning for many people.

   _____

   _____

   _____

13. After World War I, officials of the Allied countries discovered that many bodies of the soldiers could not be identified, so they did not know where to bury the soldiers. This created problems.

   _____

   _____

   _____

14. On Armistice Day, 1921, an Unknown Soldier from World War I was buried in Arlington National Cemetery. His white marble tomb and inscription were completed in 1931, and it reads, "Here rests in honored glory an American soldier known only to God."

   _____

   _____

   _____

15. On Memorial Day, 1958, unknown soldiers from both World War II and the Korean War were buried in marble-capped crypts at the head of the larger marble tomb. On Memorial Day, 1984, an unknown soldier from the Vietnam War was buried with these others, but his remains were later identified through advances in DNA testing and then removed from the Tomb of the Unknowns. This is amazing.

   _____

   _____

   _____

Chapter 8: Correct Use of Pronoun Case

Practice A
Underline the correct pronoun from the choices in parentheses.

1. Francis Thompson, an English poet of the late seventeenth century and early eighteenth century, is best known for (*his, him*) poem "The Hound of Heaven."

2. His own personal experience drove (*his, him*) to write the poem.

3. The poem can apply to you and (*I, me*) today.

4. (*It, Its*) deals with God's pursuing man.

5. The Holy Spirit is pictured as an unrelenting hound that pursues (*we, us*) to salvation.

Practice B
Underline each personal pronoun and identify it as subjective (S), objective (O), possessive (P), or as an independent possessive (IP).

_____ 6. Francis Thompson had tried to become a doctor for his career.

_____ 7. When he failed at that, Thompson went to London.

_____ 8. In London, sickness, addiction, and poverty plagued him.

_____ 9. Some of Thompson's problems may be similar to ours.

_____10. Thompson found the answer to his problems in God.

Practice C
Insert an appropriate pronoun as indicated in parentheses.

_____ 11. Wilfrid and Alice Meynell found Thompson in London, and ? helped him with his problems. (*subjective*)

_____ 12. When God helped Thompson overcome his problems, Thompson wrote ? poem "The Hound of Heaven." (*possessive*)

_____ 13. The poem describes Thompson in his search to find peace, security, and happiness outside of God; finally ? realized that these things could be found only in God. (*subjective*)

_____ 14. Thompson saw how God had used all life's circumstances to find ?. (*objective*)

_____ 15. Thompson's search for happiness may not be much different from ? or mine. (*independent possessive*)

Chapter 8: Compound Constructions, Appositives, and Comparisons Using *Than* or *As*

Practice A
Identify each sentence as correct (C) or incorrect (I).

_____ 1. In comparing Gerard Manley Hopkins with Francis Thompson, most people would say that Hopkins was a better poet than he.

_____ 2. For one thing, Thompson did not write as many poems as him.

_____ 3. Thompson and he lived at the same time.

_____ 4. However, Hopkins was about fifteen years older than he.

_____ 5. Religious poems were written by both Hopkins and he.

Practice B
Underline the correct pronoun from the choices in parentheses.

6. Hopkins used more innovative poetic structures than (*he, him*).

7. (*We, us*) readers can learn a lot about different poetic techniques through reading Hopkins's poems.

8. (*They, them*), the poets, both include nature images in their poems.

9. In "Pied Beauty," Hopkins describes the beauty of God's creation for you and (*I, me*) to read.

10. People can be pointed to God through the poems of Hopkins and (*he, him*).

Practice C
Choose the letter corresponding to the correct pronoun.

_____ 11. Like Hopkins and Thompson, George Herbert was a British poet; however, Herbert lived during an earlier time than _?_.
    A. they
    B. them

_____ 12. All of these poets—Hopkins, Thompson, and _?_—wrote religious poetry.
    A. he
    B. him

_____ 13. Most of the poems written by Hopkins and _?_ were published posthumously.
    A. he
    B. him

_____ 14. Hopkins and Thompson were not as active politically as _?_.
    A. he
    B. him

_____ 15. You and _?_ should learn more about Herbert's shape poems.
    A. I
    B. me

Chapter 8: *Who* and *Whom*, Courtesy Order, and Reflexive and Intensive Pronouns

Practice A
Identify each sentence as correct (C) or incorrect (I).

_____ 1. Whom wrote the shaped poem "Easter Wings"?

_____ 2. George Herbert wrote the poem himself in the shape of two wings.

_____ 3. The words in the poem itself form the shape of the wings.

_____ 4. How many poets do you know of whom try to write shaped poems?

_____ 5. You and your friends should try to write a shaped poem.

Practice B
Underline the correct pronoun from the choices in parentheses.

6. (*Who, Whom*) frequently used sprung meter in his poetry?

7. Hopkins (*he, himself*) wrote poems with sprung meter.

8. Hopkins came up with the term *sprung meter* (*hisself, himself*).

9. Hopkins gives you and (*I, me*) a variety of different rhythms in his poetry.

10. His poems (*them, themselves*) use sprung meter to imitate the strong accents of the way people actually speak.

Practice C
Choose the letter that corresponds to the correct pronoun.

_____ 11. Hopkins, _?_ did not publish his own poetry, was a major influence on early-twentieth-century poets.
  A. who
  B. whom

_____ 12. Of the three poets discussed, _?_ do you think is the best poet?
  A. who
  B. whom

_____ 13. In their poems, these poets did not seek to exalt _?_.
  A. theirselves
  B. themselves

_____ 14. _?_ did these men write their poetry for?
  A. Who
  B. Whom

_____ 15. You and _?_ should learn from these men.
  A. I
  B. me

Chapter 9: Showing Comparison with Modifiers

Practice A
Identify each sentence as correct (C) or incorrect (I).

_____ 1. A lighthouse is a tower with a strongest light that serves as a navigational tool.

_____ 2. Lighthouses help sailors determine their position in relation to the land and help warn them of dangerous rocks and shorelines.

_____ 3. Some lighthouses are still in operation today, although they are usually operated by automated electronic and computer navigational equipment.

_____ 4. Today, many sailors use satellites to help them navigate.

_____ 5. Before modern technology, sailors had to proceed most cautiously in dangerous waters.

Practice B
Underline the correct adjective or adverb from the choices in parentheses.

6. The Pharos, built in Alexandria, Egypt, was the *(taller, tallest)* lighthouse ever built.

7. Before an earthquake toppled the Pharos, it was *(more, most)* than 440 feet high.

8. One of the *(more, most)* famous lighthouses in the United States is the Boston lighthouse.

9. The *(older, oldest)* lighthouse in the United States, the Boston lighthouse, was built in 1716.

10. The Boston lighthouse is one of the *(better-preserved, best-preserved)* lighthouses in America.

Practice C
Write the correct form of the modifier in parentheses.

_____ 11. In 1993, the Block Island Lighthouse of Rhode Island was *(careful)* moved back from shore approximately 300 feet.

_____ 12. The move was actually *(some)* complicated than building the lighthouse.

_____ 13. The move probably made the lighthouse *(some)* widely known than it had been before.

_____ 14. Sitting over 258 feet above sea level, the lighthouse is the *(high)* lighthouse in New England.

_____ 15. In most peoples' opinions, moving the lighthouse back was *(good)* than leaving the lighthouse in a dangerous place.

Chapter 9: Problems with Modifiers

Practice A
Identify each sentence as correct (C) or incorrect (I).

_____ 1. When lighthouses were first used in the United States, the lighthouses didn't have no modern technology, so people were hired to run the lighthouses.

_____ 2. Sometimes the lighthouse keepers didn't have some way to get from the land to the lighthouse except by boat.

_____ 3. Many lighthouse keepers didn't have anywhere they could live except the lighthouse and its island.

_____ 4. Sometimes, because of inclement weather, keepers would remain stranded at the lighthouse for months.

_____ 5. All lighthouse keepers know that sometimes the sea looks calmly before a storm.

Practice B
Identify each sentence as correct (C) or incorrect (I). If the sentence is incorrect, write the correction in the blank.

_____ 6. Idawalley Zorada Lewis was a more braver lighthouse keeper than some lighthouse keepers were.

_____ 7. She was famous because there wasn't a rescue that she didn't try, and she completed many hard rescues successfully.

_____ 8. Her father had been the original lighthouse keeper, but after he had a stroke, he couldn't do the work anymore.

_____ 9. She probably worked harder than other lighthouse keepers did.

_____ 10. Because the lighthouse was much more farther than fifty yards from the mainland, Ida had to row her brother and sister to and from school each day, sometimes in very bad weather.

Practice C
Rewrite each sentence, making the modifier clear or correct.

11. We are supposed to begin studying some types of light signals today, but we have not covered none of them yet.

_____

_____

12. A fixed light is a much more steadier beam than other signals.

_____

_____

13. A flashing light is one in which the periods of darkness are more longer than the periods of light.

    _____

    _____

14. One of the most greatest practical reasons that lighthouses use different light patterns is so that sailors can distinguish the lighthouses by their light patterns.

    _____

    _____

15. When the weather grows coldly and foggy, sailors need to be able to distinguish lighthouses by their lights.

    _____

    _____

Chapter 9: Placement of Modifiers

Practice A
Identify each sentence as correct (C) or incorrect (I).

_____ 1. Involved in some Revolutionary War battles, many people today know about the Boston lighthouse.

_____ 2. When the British blockaded Boston Harbor, the minutemen attempted to swiftly blow up the Boston lighthouse to break the blockade.

_____ 3. However, the minutemen only damaged the lighthouse.

_____ 4. The British had the lighthouse almost entirely repaired when the Americans attacked the lighthouse again.

_____ 5. The Americans skillfully drove the British away and started to burn the lighthouse.

Practice B
Write the letter of the sentence in which the modifier is clear and correct.

_____ 6. A. The British who had come back to the lighthouse attacked the Americans quickly.
   B. The British who had come back to the lighthouse quickly attacked the Americans.

_____ 7. A. In the skirmish, one American soldier only died.
   B. In the skirmish, only one American soldier died.

_____ 8. A. A key navigational tool, the British also used the lighthouse as part of their blockade of Boston Harbor.
   B. A key navigational tool, the lighthouse was also part of the British blockade of Boston Harbor.

_____ 9. A. Eventually the British managed to regain control of the lighthouse completely.
   B. Eventually the British managed to completely regain control of the lighthouse.

_____ 10. A. The Americans again attacked the lighthouse, and they drove almost the British away.
   B. The Americans again attacked the lighthouse, and they almost drove the British away.

Practice C
Rewrite each sentence, making the modifiers clear and correct.

11. So the Americans wouldn't have the lighthouse, the British blew up the lighthouse merely with gunpowder as they were retreating.

_____

_____

12. Most people are aware that the rebuilt lighthouse that know history is over two hundred years old.

_____

_____

13. Located on Little Brewster Island, the official name of the lighthouse is the Boston Light.

    _____

    _____

14. A battle was fought near the lighthouse of the War of 1812, but not for possession of the lighthouse.

    _____

    _____

15. Instead of fighting over the lighthouse, the naval battle was between an American and an English ship—the USS *Chesapeake* and the HMS *Shannon*.

    _____

    _____

Chapter 10: People, Places, Constructions, Organizations, and Businesses

Practice A
Underline each word that contains a capitalization error.

1. Edward Brooke was born in washington, D.C. and graduated from howard university.

2. Brooke served in the United States army in italy in World War II and won the Bronze Star for bravery.

3. After the war, brooke earned a law degree from boston university.

4. In 1962 and 1964, he was elected attorney general of massachusetts.

5. From 1967 to 1979, he served as a massachusetts representative to the u.s. senate; he was the first black ever elected to the senate by popular vote.

Practice B
Underline each word that contains a capitalization error and write the correction in the blank. If the sentence is already correct, write C in the blank.

6. Patricia Roberts Harris graduated from Howard University in 1945 and earned a law degree from George Washington University in 1960.

_____

7. In 1965 president Lyndon B. Johnson appointed her an ambassador to luxembourg; she was the nation's first black female ambassador.

_____

8. In 1971 ibm appointed her as a director; she was the first black woman to serve as a director of a major u.s. company.

_____

9. From 1977 to 1979, she served as secretary of the Department of Housing and Urban Development.

_____

10. In 1979 Harris's department became the department of health and human services; she was the first black woman to hold a post in the U.S. cabinet.

_____

Practice C
Rewrite the following paragraph, correcting the five errors in capitalization. (Proper nouns consisting of multiple words count as one error.)

Thurgood Marshall graduated from lincoln university and studied law at Howard University; he began practicing law in 1933. From 1938 to 1950, he was chief counsel for the NAACP (national association for the advancement of colored people). In 1954 he presented the legal argument that resulted in the supreme court decision that declared segregation in public schools unconstitutional. In 1965 Marshall was appointed solicitor general of the United States. In 1967 president Lyndon B. Johnson appointed Marshall associate justice; he was the first black justice of the u.s. Supreme Court.

_____

_____

_____

_____

_____

_____

_____

_____

Chapter 10: Religious, Cultural, and Historical Terms; Titles and First Words; Proper Adjectives and Other Words

Practice A
Identify each sentence as correctly capitalized (C) or incorrectly capitalized (I).

_____ 1. Hinduism is the main religion of the country of India.

_____ 2. The main book of Hinduism is called the vedas.

_____ 3. Brahman, an impersonal world soul, is the Hindu god.

_____ 4. Hindus believe that all the gods of every religion are part of brahman.

_____ 5. Unlike Hinduism, Christianity is not an all-inclusive religion; Christianity believes in only one God and creator of all.

Practice B
Underline each word that contains a capitalization error.

6. The augsburg confession was written by Philipp Melanchthon, a friend of Martin Luther.

7. This historic document outlines the beliefs of the denomination now known as lutheran.

8. This document was written during the period in history known as the reformation.

9. A former german priest, Luther was a key figure in the reformation.

10. This document summarized what Luther believed the bible taught.

Practice C
Underline each word that contains a capitalization error and write the correction in the blank. If the sentence is already correct, write C in the blank.

_____ 11. Luther had already written his shorter catechism, which presented Scripture doctrines to children.

_____ 12. Luther had tried to reform the roman Catholic Church.

_____ 13. But the church did not want to listen to Luther's arguments, so the church excommunicated Luther in June of 1520.

_____ 14. Today, many Christians know of Martin Luther because of his hymn "A Mighty Fortress is our God."

_____ 15. I think it would be interesting to learn more about the life of Martin Luther.

Chapter 11: End Marks and Other Uses of the Period

Practice A
Identify each sentence as correctly punctuated *(C)* or incorrectly punctuated *(I)*.

_____ 1. The residence and office of the president of the United States became officially known as the White House when that name was put on President Theodore Roosevelt's stationery.

_____ 2. I wonder if the White House has any other names?

_____ 3. You should study about the history of the White House!

_____ 4. Where is the White House located?

_____ 5. The street address for the White House is 1600 Pennsylvania Avenue.

Practice B
Write the letter of the sentence that is punctuated correctly.

_____ 6. A. Wow, the White House has 132 rooms!
　　　　　　 B. Wow, the White House has 132 rooms.

_____ 7. A. Don't you think it would be nice to have a house with that many rooms to live in.
　　　　　　 B. Don't you think it would be nice to have a house with that many rooms to live in?

_____ 8. A. The president and his family don't actually live in all those rooms, do they!
　　　　　　 B. The president and his family don't actually live in all those rooms, do they?

_____ 9. A. No, their living quarters are on the second floor of the White House.
　　　　　　 B. No, their living quarters are on the second floor of the White House!

_____ 10. A. The dimensions for the main building of the White House are 52 m. × 26 m. or 170 ft. × 85 ft.
　　　　　　 B. The dimensions for the main building of the White House are 52 m × 26 m or 170 ft. × 85 ft.

Practice C
Insert the correct end marks for each sentence.

11. The first president to live in the White House was John Adams and his family

12. Why didn't George Washington live in the White House

13. Washington commissioned the building of the White House, but it wasn't completed during his presidency

14. It's awful that the first president didn't get to live in the White House

15. I wonder whether Washington really minded; he lived in a beautiful three-story home in Mount Vernon, Virginia

Chapter 11: Commas and Semicolons

Practice A
Identify each sentence as correctly punctuated (C) or incorrectly punctuated (I).

_____ 1. The third floor of the White House has the guest rooms, and rooms for the staff.

_____ 2. The Library, China Room, Vermeil Room and Map Room are all located on the ground floor while the Blue Room, Red Room, and State Dining Room are located on the first floor.

_____ 3. The formal rooms of state on the first floor are where the president and his wife receive guests aren't they?

_____ 4. While the first lady's guests usually meet the first lady in the Red Room, the president's dinner guests usually meet the president in the Blue Room.

_____ 5. The president and his wife host the most formal dinners in the elaborate, elegant State Dining Room.

Practice B
Write the letter of the sentence that is punctuated correctly.

_____ 6. A. The four main additions to the original White House are the South Portico, a porch with access to the ground floor, the North Portico, another porch on the north side of the house, the West Terrace, a patio with an entrance to the Executive Wing, and the East Terrace, a walkway with access to the East Wing.

B. The four main additions to the original White House are the South Portico, a porch with access to the ground floor; the North Portico, another porch on the north side of the house; the West Terrace, a patio with an entrance to the Executive Wing; and the East Terrace, a walkway with access to the East Wing.

_____ 7. A. James Hoban, an architect born in Ireland, won a competition sponsored by the federal government for his design for the White House.

B. James Hoban an architect born in Ireland won a competition sponsored by the federal government for his design for the White House.

_____ 8. A. During the War of 1812 when the British attacked Washington, D.C., on August 24, 1814, they burned the interior of the White House.

B. During the War of 1812 when the British attacked Washington, D.C., on August 24, 1814 they burned the interior of the White House.

_____ 9. A. James Hoban was in charge of the reconstruction of the White House, which was completed by 1817, and Hoban also helped with the design for the U.S. Capitol building, which is also in Washington, D.C.

B. James Hoban was in charge of the reconstruction of the White House, which was completed by 1817; and Hoban also helped with the design for the U.S. Capitol building, which is also in Washington, D.C.

_____ 10. A. All of the presidents since John Adams have lived in the White House. The Trumans, however, moved out of the White House from 1948 to 1952 so that the White House structure could be reinforced with concrete and steel.

B. All of the presidents since John Adams have lived in the White House. The Trumans however, moved out of the White House from 1948 to 1952 so that the White House structure could be reinforced with concrete and steel.

Practice C

Insert any missing commas into the following sentences. If the sentence is already correct, write C in the blank.

_____ 11. When the Trumans left the White House so that it could be renovated the family moved into Blair House not far from the White House.

_____ 12. Blair House still stately and majestic is a historic mansion built in 1824 by the United States Army's first surgeon general Joseph Lovell.

_____ 13. In 1836 Blair House was purchased by Francis Preston Blair Sr., a member of President Andrew Jackson's Kitchen Cabinet.

_____ 14. Jackson had called Blair to Washington, D.C., to edit the party newspaper, the *Washington Globe*.

_____ 15. Blair House a four-story yellow stucco building was at one time the official residence of the vice president; and today it is used as a guesthouse for important foreign visitors.

Chapter 11: Commas, Semicolons, and Colons

Practice A
Identify each sentence as correctly punctuated (C) or incorrectly punctuated (I).

_____ 1. Patrick Henry was born in Virginia; he attended school for only a short time because his father—a very well-educated man—tutored Patrick at home.

_____ 2. In 1760 Henry received his license to practice law; then, in 1763, the Parson's Cause, a famous lawsuit, won him recognition in Virginia as a great orator.

_____ 3. In 1764 he was elected to the Virginia House of Burgesses; where, in 1775, he made his famous speech on March 23 before the Virginia Provincial Convention.

_____ 4. The purpose of his speech was: to urge Virginia to arm its militia for defense against England; this speech may very well be one of the most famous speeches in American history.

_____ 5. This speech is famous for the following line: "I know not what course others may take, but as for me, give me liberty or give me death!"

Practice B
Write the letter of the sentence that is punctuated correctly.

_____ 6. A. Earlier, in 1765, Patrick Henry made a speech against the Stamp Act.
   B. Earlier; in 1765, Patrick Henry made a speech against the Stamp Act.

_____ 7. A. In that speech appear some other often quoted words, "Caesar had his Brutus; Charles the First his Cromwell; and George the Third—*may profit by their example. If this* be treason, make the most of it."
   B. In that speech appear some other often quoted words: "Caesar had his Brutus; Charles the First his Cromwell; and George the Third—*may profit by their example. If this* be treason, make the most of it."

_____ 8. A. In 1776 Henry began the first of five terms as the governor of the new commonwealth of Virginia: 1776, 1777, 1778, 1784, and 1785.
   B. In 1776 Henry began the first of five terms as the governor of the new commonwealth of Virginia; 1776, 1777, 1778, 1784, and 1785.

_____ 9. A. In 1796 Henry was elected governor of Virginia for the sixth time; however, he refused the office.
   B. In 1796 Henry was elected governor of Virginia for the sixth time, however, he refused the office.

_____ 10. A. Before Henry was governor the colony of Virginia elected him as a delegate to the First Continental Congress in 1774.
   B. Before Henry was governor, the colony of Virginia elected him as a delegate to the First Continental Congress in 1774.

Chapter 11: Commas, Semicolons, and Colons (continued)

Practice C
Identify the punctuation missing from each selection. In the blank write the letter that corresponds to the correct answer.

A. comma
B. semicolon
C. colon

_____ 11. In 1775 Henry was a member of the Second Continental Congress for a short time then, he became commander in chief of Virginia's military forces.

_____ 12. Henry recruited the state's quota of six thousand men for the Continental army; in addition he recruited five thousand soldiers for the state's militia.

_____ 13. Henry himself had initially opposed the ratification of the Constitution because he believed it gave too much control of the states and individuals to the federal government. When the Constitution was ratified, however he accepted it and worked hard to defend it.

_____ 14. In 1788 Henry retired from public service and returned to practicing law in 1794 he retired to his Red Hill estate near Appomattox, Virginia.

_____ 15. The title of Henry Mayer's biography about Patrick Henry seems to capture the great orator's spirit—*A Son of Thunder Patrick Henry and the American Republic.*

Chapter 12: Quotation Marks, Ellipses, and Underlining for Italics

Practice A
Identify each sentence as correctly punctuated (C) or incorrectly punctuated (I).

_____ 1. Mrs. Woodard asked the class, "Does anyone know who Edward Taylor was?"

_____ 2. Devin raised his hand and said that "Edward Taylor was a Puritan preacher and poet of the late seventeenth and early eighteenth centuries."

_____ 3. Edward Taylor wrote many poems including "Upon a Spider Catching a Fly" and "Huswifery."

_____ 4. Edward Taylor begins "Upon a Spider Catching a Fly" by identifying the spider as ". . . Thou sorrow, venom Elfe."

_____ 5. Taylor addresses the spider directly in lines 2 and 4 when he says, "Is this thy play, . . . To catch a fly"?

Practice B
Insert any missing quotation marks.

6. Although Taylor wrote some poems about personal experiences, he also wrote many poems about religion, including Meditation 1.

7. Other poems in his meditation series include Meditation 8: John 6:51 and Meditation 56: John 15:24.

8. Victoria asked, What was Taylor meditating about?

9. Good question, Victoria, Mrs. Woodard said. Does anyone know the answer?

10. Emma answered, Taylor wrote these poems when he prepared his heart for Communion by meditating on Christ's death.

Practice C
Insert any missing quotation marks or underlining for italics.

11. The collection of Taylor's meditation poems is entitled Preparatory Meditations.

12. Please notice that the vowels in the word preparatory are two a's, one e, and one o.

13. Taylor's poems were not published until after his death, but Anne Bradstreet's poems were published during her lifetime in a book called The Tenth Muse Lately Sprung Up in America.

14. The poem The Author to Her Book records Anne Bradstreet's response to seeing her poems in print.

15. Anne Bradstreet took the ship Arabella from England to Boston in 1630.

Chapter 12: Apostrophes

Practice A
Identify each sentence as correctly punctuated *(C)* or incorrectly punctuated *(I)*.

_____ 1. William Howard Taft, the twenty-seventh president of the United States, didn't really want to run for president.

_____ 2. In 1901, before he was president, Taft had served as the governor of the Philippines' to help the Filipinos become independent.

_____ 3. After his presidency, Taft was appointed as a chief justice of the Supreme Court at the beginning of the 1920's.

_____ 4. He enjoyed serving as one of the justices' on the Supreme Court.

_____ 5. Taft is the first man in the United States' history to be both a president and a Supreme Court justice.

Practice B
Underline the word that is punctuated correctly from the choices in parentheses.

6. William Taft ran for president so he (wouldnt, wouldn't) disappoint his wife, who wanted him to be president.

7. (It's, Its) very unusual for a president not to want to be president.

8. It probably (won't, willn't) surprise you to hear Mrs. Taft described as an ambitious woman.

9. At Mrs. (Tafts', Taft's) request, the mayor of Tokyo gave about three thousand cherry trees to the American people.

10. These trees were planted along the banks of (Washington's, Washingtons') Potomac River.

Practice C
Insert any missing apostrophes.

11. Taft's name *William* has two *i*s and two *l*s, and his wifes name *Nellie* has two *e*s and two *l*s.

12. Mrs. Taft suffered a stroke in 1909 and couldnt be the White House hostess anymore.

13. One of the Tafts children, Helen, helped serve as official White House hostess after her mothers stroke.

14. Its amazing that Mrs. Taft actually outlived her husband. He died in 30; she died in 43.

15. William Tafts and John F. Kennedys graves are in Arlington National Cemetery; no other U.S. presidents are buried there.

Chapter 12: Hyphens, Dashes, and Parentheses

Practice A
Identify each sentence as correctly punctuated (C) or incorrectly punctuated (I).

_____ 1. Calvin Coolidge—the thirtieth president of the United States—became president when Warren G. Harding died.

_____ 2. Coolidge was vacationing on his father's farm in Vermont when Harding died. Coolidge was the only president to be sworn into office by his own father (his father was a notary public).

_____ 3. Coolidge was then elected as president in 1924, an event making him president for most of the preGreat Depression prosperity era of the 1920s.

_____ 4. Coolidge's wife, Grace, (a former teacher at Clarke School for the Deaf) was a talkative, vivacious woman, quite the opposite of her husband who was known as Silent Cal.

_____ 5. In 1924 the Coolidges' sixteen-year-old son, Calvin Jr., died of blood poisoning from a toe blister that had developed as he was playing tennis.

Practice B
Identify the punctuation missing from each sentence. In the blank write the letter that corresponds to the correct answer.

A. hyphen
B. dash
C. parentheses

_____ 6. Iowa born Herbert Hoover was the first president born west of the Mississippi River.

_____ 7. Hoover an orphan by the time he was eight became the thirty-first president of the United States.

_____ 8. Coin laundry operator, secretary, and typist these were the three jobs that Hoover had to pay his way through college.

_____ 9. Mrs. Hoover who spoke several languages was known as a gracious hostess.

_____ 10. The Great Depression struck during Hoover's first term and probably led to his failure to be reelected as president.

Practice C
Proofread the following paragraph to find the five omissions of hyphens, dashes, and parentheses. Then insert the missing punctuation.

Eighty two days after Franklin D. Roosevelt was elected to his fourth term as president, he died, and Vice President Harry S. Truman became president. Truman was elected to a second term in 1948. In his first term as president of the United States, Truman had to make the most crucial decision that had ever faced a U.S. president, but that decision to drop the new atomic bomb on Japan probably brought a speedy end to World War II. During Truman's second term, the Trumans moved to Blair House late in 1948 the White House was in need of extensive structural repairs and remained there until March of 1952. On November 1, 1950, two would be assassins tried to invade Blair House. One gunman and one Secret Service man were killed Truman was not!

Chapter 1: Personal Letter

Compose a letter to a friend or relative, following the step-by-step instructions below.

Planning

1. Who is your audience?

2. What subjects would your audience find interesting or want to know about?

3. Circle the subjects (from your previous answer) that you intend to cover.

4. What information would you like to get from your audience?

Drafting

5. What concrete details do you want to express for each subject?

   subject _____: _____
   subject _____: _____
   subject _____: _____
   subject _____: _____
   subject _____: _____
   subject _____: _____
   subject _____: _____
   subject _____: _____

6. Remember these tips as you write:
   - Be sincere.
   - Be conversational.
   - Show interest in your reader.
   - Ask open-ended questions, not *yes/no* questions.
   - Use specific details as often as possible.

Revising

7. Reread to make sure that you said what you meant to say.

8. Revise for organization and develop each thought sufficiently.

9. Edit for grammar and punctuation but remember that you may use fragments, contractions, and other informal constructions.

10. Make a final copy.

Chapter 2A: Personal Report

Paraphrasing a Paragraph

Paragraphs 2 and 3 are paraphrases of Paragraph 1. Read each paragraph carefully and decide which paraphrase is better. Be prepared to defend your choice.

Paragraph 1

Publishing on the World Wide Web is not the mystery that people imagine. They see that a person can type a few words at one computer and instantly access information from another computer halfway across the world while, at the same time, thousands of other users are possibly seeing exactly the same information. This ability often overwhelms people, and they fear to participate in the Web. Truly, the Web is amazing, yet publishing on it is neither impossible nor fantastically difficult. Certain common elements are required: First, one needs a computer with both a Web browser and a link to the Web (usually provided by an Internet service provider, or ISP). Then, he needs to find a host computer. The host is a computer that is always on, and on which the website can be stored and with which other computers can view the site. Third, his website must have a registered name and address so that it can be found by other computers. Last, he uses an HTML editor (a program that formats the text, graphics, and links to the standard of the Internet) to design his site. While some vocabulary expansion and time investment are necessary, overall, publishing on the Web is less a work of technological magic and more a work of genuine creative exertion.

Paragraph 2

Putting things on the Web is not as hard as you think. You may wonder at the fact that you can type a few words on your keyboard and get a webpage from another country. But having your own site is just a matter of having a few simple things. You will need a computer with a Web browser, an ISP, a host computer, a registered name and address, and an HTML editor. Putting things on the Web is not magic, just creative exertion.

Paragraph 3

The Internet really is an astounding tool, and many people are amazed and even daunted by the power that it holds. However, using the Internet to publish one's own things is not as hard as it may seem. Certainly, some software and equipment are necessary, and a person will need to learn some new terms. Developing a webpage may take time, but it is not mysterious, and with the proper tools it can be done successfully and without fear.

Chapter 2B: Personal Report

Planning Sheet
Use the following form to plan and write your report.

Topic:

Purpose:

Notes:

Sources:

Thesis Statement:

Report:

Chapter 3: Response to Literature

Planning Sheet
To aid the planning process for your response to literature, answer these questions.

1. What were your initial responses to the story? (Choose as many as apply.)

Positive	*Negative*
• surprised	• saddened
• encouraged	• scared
• relieved	• insulted
• excited	• bored
• pleased	• displeased
• awed	• angered
• other _____	• other _____

2. What Scripture passages would apply to your responses? Consult a concordance if necessary.

3. In deciding which response you would like to describe, list your initial responses below. Then, beside each one, write a reason you felt the way you did. Choose one (or perhaps two or three) to write about in your response to literature.

4. Finally, select a form for your response. With help from your teacher, make a list below of possible forms. After each form, list the strengths and weaknesses of that form as they apply to responding to literature.

    • _____

    strengths:

    weaknesses:

    • _____

    strengths:

    weaknesses:

    • _____

    strengths:

    weaknesses:

Chapter 4: Cause-and-Effect Essay

Planning Sheet

1. Who is my audience?

2. What is my purpose?

3. What does my audience already know about my topic?

4. What specific aspect of my topic will my audience find most interesting?

5. What details will best achieve my purpose?

Chapter 5: Poetry and Metaphor

Getting a Second Opinion
Use this form to analyze and to make suggestions about a classmate's poem.

1. What is the metaphor in the poem?

2. What was logical or illogical about the metaphor?

3. What made the metaphor a vivid and powerful illustration? Or what caused it not to be a vivid and powerful illustration?

4. What was logical or illogical about the writer's use of line divisions?

5. Did the writer use onomatopoeia or alliteration? If so, what effect did the special techniques have?

6. What made the ending of the poem strong or weak?

7. What could be deleted from the poem to make it more compact? Or was it too compact and therefore vague?

8. Other suggestions for improvement:

Chapter 6: Eyewitness Report

Use this form to record your eyewitness report.

Date:

Time:

Place:

People:

Narrative (what happened in chronological order):

Quotations:

Details:

Personal Response:

Chapter 7A: Oral Anecdote

MW Principle

Graph the example paragraphs on page 190 to check for sentence variety. Which one follows the *MW* principle?

First Draft

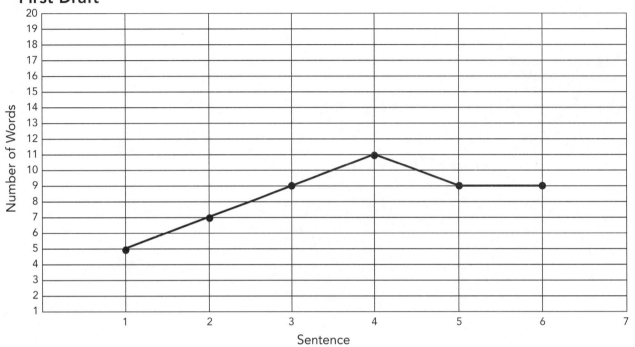

Second Draft

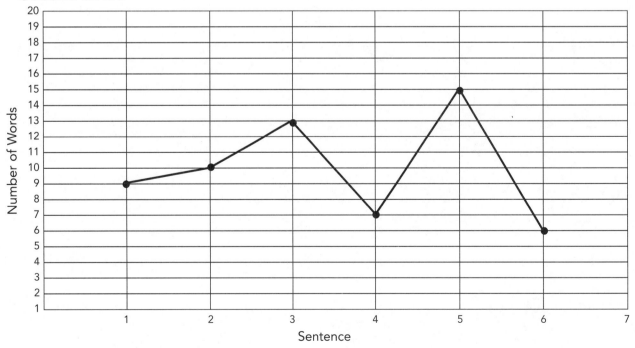

Chapter 7B: Oral Anecdote

MW Principle

Check your oral anecdote for sentence variety. Number each sentence, count the words in each sentence, and then plot the results on the graph below. If your graph does not have the shape of an *M* or a *W*, revise your anecdote to have more sentence variety.

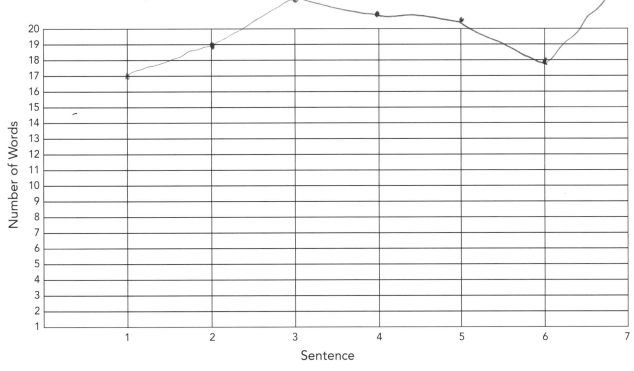

Number of Words

Sentence

Chapter 7C: Oral Anecdote

Checklist
After writing your oral anecdote, check to see whether you have included these key elements.

Topic

☐ Will your reader understand your topic clearly?

Theme

☐ Did you introduce your theme in your introduction? Though the anecdote will be conversational, it should not wander aimlessly. Make sure your theme is obvious but not awkward. Aim for a universal theme that all readers will understand.

Allusion

☐ An allusion is a reference to something outside the work itself. Have you used strong allusions that all your readers will understand?

Common Experience

☐ Have you included common experiences that the reader can relate to? Make the experiences as universal as possible.

Specific Details

☐ Did you include many specific details so that readers get an accurate mental impression of the experience?

Chapter 8: Webpage Design

Evaluating Web Writing
Rate the following criteria, using 5 as the highest possible score and 1 as the lowest.

How would you describe the navigability of the site?   1 2 3 4 5

How compact and condensed was the text?   1 2 3 4 5

How helpful was the text?   1 2 3 4 5

How available was the essential information?   1 2 3 4 5

How readable were the fonts?   1 2 3 4 5

How consistent were the layout and design of the site?   1 2 3 4 5

How would you rate the loading speed of the text and graphics? 1 2 3 4 5

How effective was the site overall at meeting its purpose?   1 2 3 4 5

Other suggestions:

Chapter 9: Short Story

Questions for Peer Response

1. What do you think is the theme of the story?

2. Does the author make his theme evident throughout the story?

3. Is the plot easy to follow?

4. Does the plot move steadily toward a climax?

5. What is the climax of the story?

6. Describe the character conflict.

7. Is the conflict resolved satisfactorily?

8. Are the characters believable? If not, what could the author change?

9. Is the dialogue realistic?

10. Is the narrative viewpoint consistently clear?

11. List one weak area in the story and suggest an improvement.

12. What is the strongest part of the story?

Chapter 10: Research Essay

Paraphrasing

Tips

- Read the selection at least twice. Then step back and verbally summarize the selection to yourself.

- Read the selection again.

- Put the selection aside and, without referring to it, write your paraphrase.

- Look at the selection and revise your paraphrase for basic meaning.

- Make sure that you have used your own words, sentence structure, and ordering of ideas.

- Avoid merely rearranging phrases or sentences; this technique does not produce a paraphrase.

- Some phrases do not necessarily need to be put in your own words because the term or expression is common knowledge and therefore not original with the author. For example, "the queen of England" would not have to be changed to "Britain's monarch."

Example

Original

During the Middle Ages a confusing system of measurements arose in Europe based on thumbs, elbows, feet, and other varying standards. After the rediscovery of Greek learning, French scientists wanted a better, more "rational" standard for describing the world around them. They decided to survey the entire meridian running from Dunkirk (the northernmost city on the coast of France) all the way to Barcelona (a southern city on the coast of Spain). Based on this survey they calculated the distance from the North Pole to the equator. One ten-millionth of this distance was called a *meter*.

France's proud accomplishment proved to be terribly inaccurate. (It was short by about two thousand meters, or 0.02 percent.) The definition of the meter was soon changed from its relationship to the earth to the length of the platinum bar that the Frenchmen had forged. Today's meter has an even more precise definition: the distance light travels in a vacuum in 1/299,792,458 of a second. Obviously, it no longer has any relationship to a measurement of the earth's surface.

(Michael Matthews, Ron Tagliapietra, and Pam Creason. GEOGRAPHY *for Christian Schools.*)

Paraphrase

The modern meter is directly related to an unchanging, accurately measurable standard: the speed of light. However, it was not always so. After the Renaissance, French scientists defined the measurement as one ten-millionth of the supposed distance from the North Pole to the equator. However, their calculations of the earth's circumference, on which this measurement was based, were not accurate. Nevertheless, the idea of a constant, "rational" unit of measure was a significant improvement over the somewhat arbitrary measurement systems of the Middle Ages.

Your Turn
Read the following paragraphs and then write your own paraphrase of them using the information in your book and at the top of the previous page.

Eratosthenes of Cyrene (ca. 276 B.C.–ca. 195 B.C.) had many talents. For instance, he drew an early map of the world, and he compiled a catalog of the stars. In mathematics he is famous for devising a method for finding prime numbers, known as Eratosthenes' sieve. He also directed the world-famous library at Alexandria. But his best-known achievement was his calculation of the circumference of the earth—seventeen hundred years before Columbus discovered America.

To achieve this great feat, Eratosthenes measured the length of shadows at noon on the first day of summer. The sun was at its height in the Egyptian city of Syene (modern Aswan), casting no shadow. But five hundred miles to the north at Alexandria, it cast a measurable shadow. Eratosthenes then drew two imaginary lines from these cities to the center of the earth. Calculating the angle between these lines, he found that Alexandria was approximately one-fiftieth of the earth's circle (a 7.2° angle) north of Syene. Thus, the earth's circumference was fifty times the distance between the two cities.

Finally, Eratosthenes calculated fifty times the 500-mile distance between the two cities. He concluded that the distance around the earth is about 25,000 miles. Today, over two thousand years later, satellite measurements have proved that Eratosthenes was amazingly close to the actual 24,860-mile circumference.

(Michael Matthews, Ron Tagliapietra, and Pam Creason. *GEOGRAPHY for Christian Schools.*)

_____

_____

_____

_____

_____

_____

_____

_____

_____

_____

_____

_____

_____

_____

_____

_____

_____

_____

_____

Chapter 11: Coordination and Subordination

Read through the sentences below, paying special attention to the key ideas. Then use coordination and subordination to rearrange and reorganize the sentences into a coherent paragraph that gives proper emphasis to the key points.

Isaac Watts lived from 1674 to 1748.

Watts was born in Southampton.

He pastored a church in London.

In 1712 he became very sick.

He became a tutor.

Watts eventually became the pastor of a Nonconformist church in London in 1702.

His illness forced him into semiretirement.

He devoted the rest of his life to writing.

He wrote several hundred hymns.

He wrote books on logic.

He wrote children's songs that were very popular.

He is known as the Father of Modern Hymnody.

Watts was a preacher, a poet, a scientist, a theologian, and a philosopher.

Watts's hymns continue to set the standard for excellence in hymns today.

The hymns of Watts are simple and precise.

Watts was born into a family of Dissenters.

Dissenters were also known as Nonconformists.

Dissenters believed that the Church of England had not separated enough from the practices of Rome.

Dissenters were not allowed to attend Cambridge or Oxford, so Watts attended a Nonconformist academy until he was twenty.

In the first two years following the completion of his formal education, Watts produced many of his great hymns.

_____

_____

_____

_____

_____

_____

_____

_____

_____

_____

Chapter 12: Persuasive Speech

Fallacies in Reasoning

But the wisdom that is from above is first pure, then peaceable, gentle, and easy to be intreated, full of mercy and good fruits, without partiality, and without hypocrisy.

James 3:17

Ad Hominem—

attacking a person rather than the issue: "Mr. Marley (Scrooge's opponent) is a greedy old miser. You shouldn't vote for him for governor!" (Mr. Scrooge takes the focus off himself by hurling insults, completely unsupported, at his opponent.)

Hasty Generalization—

basing a conclusion on too little evidence: "Vote for Mr. Scrooge—the man of choice." (One hundred people were interviewed out of the entire state, and sixty-three said they would vote for Mr. Scrooge. These sixty-three were also people who stand to gain personally if he is placed into office.)

Bandwagon or Popular Opinion—

encouraging others to join an allegedly overwhelming majority: "Everyone knows the right answer—join us in voting *yes* for Mr. Scrooge for governor!" (If you don't vote for Mr. Scrooge, the implication is that you are completely out of step with popular culture. But just who is "everyone"?)

Card Stacking—

intentionally presenting only one side of the issue: "Mr. Marley has repeatedly refused to give money to the educational system. Mr. Scrooge promises to increase educational spending." (They fail to mention that Mr. Marley was working under a tight budget at a time when the economy was down. No spending was increased in order to keep the budget balanced. His actions were actually very prudent and beneficial to the state.)

Testimonial—

citing a well-known personality as an authority on something that he or she is not qualified to speak about: "Hello. This is Mr. Local Newscaster and I've just come from lunch with Mr. Scrooge. He is a trustworthy guy, and I know he is the best choice we have. He certainly has my vote!" (The people all know Mr. Local Newscaster, but what does he know about how well Mr. Scrooge will be able to serve the people as governor?)

Chapter 13: Editorial

Choosing a Topic

Asking Questions
Use the questions below to generate more topic ideas.

Who has been in the news recently?

Who is an interesting public figure to me?

Who fights for a cause I agree/disagree with?

What forces in government am I most affected by?

What is most dangerous/helpful to people my age?

What problems does my community struggle with?

When are teenagers most likely to drop out of school?

When do children watch the most television?

When is television watching most harmful/helpful?

How do people most often get hurt?

Where do teenagers spend the most money/time?

How do schools spend the most money/time?

How does a good sibling relationship work?

How does a good friendship work?

Why are some students better learners than others?

Why are some classes more interesting than others?

Why are some things more popular than others?

Why are some people more popular than others?

Why do some people act cruelly towards animals?

Why do some people treat animals like humans?

Or choose a topic from the list you made above and explore it with your own questions. The first words are provided for you.

Who _____?

What _____?

When _____?

Where _____?

How _____?

Why _____?

Chapter 14: Journal Writing

Before you begin writing in your journal, answer the following questions. You may want to write the answers in your journal, making this your first entry, or you may use this exercise to help discover what focus your journal should take.

What is your full name?

When were you born?

Where were you born?

Where are you living now?

Where have you lived?

Do you have any brothers or sisters?

What is something unique about your family?

When were you saved?

Where were you when you realized your need for Christ?

What is God showing you about Himself right now?

Have you seen any answers to prayer lately?

What are you learning from your Bible reading?

What are some prayer requests you have?

Where do you attend church?

List three of your weaknesses and three of your strengths.

Describe a favorite memory.

PERSONAL LETTER

MESSAGE

Tone

3 Letter demonstrates a conversational tone with the reader.
2 Letter demonstrates some attempt to relate to the reader.
1 Letter demonstrates little thought for and connection with the reader.

Organization

3 Letter demonstrates preplanning and contains clear ideas.
2 Letter demonstrates preplanning but contains some random ideas.
1 Letter demonstrates little or no forethought and contains mostly random ideas.

Details

3 Letter includes several specific details.
2 Letter includes occasional, random details.
1 Letter includes generalizations and few details.

_____ **MESSAGE SCORE**

MECHANICS

Letter Form

3 Writer demonstrates correct letter form.
2 Writer demonstrates some knowledge of correct letter form.
1 Writer demonstrates little or no knowledge of correct letter form.

Grammar/Usage

3 Writer demonstrates a command of grade-level grammar skills, including agreement, verb usage, pronoun usage, and sentence structure.
2 Writer demonstrates a basic knowledge of grade-level grammar skills, including agreement, verb usage, pronoun usage, and sentence structure.
1 Writer demonstrates little or no knowledge of grade-level grammar skills.

Spelling

3 Writer uses and spells words above grade level.
2 Writer spells words on grade level.
1 Writer misspells grade-level words.

Capitalization/Punctuation

3 Writer demonstrates a command of grade-level capitalization and punctuation.
2 Writer demonstrates an understanding of grade-level capitalization and punctuation.
1 Writer misuses grade-level capitalization and/or punctuation.

_____ **MECHANICS SCORE**
_____ **TOTAL SCORE (Message plus Mechanics)**

A 19-21   B 16-18   C 13-15   D 10-12   F 7-9

Overall, this writing . . .

PERSONAL REPORT

	MESSAGE
	Purpose 3 Report has a specifically chosen topic and a clear thesis statement. 2 Report has a chosen topic but an unclear thesis statement. 1 Report has no single, clear topic and no discernible thesis statement.
	Organization 3 Report has ideas presented in a logical order with a well-drawn conclusion. 2 Report has ideas presented in random order with no obvious conclusion. 1 Report has little or no logical order.
	Support 3 Report contains well-researched, specifically stated details. 2 Report contains some interesting details. 1 Report contains few if any details.
_____	**MESSAGE SCORE**

	MECHANICS
	Grammar/Usage 3 Writer demonstrates a command of grade-level grammar skills, including agreement, verb usage, pronoun usage, and sentence structure. 2 Writer demonstrates a basic knowledge of grade-level grammar skills, including agreement, verb usage, pronoun usage, and sentence structure. 1 Writer demonstrates little or no knowledge of grade-level grammar skills.
	Spelling 3 Writer uses and spells words above grade level. 2 Writer spells words on grade level. 1 Writer misspells grade-level words.
	Capitalization/Punctuation 3 Writer demonstrates a command of grade-level capitalization and punctuation. 2 Writer demonstrates an understanding of grade-level capitalization and punctuation. 1 Writer misuses grade-level capitalization and/or punctuation.
_____	**MECHANICS SCORE**
_____	**TOTAL SCORE (Message plus Mechanics)**

A 16-18   B 14-15   C 12-13   D 10-11   F 6-9

Overall, this writing . . .

RESPONSE TO LITERATURE

		MESSAGE
1		**Relationship** 3 Response shows a clear relationship between the writer's experience and the literature. 2 Response shows a sufficient relationship between the writer's experience and the literature. 1 Response shows little or no relationship between the writer's experience and the literature.
2		**Organization** 3 Response begins with a synopsis of the literature and concludes by summarizing the writer's response. 2 Response begins with a general reference to the literature and has no specific conclusion. 1 Response begins with little or no reference to the literature and has no apparent conclusion.
1		**Support** 3 Response contains specific details in a logical order. 2 Response contains a few supporting details. 1 Response contains few if any supporting details.
4		**MESSAGE SCORE**

		MECHANICS
2		**Grammar/Usage** 3 Writer demonstrates a command of grade-level grammar skills, including agreement, verb usage, pronoun usage, and sentence structure. 2 Writer demonstrates a basic knowledge of grade-level grammar skills, including agreement, verb usage, pronoun usage, and sentence structure. 1 Writer demonstrates little or no knowledge of grade-level grammar skills.
2		**Spelling** 3 Writer uses and spells words above grade level. 2 Writer spells words on grade level. 1 Writer misspells grade-level words.
3		**Capitalization/Punctuation** 3 Writer demonstrates a command of grade-level capitalization and punctuation. 2 Writer demonstrates an understanding of grade-level capitalization and punctuation. 1 Writer misuses grade-level capitalization and/or punctuation.
7		**MECHANICS SCORE** **TOTAL SCORE (Message plus Mechanics)**

A 16-18   B 14-15   C 12-13   D 10-11   F 6-9

Overall, this writing . . .

CAUSE–AND–EFFECT ESSAY

MESSAGE
Purpose
3 Essay has a specifically chosen topic and a clear audience.
2 Essay has a chosen topic but an unclear audience.
1 Essay has no clear topic and an unclear audience.
Clarity
3 Essay demonstrates a clear cause-and-effect relationship with an obviously defined order.
2 Essay demonstrates a basic cause-and-effect relationship with some sense of order.
1 Essay demonstrates little or no cause-and-effect relationship with little or no sense of order.
Expression
3 Essay displays excellent use of transitions, good supporting examples, and a specifically designed conclusion.
2 Essay displays some use of transitions, some supporting examples, and a sense of conclusion.
1 Essay displays little or no use of transitions, few if any supporting examples, and/or no sense of conclusion.
MESSAGE SCORE

MECHANICS
Grammar/Usage
3 Writer demonstrates a command of grade-level grammar skills, including agreement, verb usage, pronoun usage, and sentence structure.
2 Writer demonstrates a basic knowledge of grade-level grammar skills, including agreement, verb usage, pronoun usage, and sentence structure.
1 Writer demonstrates little or no knowledge of grade-level grammar skills.
Spelling
3 Writer uses and spells words above grade level.
2 Writer spells words on grade level.
1 Writer misspells grade-level words.
Capitalization/Punctuation
3 Writer demonstrates a command of grade-level capitalization and punctuation.
2 Writer demonstrates an understanding of grade-level capitalization and punctuation.
1 Writer misuses grade-level capitalization and/or punctuation.
MECHANICS SCORE
TOTAL SCORE (Message plus Mechanics)

A 16-18   B 14-15   C 12-13   D 10-11   F 6-9

Overall, this writing . . .

POETRY AND METAPHOR

	MESSAGE
	Figurative Language 3 Poem uses metaphors to make strong comparisons. 2 Poem uses metaphors to make adequate comparisons. 1 Poem uses metaphors to make weak comparisons or does not use metaphors at all.
	Convention 3 Poem is written in lines containing abundant condensed speech and a strong variety of word order. 2 Poem is written in lines containing some condensed speech and some variety of word order. 1 Poem is written in lines, but it lacks condensed speech and variety in word order.
	Sound 3 Poem consistently uses sound devices effectively. 2 Poem sometimes uses sound devices effectively. 1 Poem does not use sound devices.
_____	**MESSAGE SCORE**

	MECHANICS
	Grammar/Usage 3 Writer demonstrates a command of grade-level grammar skills, including agreement, verb usage, pronoun usage, and sentence structure. 2 Writer demonstrates a basic knowledge of grade-level grammar skills, including agreement, verb usage, pronoun usage, and sentence structure. 1 Writer demonstrates little or no knowledge of grade-level grammar skills.
	Spelling 3 Writer uses and spells words above grade level. 2 Writer spells words on grade level. 1 Writer misspells grade-level words.
	Capitalization/Punctuation 3 Writer demonstrates a command of grade-level capitalization and punctuation. 2 Writer demonstrates an understanding of grade-level capitalization and punctuation. 1 Writer misuses grade-level capitalization and/or punctuation.
_____ _____	**MECHANICS SCORE** **TOTAL SCORE (Message plus Mechanics)**

A 16-18   B 14-15   C 12-13   D 10-11   F 6-9

Overall, this writing . . .

RUBRICS

EYEWITNESS REPORT

	MESSAGE
	Response 3 Report evidences a personal, intimate connection with the event. 2 Report evidences a distant connection with the event. 1 Report evidences only an objective view of the event.
	Organization 3 Report displays strong chronological order. 2 Report displays adequate chronological order. 1 Report displays no discernible chronological order.
	Details 3 Report includes abundant, accurate details, engaging the reader's five senses. 2 Report includes sufficient, valid details, engaging some of the reader's five senses. 1 Report includes inadequate and/or inaccurate details, engaging one, two, or none of the reader's five senses.
_____	**MESSAGE SCORE**

	MECHANICS
	Grammar/Usage 3 Writer demonstrates a command of grade-level grammar skills, including agreement, verb usage, pronoun usage, and sentence structure. 2 Writer demonstrates a basic knowledge of grade-level grammar skills, including agreement, verb usage, pronoun usage, and sentence structure. 1 Writer demonstrates little or no knowledge of grade-level grammar skills.
	Spelling 3 Writer uses and spells words above grade level. 2 Writer spells words on grade level. 1 Writer misspells grade-level words.
	Capitalization/Punctuation 3 Writer demonstrates a command of grade-level capitalization and punctuation. 2 Writer demonstrates an understanding of grade-level capitalization and punctuation. 1 Writer misuses grade-level capitalization and/or punctuation.
_____	**MECHANICS SCORE**
_____	**TOTAL SCORE (Message plus Mechanics)**

A 16-18   B 14-15   C 12-13   D 10-11   F 6-9

Overall, this writing . . .

ORAL ANECDOTE

	MESSAGE
	Universality 3 Anecdote contains allusions and common experiences that clearly demonstrate universality. 2 Anecdote contains allusions and common experiences that are appropriate. 1 Anecdote does not contain allusions and common experiences, or they do not demonstrate universality.
	Style 3 Anecdote uses a conversational tone and has an attention-getting opening and a dramatic ending. 2 Anecdote uses a mixture of conversational and formal tone and has an appropriate opening and ending. 1 Anecdote uses a formal tone and has a weak opening and a nondramatic ending.
	Details 3 Anecdote includes abundant, accurate details. 2 Anecdote includes sufficient, valid details. 1 Anecdote includes inadequate and/or inaccurate details.
_____	**MESSAGE SCORE**

	MECHANICS
	Grammar/Usage 3 Writer demonstrates a command of grade-level grammar skills, including agreement, verb usage, pronoun usage, and sentence structure. 2 Writer demonstrates a basic knowledge of grade-level grammar skills, including agreement, verb usage, pronoun usage, and sentence structure. 1 Writer demonstrates little or no knowledge of grade-level grammar skills.
	Spelling 3 Writer uses and spells words above grade level. 2 Writer spells words on grade level. 1 Writer misspells grade-level words.
	Capitalization/Punctuation 3 Writer demonstrates a command of grade-level capitalization and punctuation. 2 Writer demonstrates an understanding of grade-level capitalization and punctuation. 1 Writer misuses grade-level capitalization and/or punctuation.
_____ _____	**MECHANICS SCORE** **TOTAL SCORE (Message plus Mechanics)**

A 16-18   B 14-15   C 12-13   D 10-11   F 6-9

Overall, this writing . . .

WEBPAGE DESIGN

	MESSAGE
	Purpose 3 Webpage clearly has a specifically chosen audience, topic, and form. 2 Webpage contains some evidence of a specifically chosen audience, topic, and form. 1 Webpage contains little or no evidence of a specifically chosen audience, topic, and/or form.
	Organization 3 Webpage displays good organization. 2 Webpage displays some organization. 1 Webpage displays only mediocre organization.
	Delivery 3 Webpage demonstrates effective writing and good choices of color and graphics. 2 Webpage demonstrates adequate writing and acceptable choices of color and graphics. 1 Webpage demonstrates inadequate writing and poor choices of color and graphics.
_____	**MESSAGE SCORE**

	MECHANICS
	Grammar/Usage 3 Writer demonstrates a command of grade-level grammar skills, including agreement, verb usage, pronoun usage, and sentence structure. 2 Writer demonstrates a basic knowledge of grade-level grammar skills, including agreement, verb usage, pronoun usage, and sentence structure. 1 Writer demonstrates little or no knowledge of grade-level grammar skills.
	Spelling 3 Writer uses and spells words above grade level. 2 Writer spells words on grade level. 1 Writer misspells grade-level words.
	Capitalization/Punctuation 3 Writer demonstrates a command of grade-level capitalization and punctuation. 2 Writer demonstrates an understanding of grade-level capitalization and punctuation. 1 Writer misuses grade-level capitalization and/or punctuation.
_____	**MECHANICS SCORE**
_____	**TOTAL SCORE (Message plus Mechanics)**

A 16-18 B 14-15 C 12-13 D 10-11 F 6-9

Overall, this writing . . .

SHORT STORY

	MESSAGE
	Elements 3 Story demonstrates excellent development of the six story elements. 2 Story demonstrates some development of the six story elements. 1 Story demonstrates little or no development of the six story elements.
	Content 3 Story contains excellent use of dialogue and/or figurative language. 2 Story contains some use of dialogue and/or figurative language. 1 Story contains little or no use of dialogue and/or figurative language.
	Style (showing v. telling) 3 Story contains many details showing the characters' emotions and motives. 2 Story contains some details showing the characters' emotions and motives. 1 Story contains few if any details showing the characters' emotions and motives.
_____	**MESSAGE SCORE**

	MECHANICS
	Grammar/Usage 3 Writer demonstrates a command of grade-level grammar skills, including agreement, verb usage, pronoun usage, and sentence structure. 2 Writer demonstrates a basic knowledge of grade-level grammar skills, including agreement, verb usage, pronoun usage, and sentence structure. 1 Writer demonstrates little or no knowledge of grade-level grammar skills.
	Spelling 3 Writer uses and spells words above grade level. 2 Writer spells words on grade level. 1 Writer misspells grade-level words.
	Capitalization/Punctuation 3 Writer demonstrates a command of grade-level capitalization and punctuation. 2 Writer demonstrates an understanding of grade-level capitalization and punctuation. 1 Writer misuses grade-level capitalization and/or punctuation.
_____ _____	**MECHANICS SCORE** **TOTAL SCORE (Message plus Mechanics)**

A 16-18   B 14-15   C 12-13   D 10-11   F 6-9

Overall, this writing . . .

RESEARCH ESSAY

MESSAGE

Introduction

3 Introduction contains interesting remarks about the topic, leading to a clear and concise thesis statement.

2 Introduction contains some general remarks about the topic and contains a thesis statement.

1 Introduction contains random remarks about the topic and contains no discernible thesis statement.

Body of Essay

3 Essay development shows a logical arrangement of ideas as well as effective support.

2 Essay development shows a good arrangement of ideas with some support.

1 Essay development shows little or no effective arrangement of ideas and/or little or no support.

Conclusion

3 Conclusion contains a restatement of the thesis and comments that are of interest or are important to the reader.

2 Conclusion contains a general reference to the thesis along with general sentences related to the topic.

1 Conclusion contains little or no reference to the thesis along with random comments.

Research

3 Essay contains abundant information from research and demonstrates accurate citations of sources.

2 Essay contains some information from research and demonstrates accurate citations of sources.

1 Essay contains little or no information from research and/or contains incorrect or incomplete citations of sources.

_____ **MESSAGE SCORE**

MECHANICS

Works Cited Page

3 Writer demonstrates a command of correct and complete format.

2 Writer demonstrates a basic knowledge of correct format.

1 Writer demonstrates little or no knowledge of correct format.

Grammar/Usage

3 Writer demonstrates a command of grade-level grammar skills, including agreement, verb usage, pronoun usage, and sentence structure.

2 Writer demonstrates a basic knowledge of grade-level grammar skills, including agreement, verb usage, pronoun usage, and sentence structure.

1 Writer demonstrates little or no knowledge of grade-level grammar skills.

Spelling

3 Writer uses and spells words above grade level.

2 Writer spells words on grade level.

1 Writer misspells grade-level words.

Capitalization/Punctuation

3 Writer demonstrates a command of grade-level capitalization and punctuation.

2 Writer demonstrates an understanding of grade-level capitalization and punctuation.

1 Writer misuses grade-level capitalization and/or punctuation.

_____ **MECHANICS SCORE**

_____ **TOTAL SCORE (Message plus Mechanics)**

A 21–24   B 18–20   C 15–17   D 12–14   F 8–11

COORDINATION AND SUBORDINATION

	MESSAGE
	Purpose 3 Writing has a clear sense of audience and uses appropriate terminology. 2 Writing has an unclear sense of audience and uses acceptable terminology. 1 Writing has no clear sense of audience and/or uses unacceptable terminology.
	Content 3 Writing provides accurate and abundant details. 2 Writing provides sufficient details. 1 Writing provides few if any details.
	Balance 3 Writing demonstrates an effective balance between coordination and subordination. 2 Writing demonstrates an acceptable amount of both coordination and subordination. 1 Writing fails to demonstrate an acceptable amount of coordination and subordination.
_____	**MESSAGE SCORE**

	MECHANICS
	Grammar/Usage 3 Writer demonstrates a command of grade-level grammar skills, including agreement, verb usage, pronoun usage, and sentence structure. 2 Writer demonstrates a basic knowledge of grade-level grammar skills, including agreement, verb usage, pronoun usage, and sentence structure. 1 Writer demonstrates little or no knowledge of grade-level grammar skills.
	Spelling 3 Writer uses and spells words above grade level. 2 Writer spells words on grade level. 1 Writer misspells grade-level words.
	Capitalization/Punctuation 3 Writer demonstrates a command of grade-level capitalization and punctuation. 2 Writer demonstrates an understanding of grade-level capitalization and punctuation. 1 Writer misuses grade-level capitalization and/or punctuation.
_____	**MECHANICS SCORE**
_____	**TOTAL SCORE (Message plus Mechanics)**

A 16-18   B 14-15   C 12-13   D 10-11   F 6-9

Overall, this writing . . .

PERSUASIVE SPEECH

	MESSAGE
	Introduction and Conclusion 3 Speech contains an interesting introduction and a powerful conclusion. 2 Speech contains an introduction and a conclusion. 1 Speech contains no clear introduction and/or conclusion.
	Logic 3 Speech provides specific evidence and contains no fallacies in reasoning. 2 Speech provides some evidence and contains few fallacies in reasoning. 1 Speech provides little or no evidence and contains significant fallacies in reasoning.
	Presentation 3 Speech is presented with confidence and appeal. 2 Speech is presented adequately. 1 Speech is presented poorly.
_____	**MESSAGE SCORE**

	MECHANICS
	Grammar/Usage 3 Writer demonstrates a command of grade-level grammar skills, including agreement, verb usage, pronoun usage, and sentence structure. 2 Writer demonstrates a basic knowledge of grade-level grammar skills, including agreement, verb usage, pronoun usage, and sentence structure. 1 Writer demonstrates little or no knowledge of grade-level grammar skills.
	Spelling 3 Writer uses and spells words above grade level. 2 Writer spells words on grade level. 1 Writer misspells grade-level words.
	Capitalization/Punctuation 3 Writer demonstrates a command of grade-level capitalization and punctuation. 2 Writer demonstrates an understanding of grade-level capitalization and punctuation. 1 Writer misuses grade-level capitalization and/or punctuation.
_____	**MECHANICS SCORE**
_____	**TOTAL SCORE (Message plus Mechanics)**

A 16-18   B 14-15   C 12-13   D 10-11   F 6-9

Overall, this writing . . .

EDITORIAL

	MESSAGE
	Purpose 3 Editorial has a specific main point and exhibits predetermined organization. 2 Editorial has a general main point and exhibits some organization. 1 Editorial has no clear main point and exhibits little or no organization.
	Persuasion 3 Editorial contains specific reasons in support of the main point. 2 Editorial contains generalities in support of a general idea. 1 Editorial contains little or no support for the topic.
	Appeal 3 Editorial targets a specific audience and uses a friendly tone. 2 Editorial has a general audience and exhibits an uncertain tone. 1 Editorial has little or no sense of audience and exhibits an argumentative tone.
_____	**MESSAGE SCORE**

	MECHANICS
	Grammar/Usage 3 Writer demonstrates a command of grade-level grammar skills, including agreement, verb usage, pronoun usage, and sentence structure. 2 Writer demonstrates a basic knowledge of grade-level grammar skills, including agreement, verb usage, pronoun usage, and sentence structure. 1 Writer demonstrates little or no knowledge of grade-level grammar skills.
	Spelling 3 Writer uses and spells words above grade level. 2 Writer spells words on grade level. 1 Writer misspells grade-level words.
	Capitalization/Punctuation 3 Writer demonstrates a command of grade-level capitalization and punctuation. 2 Writer demonstrates an understanding of grade-level capitalization and punctuation. 1 Writer misuses grade-level capitalization and/or punctuation.
_____	**MECHANICS SCORE**
_____	**TOTAL SCORE (Message plus Mechanics)**

A 16-18   B 14-15   C 12-13   D 10-11   F 6-9

Overall, this writing . . .

	MESSAGE
	Tone 3 Entries demonstrate an informal, conversational tone. 2 Entries demonstrate an acceptable tone. 1 Entries demonstrate little or no sense of proper journalistic tone.
	Content 3 Entries contain personal feelings/thoughts or real-life events. 2 Entries contain some personal thoughts or ideas. 1 Entries contain random ideas with little if any personal thought.
	Details 3 Entries contain several specific details. 2 Entries contain general ideas with some details. 1 Entries contain few if any details.
_____	**MESSAGE SCORE**

	MECHANICS
	Grammar/Usage 3 Writer demonstrates a command of grade-level grammar skills, including agreement, verb usage, pronoun usage, and sentence structure. 2 Writer demonstrates a basic knowledge of grade-level grammar skills, including agreement, verb usage, pronoun usage, and sentence structure. 1 Writer demonstrates little or no knowledge of grade-level grammar skills.
	Spelling 3 Writer uses and spells words above grade level. 2 Writer spells words on grade level. 1 Writer misspells grade-level words.
	Capitalization/Punctuation 3 Writer demonstrates a command of grade-level capitalization and punctuation. 2 Writer demonstrates an understanding of grade-level capitalization and punctuation. 1 Writer misuses grade-level capitalization and/or punctuation.
_____	**MECHANICS SCORE**
_____	**TOTAL SCORE (Message plus Mechanics)**

A 16-18   B 14-15   C 12-13   D 10-11   F 6-9

Overall, this writing . . .

Chapter 1 Pretest: Parts of Speech

I. Nouns and Pronouns
Underline each noun once and each pronoun twice.

1. *The Four Seasons* is one of my favorite orchestral pieces.

2. Who knows whether it was the Italian composer Antonio Vivaldi who wrote that?

3. Vivaldi himself lived from 1678 to 1741, but the music he wrote lives on today.

4. All of the music Vivaldi composed is in the baroque style.

5. Regular rhythm and elaborate melody complement each other in baroque music.

II. Verbs
Underline each verb and identify it as *action* or *state-of-being*.

action   6. Vivaldi did influence Bach.

action   7. A progressive musician, Vivaldi developed the concerto.

state-of-being   8. The concerto is a composition for a small orchestra with a solo lead instrument.

action   9. My friend George has heard all 230 Vivaldi violin concertos.

state-of-being   10. Vivaldi remained a prolific composer for many years.

III. Adjectives
Underline each adjective. Then draw an arrow from each adjective to the word it modifies.

11. Some consider the Italian composer and violinist superb.

12. Vivaldi's baroque compositions are brilliant.

13. His early training was from his father, who was also a competent violinist.

14. Then Vivaldi, talented and dedicated, studied with Giovanni Legrenzi, a violin master.

15. Legrenzi composed several operas, and he is famous for his trio sonatas.

IV. Adverbs

Underline each adverb. Then draw an arrow from each adverb to the word it modifies.

16. <u>Later</u>, in 1703, Vivaldi was ordained as a priest; <u>however</u>, he gave his life <u>wholeheartedly</u> to music.

17. Vivaldi had <u>very</u> red hair, which <u>eventually</u> earned him the nickname "the Red Priest."

18. Vivaldi did <u>not</u> conduct a mass because a chronic illness <u>unfortunately</u> made breathing <u>very</u> difficult.

19. <u>Also</u> in 1703, he was appointed violin master at the Pietà, an orphanage for girls, and there he <u>enthusiastically</u> taught the violin and <u>industriously</u> wrote music.

20. For the rest of his life, Vivaldi <u>constantly</u> remained in contact with the Pietà.

V. Prepositions

Underline the prepositions once and the object of each preposition twice.

21. <u>In</u> <u>1711</u> Vivaldi published his first influential concertos <u>for</u> string <u>orchestra</u>.

22. <u>After</u> a few <u>years</u>, the choirmaster <u>of</u> the <u>Pietà</u> left, vacating a position Vivaldi helped to fill.

23. <u>At</u> this <u>time</u> Vivaldi began writing vocal pieces <u>for</u> the <u>choir</u>.

24. These successful sacred works written <u>during</u> this <u>time</u> earned him commissions <u>from</u> several other <u>institutions</u>.

25. His first opera was produced <u>in</u> <u>Vicenza</u> <u>in</u> <u>1713</u>.

VI. Conjunctions and Interjections

Underline each conjunction once. Then identify each conjunction as *coordinating*, *correlative*, or *subordinating*. Underline each interjection twice.

<u>*subordinating*</u>   26. <u>Well</u>, Vivaldi preferred to work as a freelance composer <u>because</u> he preferred the flexibility it offered.

<u>*coordinating*</u>   27. In the 1720s Vivaldi lived in Venice <u>but</u> frequently traveled throughout Europe to supply music to various customers <u>and</u> patrons.

<u>*correlative*</u>   28. <u>Wow</u>! Vivaldi wrote <u>not only</u> for the violin <u>but also</u> for woodwind instruments.

<u>*subordinating*</u>   29. <u>While</u> Vivaldi's music declined in popularity before his death, many of his compositions, such as *The Four Seasons,* are very popular today.

<u>*coordinating*</u>   30. Melodic <u>and</u> powerful, *The Four Seasons* is a programmatic piece describing a landscape.

Name_____

Chapter 2 Pretest: Sentences

I. Finding the Subjects and Predicates

Underline the subject once and the predicate twice. If the subject of the sentence is understood, write the understood *you* to the left of the number.

1. Have you heard John Rutter's *Requiem?*

2. Here is a Rutter recording.

You 3. Listen to this.

4. Rutter's *Requiem* was composed in 1985 and was first performed in October of that year.

5. The seven sections of the work have an archlike structure.

6. The first and last movements take the form of prayers on the behalf of all humanity.

7. The second and sixth sections are psalms.

8. The third section and the fifth movement are personal prayers to Christ.

9. The very center of the work, the fourth section, affirms the holiness and glory of God.

You 10. Tell me your opinion of it.

II. Identifying Types of Sentences

Identify each sentence as *declarative, exclamatory, imperative,* or *interrogative.* Insert the appropriate end punctuation for each sentence.

_____*interrogative*_____ 11. What is a requiem?

_____*declarative*_____ 12. It is a hymn, composition, or service in memory of the dead.

_____*declarative*_____ 13. The word *requiem* comes from the Latin word *requiēs,* meaning "rest."

_____*interrogative*_____ 14. Did you know this musical tradition began around A.D. 1200?

_____*declarative*_____ 15. In A.D. 998 the abbot of Cluny instituted the Requiem Mass, which became more common when the Catholic Church officially embraced the doctrine of purgatory two hundred years later.

_____*interrogative*_____ 16. What does the Catholic service have to do with the musical compositions?

_____*imperative*_____ 17. Keep reading.

_____*declarative*_____ 18. The Requiem Mass, given on All Souls' Day, November 2, is a prayer for Christ to free the deceased from purgatory and to grant them eternal rest in heaven.

_____*declarative*_____ 19. The Bible does not support the existence of purgatory, by the way.

_____*exclamatory*_____ 20. This study of music history is fascinating!

III. Analyzing Sentence Patterns

Label the sentence patterns *S-InV*, *S-TrV-DO*, *S-TrV-IO-DO*, *S-LV-PN*, *S-LV-PA*, *S-TrV-DO-OC*, or *S-be-Advl*. If the adverbial is a prepositional phrase, underline it.

                                   S   **TrV**   **DO**

21. Several other famous composers wrote requiems.

               S   **LV**   **PA**

22. Mozart's *Requiem* was not complete at his death in 1791.

            S   **TrV**   **IO**   **DO**

23. His pupil Süssmayr gave the unfinished work an ending.

    S   **TrV**   **DO**   **OC**

24. Many consider Süssmayr's ending the best.

       S   **InV**

25. Some works known as requiems differ from true requiems.

           S   **TrV**   **DO**

26. Brahms's *German Requiem* does not use the Latin text.

                          S LV   **PN**

27. A commemoration for someone deceased, it is still a requiem.

   S   **TrV DO**

28. Brahms wrote it for his mother.

       S   **TrV**   **DO**

29. Brahms's requiem, like Rutter's, contains biblical texts.

     S   **be**   **Advl**

30. His recording is <u>on my desk</u>.

Chapter 3 Pretest: Phrases

I. Prepositional Phrases

Underline each prepositional phrase. Draw an arrow from each prepositional phrase to the word it modifies.

1. Africa is the continent with the second largest land area and the third largest population.

2. This vast continent contains an amazing variety of wild animals.

3. In the east, buffalo, antelope, giraffes, and zebras roam the plains.

4. A few large elephant herds live in the east and the southeast.

5. Baboons can be found throughout Africa.

II. Misplaced Prepositional Phrases

Underline each misplaced prepositional phrase. Then rewrite each sentence with the prepositional phrase in its correct location.

6. The photographer pointed his camera at the baboons with the expensive equipment.

   The photographer with the expensive equipment pointed his camera at the baboons.

7. The camera in the tree awakened the baboon.

   The camera awakened the baboon in the tree.

8. Sitting perfectly still, the baboon carefully watched the photographer with his eyes half open.

   Sitting perfectly still with his eyes half open, the baboon carefully watched the photographer.

9. The photographer nervously snapped another photo of the baboon with shaking hands.

   With shaking hands, the photographer nervously snapped another photo of the baboon.

10. In one rapid motion, the baboon grabbed a piece of fruit and hurled it at the intrusive photographer from the tree.

    In one rapid motion, the baboon grabbed a piece of fruit from the tree and hurled it at the intrusive photographer.

Chapter 3 Pretest: Phrases (continued)

III. Appositive Phrases
Underline each appositive or appositive phrase. Then identify the word that each appositive renames.

Baboons   11. Baboons, <u>a type of large monkey</u>, have canine teeth and doglike muzzles.

diet   12. These animals have an interesting diet: <u>eggs, fruit, grass, insects, and roots</u>.

Mandrills   13. Mandrills, <u>large and colorful monkeys</u>, are very similar to baboons.

males   14. The colorful males protect the pack <u>themselves</u>.

mandrill   15. Not much is known about the mandrill, <u>a shy and quick creature</u>.

IV. Verbal Phrases
Underline each verbal or verbal phrase. Then identify each verbal or verbal phrase as a gerund (G), a participle (P), or an infinitive (I).

P   16. In central and southern Africa, Black and White rhinoceros are <u>endangered</u> species.

G   17. <u>Selling rhinoceros' horns</u> brings poachers money on the black market.

G   18. Tribes in Yemen use the horns for <u>the making of dagger handles</u>.

P   19. African elephants are the largest <u>living</u> land animals.

I   20. Hunters kill the African elephants <u>to take their tusks</u>.

G   21. The elephants' valuable ivory tusks invite <u>poaching</u>.

I   22. The pygmy hippopotamus is an animal <u>to be protected</u> if the species is <u>to last</u>.

I   23. The number of pygmy hippopotamuses is starting <u>to decline rapidly</u>.

G   24. <u>Selling the hippo meat</u> brings a large profit to the hunters.

I   25. Cheetahs are hunted <u>to secure their rare fur</u>.

P   26. <u>Considered a magnificent and bizarre creature</u>, the giraffe can be found only in the arid plains of Africa.

P   27. <u>Living up to twenty-five years</u>, giraffes may reach eighteen feet tall and may weigh as much as three thousand pounds.

G   28. <u>Having never seen giraffes before</u> caused people's assumption that the animals were a cross between a leopard and a camel.

I   29. Giraffes like <u>to eat foliage from acacia trees</u>.

I   30. A testimony to the creativity of God, the unique and graceful giraffe is a wonderful creature <u>to see</u>.

V. Misplaced and Dangling Participial Phrases
Underline each misplaced or dangling participial phrase. Then rewrite each sentence correctly.

31. Living in a wide variety of habitats, the African mainland contains many leopards.

    The African mainland contains many leopards living in a wide variety of habitats.

32. Having highly prized fur, hunters kill leopards.

    Hunters kill leopards having highly prized fur.

33. Hunting them as game, the Cape Mountain zebra has become an endangered species.

    Hunting them as game, poachers have made the Cape Mountain zebra an endangered species.

34. Declining rapidly in number, farmland is taking over the habitat of pygmy chimpanzees.

    Farmland is taking over the habitat of pygmy chimpanzees, declining rapidly in number.

35. Hunters are the most dangerous predators of African wildlife, seeking material gain.

    Hunters seeking material gain are the most dangerous predators of African wildlife.

Chapter 4 Pretest: Clauses

I. Distinguishing Independent and Dependent Clauses
Place parentheses around each dependent clause. Some sentences may not contain a dependent clause.

1. The World Cup is played once every four years.

2. It is the ultimate prize (that the world of soccer offers.)

3. Each country sends its national team, (whose players have been playing together for years.)

4. The World Cup has been played every four years since 1930.

5. Each time (it is played,) the drama of the event is new and different.

II. Kinds of Dependent Clauses
Identify each italicized group of words as an adjective clause (Adj), an adverb clause (Adv), or a noun clause (Noun).

__Adv__ 6. *Because soccer is a popular sport,* many countries submit teams to the event.

__Adj__ 7. Only the countries *that cooperate with FIFA* can play in the World Cup.

__Adj__ 8. FIFA is the international body *that governs the World Cup, as well as soccer in general, around the globe.*

__Adv__ 9. FIFA is an acronym, *since the letters correspond to the first letters of its longer name: the Fédération Internationale de Football Association.*

__Noun__ 10. *That it was established in 1904* is often surprising to people.

III. Adjective Clauses
A. Place parentheses around each adjective clause.
B. Underline each relative pronoun once.
C. Underline each relative adverb twice.
D. In the blank write the word that the adjective clause modifies.

__Soccer__ 11. Soccer, (which is now played by more nations than any other team sport,) is also one of the world's oldest sports.

__England__ 12. In A.D. 217, the first recorded soccer game was played in England, (where the natives had just won a battle over the invading Romans.)

__celebration__ 13. It was part of a victory celebration (that they had.)

__reason__ 14. The people apparently enjoyed the game immensely, and this is the reason (why it soon became an annual event.)

__fans__ 15. By the late twentieth century, the fans (who loved soccer) had made it popular enough for the illustrious World Cup and the Olympics.

IV. Adverb Clauses

Place parentheses around each adverb clause. Underline each subordinating conjunction. In the blank write the word that the adverb clause modifies.

are 16. (<u>Although</u> the sport is popular around the world,)soccer teams from Europe and South America are traditionally the best.

has won 17. Brazil has won the World Cup many times,(<u>while</u> the United States has never won it.)

led 18. The world-renowned Pelé led Brazil to many titles in the 1960s and 1970s (<u>because</u> he had amazing ball-handling skills.)

can recognize 19. (<u>Inasmuch as</u> Italy too has sported great teams,)one can recognize the great love of the game in that country also.

has been 20. England's soccer tradition,(<u>if</u> it has not been dominant,)has certainly been long and rich.

V. Noun Clauses

A. Place parentheses around each noun clause.
B. Identify the function of each noun clause as subject *(S)*, predicate noun *(PN)*, direct object *(DO)*, indirect object *(IO)*, object of the preposition *(OP)*, or appositive *(App)*.
C. Underline each subordinating conjunction once.
D. Underline each indefinite relative pronoun twice.

DO 21. Some people do not realize(<u>that</u> some teams tend to dominate the World Cup more than others.)

PN 22. One reason for the dominance is(<u>that</u> the sport is extremely important in the countries with successful teams.)

OP 23. Many fans follow their team to(<u>wherever</u> it is playing.)

App 24. One angry fan assaulted a police officer for a very petty reason,(<u>that</u> he was not able to obtain a ticket to see his team play.)

S 25. (<u>Who</u> started the 1969 Soccer War between El Salvador and Honduras)is still a mystery.

Chapter 4 Pretest: Clauses (continued)

VI. Using Independent and Dependent Clauses
Identify each sentence as simple (S), compound (Cd), complex (Cx), or compound-complex (Cd-Cx).

Cd 26. France also has produced a dominant European team on occasion, but it could not win the World Cup until 2000.

S 27. The English professional league, with its colorful cast of characters, is famous around the world.

Cx 28. In the United States, where American football, a derivative of rugby, dominates, soccer has taken a back seat.

Cd-Cx 29. My uncle showed me where to strike the ball when I am shooting, and he demonstrated the kick himself.

Cx 30. He played as a forward in Scotland when he was younger.

VII. Avoiding Errors
Identify each group of words as a sentence (S), a fragment (F), a comma splice (CS), or a fused sentence (FS).

S 31. Because my uncle started playing when he was very young, he became a professional soccer player upon graduation from high school.

F 32. Although he is very quick with the ball even now.

CS 33. His shot is still very powerful and accurate, it was even better when he was younger, however.

FS 34. He twisted his ankle in a match in Scotland then he decided to retire and return to the United States.

CS 35. Now he coaches Little League soccer at a YMCA, he started doing that about five years ago.

Chapter 5 Pretest: Agreement

I. Subjects and Predicates

Underline the subject(s) in each sentence. Then underline the correct verb from the choices in parentheses.

1. There (is, _are_) many eye _disorders_ resulting in a partial loss of sight.

2. Either an age-related _disease_ or a genetic _mutation_ (_causes_, cause) blindness.

3. Stargardt's _disease_, a form of macular degeneration, (_occurs_, occur) rarely.

4. What (_is_, are) the _cause_ of Stargardt's disease?

5. This particular _type_ of macular degeneration (_is_, are) genetic.

6. Both _teenagers_ and young _children_ (develops, _develop_) Stargardt's.

7. A mutated _gene_ (_causes_, cause) the transport protein to malfunction.

8. The _eye_, in processing light, (_produces_, produce) a byproduct called spent retinal.

9. In a pair of healthy eyes, the transport _proteins_ (is, _are_) the removers of the spent retinal, carrying the waste away from the eye.

10. _Eyes_ with Stargardt's (retains, _retain_) the byproduct, a malfunction causing deposits to form on the retina with a high concentration on the macula.

II. Problem Nouns and Pronouns

Underline the subject(s) in each sentence. Then underline the correct verb from the choices in parentheses.

11. _Anybody_ with healthy eyes (_uses_, use) his macula, a small tissue on the retina, for clear, detailed central vision.

12. _Someone_ with Stargardt's (_has_, have) a hard time recognizing people's faces and reading small print.

13. _Little_ (_is_, are) known about Stargardt's.

14. There (is, _are_) no known _cures_ for Stargardt's.

15. _Eyeglasses_ (is, _are_) helpful.

16. One _pair_ of her glasses (_is_, are) for reading.

17. _Many_ (uses, _use_) magnifiers and other low-vision aids to read.

18. _The American Heritage Dictionary_ (_defines_, define) blindness as "having a maximal visual acuity of the better eye, after correction by refractive lenses, of one-tenth normal vision or less."

19. Legal _blindness_ (_prohibits_, prohibit) driving.

20. _Eleven years_ (has, _have_) passed since Danielle's diagnosis.

III. Pronoun-Antecedent Agreement
Write the correct pronoun to complete each sentence.

_____**their**_____ 21. Both Dianna and Deborah have lost some of _?_ sight because of Stargardt's disease.

_____**her**_____ 22. Neither Dianna nor Deborah has allowed the loss of sight to limit _?_.

_____**her**_____ 23. God has blessed the sisters, giving each of the girls _?_ own talents.

_____**her**_____ 24. Deborah is a track star and the starting center of _?_ soccer team.

_____**she**_____ 25. Dianna rides horses, and _?_ has acted in major roles in several plays.

_____**them**_____ 26. No matter how imperfect eyes with Stargardt's may seem, God created _?_ in His absolute sovereignty.

_____**His**_____ 27. God has lovingly promised to supply _?_ sufficient grace.

_____**his**_____ 28. Everybody needs God's strength to overcome _?_ weaknesses, both spiritual and physical.

_____**he**_____ 29. No matter what someone struggles with, _?_ can look to God for help and comfort.

_____**Him**_____ 30. God is glorified when we admit our inadequacy and lean wholly on _?_.

Chapter 6 Pretest: Verb Use

I. Auxiliaries and Principal Parts

Underline each complete verb. Then write *Aux* above each auxiliary. Be prepared to identify the principal part of the verb and to tell whether the verb is regular or irregular.

1. What <u>does</u> *(Aux)* the word *inventor* <u>mean</u> to you?

2. Many people immediately <u>think</u> of Thomas Edison or Alexander Graham Bell.

3. However, people <u>are</u> *(Aux)* <u>inventing</u> new things even today.

4. Professional inventors <u>have</u> *(Aux)* often <u>worked</u> for companies to make new or improved products.

5. Some inventors <u>wrote</u> about their research and its results.

II. Simple and Perfect Tenses

Identify each italicized verb as *present, past, future, present perfect, past perfect,* or *future perfect.*

_____**past**_____ 6. Many famous inventors *began* their careers early.

_____**present perfect**_____ 7. The NCIIA, an association to help collegiate inventors get their works off the ground, *has awarded* many cash prizes to inventors for high-quality work.

_____**present**_____ 8. Also, some young minds *work* with companies to create practical products for commercial sale.

_____**past perfect**_____ 9. Once the inventor *had made* his invention, he was quick to obtain a patent.

_____**future**_____ 10. The patent *will protect* his invention from being copied by someone else.

III. Progressive Tenses

Identify each italicized verb as *present progressive, past progressive, future progressive, present perfect progressive, past perfect progressive,* or *future perfect progressive.*

__**present progressive**__ 11. Joey's new automatic garage door opener *is developing* into a real improvement.

__**present perfect progressive**__ 12. In his tests, it *has been opening* regularly when the sensor installed on the car approached.

__**future perfect progressive**__ 13. By next month, he *will have been working* on the system for two years.

__**past progressive**__ 14. When the car had moved far enough inside and the engine had been turned off, the door *was closing* just as it should.

__**future progressive**__ 15. Soon, a company *will be manufacturing* his invention.

IV. Voice
Underline the verb in each clause. Then identify the verb as either *active* or *passive*.

_____*active*_____ 16. Joey promptly <u>obtained</u> a patent for his work.

_____*passive*_____ 17. A patent attorney <u>was called</u>, and all the work <u>was handled</u> for him.

_____*active*_____ 18. The attorney <u>did charge</u> an expensive fee.

_____*active*_____ 19. Hopefully, the invention <u>will pay</u> for the patent and the attorney fees.

_____*passive*_____ 20. Now a new glow mechanism for bicycles, capable of covering the entire bike, <u>is being developed</u> by Joey.

V. Mood
Identify the mood of the italicized verb as *indicative*, *imperative*, or *subjunctive*.

_____*subjunctive*_____ 21. If he *had been able* to finish it by December, it would have been in the stores by next summer.

_____*indicative*_____ 22. If I buy one, it *will be* the neon green color.

_____*imperative*_____ 23. Never *go riding* at night without reflectors!

_____*indicative*_____ 24. Now, with reflectors and Joey's new nighttime glow mechanism, the entire bike *will glow* like fire.

_____*imperative*_____ 25. Even though he has just started to work on it, *tell* him I will buy one when he's done.

Chapter 7 Pretest: Pronoun Reference

I. Ambiguous and Remote Reference
Underline each pronoun that refers to an ambiguous or remote antecedent. Then rewrite the problem sentence correctly, replacing the unclear pronoun with the intended antecedent. *(Answers may vary.)*

1. The ancestors of the people living in the Philippines are from Indonesia and Malaysia. <u>They</u> are called Filipinos.

   People living in the Philippines are called Filipinos.

2. Farming, which involves wealthy landowners and laborers, is a major industry in the Philippines. <u>They</u> make up about 40 percent of the Filipino working population.

   Farm laborers make up about 40 percent of the Filipino working population.

3. A close relationship with family members is very important in the Philippines, and Filipinos keep in contact with many distant relatives. <u>It</u> includes distant cousins and extended family members.

   This close relationship includes distant cousins and extended family members.

4. Small rural homes often have wooden walls and thatched roofs, but wealthy city families live in large homes. <u>They</u> are often surrounded by a wall.

   Large city homes are often surrounded by a wall.

5. Gardening is popular in the Philippines, and Filipinos love growing flowers wherever they can. <u>It</u> is done in both rural and urban areas.

   Gardening is done in both rural and urban areas.

Chapter 7 Pretest: Pronoun Reference (continued)

II. Reference to an Implied Noun or to a Noun That Is a Modifier
Rewrite each sentence to correct any unclear pronoun reference. (Answers will vary.)

6. If you visit the Philippines, you will probably notice that their food is often highly seasoned.

   If you visit the Philippines, you will probably notice that the Filipino's food is often highly seasoned.

7. In a popular chicken and pork dish called *adobe,* it is cooked in soy sauce and vinegar.

   In a popular dish called adobe, *chicken and pork are cooked in soy sauce and vinegar.*

8. The abundance of Western clothing worn in the Philippines shows their influence on Filipino culture.

   The abundance of Western clothing worn in the Philippines shows the influence of the West on

   Filipino culture.

9. The Philippine Constitution gives them freedom of worship.

   The Philippine Constitution gives Filipinos freedom of worship.

10. About 85 percent of Filipinos are Roman Catholic, and it is more widespread in the Philippines than in any other Asian country.

    About 85 percent of Filipinos are Roman Catholic, and Roman Catholicism is more widespread

    in the Philippines than in any other Asian country.

III. Indefinite Reference of Personal Pronouns
Rewrite each sentence to correct any unclear pronoun reference. (Answers will vary.)

11. They say that the literacy rate in the Philippines is 90 percent.

    Statistics report that the literacy rate in the Philippines is 90 percent.

12. In the Philippines, about 30 percent of them go to college.

    In the Philippines, about 30 percent of Filipinos go to college.

13. In most schools and universities, they teach English as well as Filipino.

    In most schools and universities, instructors teach English as well as Filipino.

14. If you want to learn about Filipino political literature in the 1900s, you should read works by José Rizal.

    A person who wants to learn about Filipino political literature in the 1900s should read works by

    José Rizal.

15. In these works, it talks about the need for national independence.

    These works discuss the need for national independence.

IV. Reference to a Broad Idea

Rewrite each problem sentence to correct any unclear pronoun reference. If the sentence is already clear, write C in the blank. *(Answers will vary.)*

16. The well-known Mayon volcano is located in the Philippines. This is a beautiful sight.

    A view of the volcano is a beautiful sight.

17. Mount Mayon's volcanic cone is perfectly shaped, and it is one of the most beautiful volcanic cones in the world.

    C

18. The area surrounding the volcano is mostly flat; this allows the cone to be seen for miles.

    The area surrounding the volcano is mostly flat; this landscape allows the cone to be seen for miles.

19. The volcano has erupted over forty times in the past four hundred years, and it can be devastating.

    The volcano has erupted over forty times in the past four hundred years; the effects of the eruptions

    can be devastating.

20. Mount Mayon erupted on July 25, 2001, and this caused about forty-six thousand people to be evacuated.

    Mount Mayon erupted on July 25, 2001, and the eruption caused about forty-six thousand people to be

    evacuated.

Chapter 8 Pretest: Pronoun Use

I. Pronoun Case: Personal Pronouns
Underline each personal pronoun and identify it as subjective (S), objective (O), possessive (P), or independent possessive (IP).

_____**S**_____ 1. Because lions, tigers, and ligers are large cats, <u>they</u> interest many people.

_____**O**_____ 2. The guide told <u>us</u> that tigers, like other cats, are not extremely sociable animals.

_____**S**_____ 3. <u>They</u> prefer to hunt and live alone.

_____**P**_____ 4. Lions travel in <u>their</u> prides, which sometimes contain as many as thirty lions.

_____**IP**_____ 5. Many adult lions have spots that are faded and hard to see; a liger's spots are more visible than <u>theirs</u>.

II. Pronoun Case: Compounds, Appositives, and Comparisons
Underline the correct pronoun from the choices in parentheses.

6. This wildlife preserve has both lions and tigers. Although he is an expert on lions, our guide enjoys the tigers as much as *(they, <u>them</u>)*.

7. Our guide told the first-time visitors—Judy and *(I, <u>me</u>)*—that the Gir Forest region of India is the only area of the world where the habitats of lions and tigers overlap.

8. *(<u>We</u>, Us)* students were surprised to see a liger, a hybrid of a lion and a tiger, at the park.

9. Because this liger has a lionlike mane, Judy told Mom and *(I, <u>me</u>)* that it was a lion.

10. Tigers are not known to roar; ligers roar much better than *(<u>they</u>, them)*.

III. Pronoun Case: *Who* vs. *Whom*
Underline the correct pronoun from the choices in parentheses.

11. *(<u>Who</u>, Whom)* asked the guide about this liger?

12. The guide *(who, <u>whom</u>)* we met this morning said that nearly all hybrids are sterile.

13. *(<u>Who</u>, Whom)* do you think is the more knowledgeable guide?

14. The visitor *(<u>who</u>, whom)* asked about the name of the exhibit is my neighbor.

15. The contributors for *(who, <u>whom</u>)* the liger exhibit is named have donated money to the wildlife preserve.

IV. Courtesy Order and Correct Use of Reflexive and Intensive Pronouns
Underline the correct pronoun or pronouns from the choices in parentheses.

16. Between (*you and me*, *me and you*), facing a lion alone in the wild would be a hair-raising experience!

17. Lions (*they*, *themselves*) can weigh 400 pounds, and tigers often weigh 650 pounds, but the sign says that this liger weighs approximately 800 pounds!

18. You should be careful not to allow (*you*, *yourself*) to get too close to that wall.

19. Mom took a picture of Judy and (*me*, *myself*) in front of the liger exhibit.

20. We will take (*you and D'Andre*, *D'Andre and you*) to the wildlife preserve next month.

Chapter 9 Pretest: Adjective and Adverb Use

I. Comparison with Adjectives
Write the correct form of the adjective in parentheses.

__*more interesting*__ 1. Tom finds his world history class (*interesting*) than his biology class.

__*biggest*__ 2. His class is studying one of the (*big*) wars of all time.

__*most fascinating*__ 3. The teacher gave the (*fascinating*) presentation of the Hundred Years' War that Tom had ever heard.

__*long*__ 4. The war was (*long*), lasting from 1337 to 1453.

__*longer*__ 5. There is not a (*long*) war recorded in history.

II. Comparison with Adverbs
Write the correct form of the adverb in parentheses.

__*slowly*__ 6. For a long time before the war, tension between England and France mounted (*slowly*).

__*constantly*__ 7. They battled (*constantly*) over English holdings in France.

__*more regularly*__ 8. One valuable territory, Flanders, profited England (*regularly*) than other territories because of its thriving wool trade.

__*persistently*__ 9. France (*persistently*) tried to gain control of Flanders.

__*the most offensively*__ 10. From France's perspective, the English acted (*offensively*) when England's King Edward III claimed the throne of France.

III. Irregular Comparison of Adjectives and Adverbs
Underline the correct adjective or adverb from the choices in parentheses.

11. The English won (*more*, *most*) battles over the French than the French won over the English.

12. The French fought (*bad*, *badly*) but still managed to win the war.

13. Unlike the English, the French were supplied (*good*, *well*).

14. One of the (*worse*, *worst*) French defeats was at the battle of Crécy.

15. Even though the English were greatly outnumbered, they performed (*good*, *well*) because they were well organized and had the aid of new weaponry—the cannon and the longbow.

IV. Problems with Modifiers
Rewrite each sentence to make the modifiers clear and correct.

16. After an even more worse French defeat in 1356, a treaty in 1360 ended the first phase of the war.

    After an even worse French defeat in 1356, a treaty in 1360 ended the first phase of the war.

17. The political scene in England remained unstably after the Peasants' Revolt in 1381.

    The political scene in England remained unstable after the Peasants' Revolt in 1381.

18. Becoming more weaker from a lack of resources, the English gradually lost much of the land they had in France.

    Becoming weaker from a lack of resources, the English gradually lost much of the land they had

    in France.

19. King Henry V of England, whose determined spirit could not be stopped by no one, won a decisive victory over France at the battle of Agincourt.

    King Henry V of England, whose determined spirit could not be stopped by anyone, won a decisive

    victory over France at the battle of Agincourt.

20. Despite Henry V's marriage to Princess Catherine of France, French and English relations remained tenuously.

    Despite Henry V's marriage to Princess Catherine of France, French and English relations remained

    tenuous.

Chapter 9 Pretest: Adjective and Adverb Use (continued)

V. Placement of Modifiers
Rewrite each sentence to make the modifiers clear and correct. *(Answers may vary.)*

21. Henry V's dying quickly caused war to erupt again.

    Henry V's dying caused war to erupt again quickly.

    _____

    _____

22. Rallying around the French peasant Joan of Arc, the tides began to turn in favor of the French troops.

    The tides began to turn in favor of the French troops, rallying around the French peasant Joan of Arc.

    _____

    _____

23. By 1453 the English only had one holding left in Europe, a territory they later lost in 1458.

    By 1453 the English had only one holding left in Europe, a territory they later lost in 1458.

    _____

    _____

24. After the war English kings were able to without distraction focus on building a strong nation.

    After the war English kings were able to focus without distraction on building a strong nation.

    _____

    _____

25. As a result of the war, the nobility began to lose gradually its power as the centralized government gained strength.

    As a result of the war, the nobility gradually began to lose its power as the centralized government

    gained strength.

    _____

Chapter 10 Pretest: Capitalization

I. People and Places
Underline each word containing a capitalization error.

1. There are unique facts about the various states of the <u>united states</u> of <u>america</u>.

2. Arizona is located in the <u>Southwest</u> part of the United States.

3. My neighbor's hometown, <u>tucson</u>, <u>arizona</u>, is famous for its association with astronomy.

4. On <u>kitt peak</u> near <u>tucson</u> is the largest solar telescope in the world.

5. In <u>flagstaff</u>, <u>arizona</u>, in 1930, <u>mr</u>. Clyde W. Tombaugh discovered <u>pluto</u>.

II. Constructions, Organizations, and Businesses
Underline each word containing a capitalization error.

6. The world's first <u>Metal-frame Skyscraper</u> was officially known as the <u>home insurance building</u>; it was constructed in Chicago, Illinois, in 1884 and 1885.

7. In 1942 the first controlled nuclear chain reaction took place at the <u>university</u> of <u>chicago</u>.

8. In Fort Wayne, Indiana, on May 4, 1871, the first professional baseball game was played; the <u>fort wayne kekiongas</u> defeated the <u>cleveland forest citys</u>, 2-0.

9. On May 30, 1911, the first long-distance automobile race in the United States took place in Indiana at the <u>indianapolis motor speedway</u>.

10. The <u>minnesota manufacturing</u> and <u>mining company</u> began producing transparent cellophane tape in 1930; the tape was invented and patented by Richard Gurley Drew of St. Paul.

III. Religious, Cultural, and Historical Terms
Underline each word containing a capitalization error.

11. The first American to win the <u>nobel prize</u> for literature was Sinclair Lewis, who had been born in Sauk Centre, Minnesota, in 1885.

12. In <u>october</u> of 1908, the Gideons first placed Bibles in the Superior Hotel in Iron Mountain, now called Superior, Montana.

13. <u>custer's last stand</u> took place in 1876, when Lt. Col. George A. Custer and about 210 of his troops were killed in Montana in the <u>battle</u> of <u>little bighorn</u>.

14. As the capital of New Mexico, Santa Fe ranks as the oldest seat of government in the United States; Santa Fe was founded as the capital of the <u>spanish</u> province in 1609 or 1610.

15. Independence Hall in Philadelphia, Pennsylvania, is a very famous building because both the <u>declaration</u> of <u>independence</u> and the <u>constitution</u> of the <u>united states</u> were adopted there.

IV. Titles and First Words
Underline each word containing a capitalization error.

16. Published by Andrew Bradford of Philadelphia, Pennsylvania, the first magazine in the American colonies appeared on February 13, 1741; however, the _american_ _magazine:_ _a_ _monthly_ _view_ of the _british_ _colonies_ lasted for only three months.

17. One of Connecticut's chief newspapers, known as the _hartford_ _courant,_ began publication in 1764 and has been published continuously, a time span longer than any other newspaper in the United States.

18. Published in Hartford, Connecticut, in 1796, the book _american_ _cookery_ by Amelia Simmons was the first cookbook written by an American.

19. In September of 1814, during the War of 1812, Francis Scott Key wrote "the star-spangled banner," which became the national anthem of the United States.

20. when he wrote the poem, Key was watching the British bombard Baltimore, Maryland's Fort McHenry.

V. Proper Adjectives and Other Words
Underline each word containing a capitalization error.

21. Log cabins, which were first built in the United States at the mouth of the Delaware River, are actually swedish and finnish in their origin.

22. Delaware's northern boundary with Pennsylvania is a u-shaped boundary, forming the arc of a perfect circle; no other state has such a boundary.

23. Did i tell you that Delaware was the very first state to ratify the United States Constitution on December 7, 1787?

24. The oldest highway in the United States is a european highway called the Royal Highway. Europeans built it in New Mexico in the 1500s.

25. Perhaps this review of United States history will help you earn an a on your next test.

Chapter 11 Pretest: Punctuation

I. End Marks
Insert any missing periods or decimal points, question marks, or exclamation points.

1. The Mongols created the largest empire in world history.

2. Did you know that their empire stretched from the East China Sea to the Mediterranean Sea?

3. Genghis Khan ruled during the AD. 1200s.

4. Many Mongol men were shorter than 5 ft. 2 in. tall.

5. Hunting and fighting were the Mongol way of life, for both men and women.

II. Commas in a Series and After Introductory Elements
Insert any missing commas. If the sentence is already correct, write C in the blank.

_____ 6. *Yurts, ordus,* and *Tartars* are all words that come from the Mongol Empire.

___C___ 7. Yurts were round felt tents made by the women.

_____ 8. Ordus were camps led by Mongol generals, and the word *horde* comes from *ordu.*

_____ 9. Frightened by the approaching invaders, Europeans gave them the nickname Tartars.

_____ 10. Originally, Mongols were a nomadic group of people, but some Mongol empires became more stationary in places such as China and India.

III. Commas to Separate; in Letters; and with Quotations, Dates, and Addresses
Insert any missing commas. If the sentence is already correct, write C in the blank.

_____ 11. Dear Grandson,
I wonder if you have ever heard of the ruler Genghis Khan.

___C___ 12. Genghis Khan was the founder of the Mongol nation, wasn't he?

_____ 13. He wanted to unite the world into one empire; he conquered most of Asia, beginning near what is Beijing, China, today.

_____ 14. He united his people to fight under his law code, the Great Yasa, which required loyalty above all else.

_____ 15. "We must conquer the world," Genghis Khan would tell his people.

IV. Incorrect Commas
Circle any incorrect commas. If the sentence is already correct, write C in the blank.

_____ 16. The Mongols believed that both loyalty, and horses were important.

_____ 17. The Taj Maha₍₎was built by a ruler of the Mughul dynasty, the Mongol empire in India.

_____ 18. Shamanism was the major religion of the Mongols, while₍₎Nestorianism was also a prominent religion.

___*C*___ 19. "In Xanadu did Kubla Khan / A stately pleasure dome decree" begins Samuel Taylor Coleridge's poem.

_____ 20. In December₍₎2001 we learned about the Mongols' system of warfare.

V. Semicolons
Insert any missing semicolons.

21. Arrow riders had an important job; they had to take messages from one part of the empire to another.

22. Pretend retreat worked well for the Mongols; the townspeople would be attacked as they came out to loot the apparently abandoned camp.

23. Siege warfare was used to starve out townspeople of walled cities; however, this method was sometimes not as effective as an all-out attack.

24. Silk, made from silkworms and unable to be penetrated by arrows; felt, made by crushing and bonding fur and threads; and leather, made from horsehide for shields and armor, were common fabrics of the Mongol people.

25. The great Mongol empires were as follows: Genghis Khan's original empire; Batu Khan's Golden Horde in Russia; Kublai Khan's Yuan dynasty in China; Tamerlane's empire in the Middle East; and Akbar's Mughul empire in India.

VI. Colons
Insert any missing colons. If the sentence is already correct, write C in the blank.

_____ 26. Although Mongol warriors relied on their horses, Proverbs 21:31 says, "The horse is prepared against the day of battle: but safety is of the Lord."

_____ 27. O Great Khan:
We are writing to you to inquire of the state of your empire.

_____ 28. Today central Asia is made up of the following countries: Tibet, Qinghai, Xinjiang Uygur, Kazakhstan, Kyrgyzstan, Mongolia, Tajikistan, Turkmenistan, and Uzbekistan.

___*C*___ 29. Next, we will hear what the Great Khan said: "The punishment for horse stealing will be death."

_____ 30. *Genghis Khan:Universal Ruler* is the title of the next book I will read about the Mongols.

Chapter 12 Pretest: More Punctuation

I. Quotation Marks

Insert any missing quotation marks. Circle any unnecessary quotation marks. If the sentence is already correct, write *C* in the blank.

__*C*__ 1. "Have you read any of the Narnia series?" my teacher asked.

_____ 2. "They were written by C. S. Lewis, right?" was my reply.○

_____ 3. "What," demanded Rochelle, "do the initials C. S. stand for?"

_____ 4. "*Clive Staples:* at least that's what the essay 'C. S. Lewis: A Modest Literary Biography,' by Dr. Bruce Edwards says."

__*C*__ 5. "I wonder why his mother named him Clive Staples," I said. "What do you think?"

II. Ellipses

Read the paragraph and determine whether the quotations following it are correct. Write the letter of the quotation that is properly punctuated.

C. S. Lewis was born in Belfast, Ireland (now Northern Ireland), on November 29, 1898. He fought during World War I in France and was wounded in battle. Later he attended University College, Oxford, and eventually became a professor of medieval and Renaissance literature. Overall, he wrote about forty works of literature. These include works of science fiction, autobiography, children's literature, Christian apologetics, satire, and allegory. His science fiction trilogy, considered by some to be one of the best trilogies in this genre, was a new phenomenon in literature when he wrote it. He wrote the last novel in his science fiction series in 1945.

__*A*__ 6. A. "C. S. Lewis was born in Belfast . . . on November 29, 1898."
   B. "C. S. Lewis was born in Belfast, . . . on November 29, 1898."
   C. "C. S. Lewis was born in Belfast...on November 29, 1898."

__*C*__ 7. A. "He fought during World War I in France and was wounded in battle".
   B. "He fought during World War I in France and was wounded in battle"
   C. "He fought during World War I in France and was wounded in battle."

__*B*__ 8. A. "Later he attended University College, Oxford, and. . .he wrote about forty works of literature."
   B. "Later he attended University College, Oxford, and . . . he wrote about forty works of literature."
   C. "Later he attended University College, Oxford, and...he wrote about forty works of literature."

__*A*__ 9. A. "Overall, he wrote about forty works of literature. . . . He wrote the last novel in his science fiction series in 1945."
   B. "Overall, he wrote about forty works of literature . . . He wrote the last novel in his science fiction series in 1945."
   C. "Overall, he wrote about forty works of literature....He wrote the last novel in his science fiction series in 1945."

___B___ 10. A. The passage notes that "many literary writings in many different genres were composed by Lewis."

               B. The passage notes that many literary writings in many different genres were composed by Lewis.

               C. The passage notes that "many literary writings" in many different genres were composed by Lewis.

III. Underlining for Italics

Underline any words that should be italicized or that are italicized incorrectly. If the sentence is already correct, write _C_ in the blank.

_____ 11. Lewis wrote a poem called _French Nocturne,_ which reveals the feelings of a soldier during a quiet night on a battlefield in France.

_____ 12. Lewis wrote the book <u>Mere Christianity</u>, originally a collection of radio talks aired by the <u>_British Broadcasting Company_</u>.

_____ 13. He was also an expert in English literature, and as an expert he was familiar with Spenser's _Faerie Queene_ and Milton's epic <u>Paradise Lost</u>.

_____ 14. Upon examining his correspondence, one can easily see that Lewis was a <u>bel esprit</u>.

___C___ 15. He had a beautiful writing style that appealed even to children; _The Horse and His Boy_ is the name of one his books written for children.

IV. Apostrophe

Insert any missing apostrophes. Underline any words that contain unnecessary apostrophes. If the sentence is already correct, write _C_ in the blank.

___C___ 16. During one of the battles of '18, Lewis was wounded and forced to leave the war.

_____ 17. Lewis eventually recuperated and was sent back to the war until <u>its'</u> end in '19.

_____ 18. Lewis's first published work was "Death in Battle."

_____ 19. Someone's reading of Lewis's works would be aided by a basic understanding of classical literature.

_____ 20. It was Jack (Lewis's nickname) and his brother's plight to lose <u>their'</u> mother at an early age.

V. Hyphen

Insert any missing hyphens. Underline any words that contain unnecessary hyphens. If the sentence is already correct, write C in the blank.

_____ 21. Lewis led an <u>extra-ordinary</u> life that included the grief of losing a close friend in World War I.

_____ 22. Lewis wrote a variety of thought‸provoking works; and he once feared that others considered him not "a single author . . . [but] a man who impersonates half a dozen authors."

___C___ 23. He always loved to read: from childhood until he died at the age of sixty-five.

_____ 24. He often read books that would have been too hard for many other children to under‸ stand.

_____ 25. Since he had few friends to play with, he would often spend from <u>8:00-to-5:00</u> in his father's old library.

VI. Dashes and Parentheses

Insert any missing dashes or parentheses. (Answers may vary.)

26. His mother died when he was only ten years old‸the same year Jack and his brother were sent to Wynyard School in England.

27. The two Lewises always looked forward(school life was hard!)to vacation time.

28. In his later life(after his war experiences), Lewis was considered to be a kind friend of children.

29. He wrote *The Chronicles of Narnia*‸perhaps his most famous work‸for young readers.

30. This series(though it was written for children)contains symbolism that even some adults may not notice.

Teaching Help 2A: Finding the Subjects and Predicates

Underline the complete subject once and the complete predicate twice. Write the simple subject in the first blank. (If the subject is understood, write *you* in the blank.) Write the simple predicate in the second blank.

word	1. Is the <u>word *treasure*</u> used in the Bible?
Is used	
references	2. There are at least ninety-seven references to the word *treasure* (or *treasures*) in God's Word.
are	
God	3. In Job 38:22, God speaks of the treasures contained in the snow and the hail.
speaks	
Shishak	4. Shishak, the Egyptian king, descended upon Jerusalem and seized the
descended/seized	treasure from the king's house as well as from the Lord's house. (I Kings 14:25-26)
Some	5. Some of the leaders in Nehemiah's day contributed much "to the treasure of
contributed	the work" of the Lord. (Nehemiah 7:71)
treasure	6. "In the house of the righteous is much treasure." (Proverbs 15:6)
is	
man/woman	7. The godly man or woman will diligently search for wisdom.
will search	
reference	8. The most famous reference to *treasure* in the Bible is, of course, the one
is	about accumulating treasure in heaven.
Moses	9. Moses considered persecution for God's sake greater treasure than monetary
considered	riches.
You	10. Study more for yourself about the use of *treasure* in God's precious Word.
Study	

Teaching Help 2B: Analyzing Sentence Patterns

Label the sentence patterns *S-InV, S-TrV-DO, S-TrV-IO-DO, S-LV-PN, S-LV-PA, S-TrV-DO-OC,* **or** *S-be-Advl.* **If the adverbial is a prepositional phrase, underline it.**

     S   **InV**
1. Members of an Amish community often marry at an early age.

        S   **TrV**   **IO**   **DO**
2. An Amish young man gives his fiancée a practical gift instead of a diamond ring.

          S   **TrV**   **DO**
3. Before the wedding, the couple must "publish" their engagement at a special church service.

        S   **TrV**   **DO**
4. The wedding ceremony quickly follows this published announcement.

      S   **InV**
5. These weddings occur in the bride's house.

                      S   **LV** **PA**
6. In contrast to a non-Amish wedding, an Amish wedding is long (three or four hours).

        S   **be**   **Advl**
7. All Amish weddings are <u>of the same style and length</u>.

                          S   **TrV**   **DO** **OC**   **OC**
8. Instead of wearing a traditional white gown, an Amish bride makes her dress blue or purple.

                    S   **S**   **LV**   **PN**
9. Sometimes, during the rest of the day, the bride and groom will become matchmakers for their

unmarried friends.

             S   **TrV**   **DO**   **DO**
10. A traditional Amish wedding dinner includes roast chicken, mashed potatoes with gravy, creamed
   DO   **DO**   **DO**   **DO**
   celery, coleslaw, applesauce, and many desserts.

© 2002 BJU Press. Reproduction prohibited.

Teaching Help 3: Misplaced and Dangling Participial Phrases

Rewrite each sentence to avoid dangling or misplaced participial phrases. *(Answers may vary.)*

1. The rookie ran onto the football field grinning nervously.

    Grinning nervously, the rookie ran onto the football field.

2. Pacing back and forth along the sidelines, orders were shouted to the players.

    Pacing back and forth along the sidelines, the head coach shouted orders to the players.

3. Approaching the line of scrimmage, the news media focused on the rookie quarterback.

    The news media focused on the rookie quarterback approaching the line of scrimmage.

4. Strapping on his helmet, the crowd got almost quiet as the player took his position.

    Strapping on his helmet, the player took his position as the crowd got almost quiet.

5. Passing the ball to the receiver in the end zone, a tough offensive line would be necessary.

    Passing the ball to the receiver in the end zone, the quarterback was protected by a tough offensive line.

6. Hurrying onto the field, everyone's eyes were glued to the rookie.

    Hurrying onto the field, the rookie had everyone's attention.

7. Crouched behind the center, every fan eyed the young quarterback.

    Every fan eyed the young quarterback crouched behind the center.

8. Ricocheting from player to player, the lineman scrambled for the fumbled football.

    The lineman scrambled for the fumbled football ricocheting from player to player.

9. Grabbing wildly, the football was too slippery.

    Grabbing wildly, even the best players could not hold the slippery football.

10. Running the ball into the end zone, the clock ticked off the closing seconds of the game.

    Running the ball into the end zone, the rookie quarterback glanced back to watch the clock tick off the closing seconds of the game.

Teaching Help 4B: Avoiding Sentence Errors

Rewrite the paragraph below, paying special attention to errors created by any misplaced commas. In the score box, keep track of how many correct sentences, fragments, comma splices, and fused sentences you find.

Correct Sentence	Fragment	Comma Splice	Fused Sentence
3	4	2	2

Ancient Egyptian civilization is fascinating, the discovery of the tomb of King Tut was a great archeological find, it deepened appreciation for Egyptian culture. Egypt's kings, called pharaohs. Buried secretly with great amounts of treasure. In the middle of the fourteenth century B.C., a nine-year-old boy became pharaoh Tutankhamen ruled for ten years before he died and was buried in the Valley of the Kings at Thebes. His tomb was soon discovered and robbed. Then rubble from a nearby building project soon covered King Tut's tomb it lay untouched until 1922. British archeologists found the tomb. Soon excavated its many treasures. Though thieves had carried away some of the treasure. An overwhelming amount still remained untouched.

Ancient Egyptian civilization is fascinating. The discovery of the tomb of King Tut was a great archeological find, and it deepened appreciation for Egyptian culture. Egypt's kings, called pharaohs, were buried secretly with great amounts of treasure. In the middle of the fourteenth century B.C., a nine-year-old boy became pharaoh. Tutankhamen ruled for ten years before he died and was buried in the Valley of the Kings at Thebes. His tomb was soon discovered and robbed. Then rubble from a nearby building project soon covered King Tut's tomb. It lay untouched until 1922. British archeologists found the tomb and soon excavated its many treasures. Though thieves had carried away some of the treasure, an overwhelming amount still remained untouched.

Teaching Help 5: Agreement

Underline each relative pronoun. Then underline the correct verb from the choices in parentheses.

1. Here is the sheet <u>that</u> (*<u>gives</u>, give*) the instructions.

2. Where are the campers <u>who</u> (*has, <u>have</u>*) lost their way?

3. Elise is one of the campers <u>who</u> (*knows, <u>know</u>*) where the picnic shelter is located.

4. Give them the maps, <u>which</u> (*is, <u>are</u>*) necessary for finding the cabin.

5. This is the path <u>that</u> (*<u>confuses</u>, confuse*) many people.

6. It is the only one of the paths <u>that</u> (*<u>was</u>, were*) not marked clearly.

Teaching Help 7A: Pronoun Reference I

Answer each question by following the instructions given after each sentence.

1. Jeremiah told Bret that he had a healthy Akita.

   Who owns the healthy Akita?

   Rewrite the sentence, making it clear that the dog belongs to Bret.

   Jeremiah told Bret, "You have a healthy Akita."

2. Akitas are Japanese hunting dogs that at one time could be owned only by royalty. They were used for hunting bears and other large animals.

   Were the royalty used to hunt bears?

   Rewrite the sentence, making the Akitas the agent used for hunting.

   The hunting dogs were used for hunting bears and other large animals.

3. Jeremiah told Bret his dog had the head of a bear.

   Is the scary-looking dog Bret's or Jeremiah's?

   Rewrite the sentence so that Bret owns the dog.

   Bret told Jeremiah, "My dog's head looks like a bear's head!"

4. Akitas are still revered by the Japanese people today. They are loved for their loyalty and service as reliable guardians. In the presence of other dogs, they can become aggressive.

   Who becomes aggressive?

   Rewrite the last sentence so that there is no question about the agent of aggression.

   In the presence of other dogs, Akitas can become aggressive.

5. Lately, Akitas have been overbred. This has resulted in many overly aggressive, dangerous animals. Sometimes these dangerous animals have to be put to death. Sadly, it has happened to other breeds as well, such as Dalmatians.

   What is the sad thing that has happened?

   Rewrite the sentence so that it is clear what careless action has hurt the breed.

   Sadly, overbreeding has happened to other breeds as well, such as Dalmatians.

Name_____

Teaching Help 7B: Pronoun Reference II

Rewrite the sentences, correcting the pronoun reference problems.

1. Jocelyn arranged a place and time to meet so they could make the trip together to the Dillard House in Dillard, Georgia.

   Jocelyn arranged a place and time to meet so she and her family could make the trip together to the

   Dillard House in Dillard, Georgia.

2. Jocelyn's family took her dad's car, who had just taken it in for a tune-up.

   Jocelyn's family took the car that her dad had just taken in for a tune-up.

3. The Dillard House is located on a plateau in the Little Tennessee River Valley, and it is breathtaking.

   The Dillard House is located on a plateau in the Little Tennessee River Valley, and the view is

   breathtaking.

4. The Blue Ridge Mountains rise with a serene beauty around the valley, and it creates a peaceful backdrop for the restaurant and resort.

   The Blue Ridge Mountains rise with a serene beauty around the valley, and the scenery creates a

   peaceful backdrop for the restaurant and resort.

5. At the Dillard House, they serve fantastic meals of authentic Southern cooking.

   The Dillard House serves fantastic meals of authentic Southern cooking.

Teaching Help 8: Compound Constructions

Insert a correct pronoun to complete each sentence. *(Answers may vary.)*

1. My friend and ___*I*___ ran in a 5-K (a five-kilometer race) last week.

2. A T-shirt was given to him and ___*me*___.

3. They took his and ___*my*___ picture while we were running.

4. My family and ___*his*___ came to watch us.

5. When I crossed the finish line, I heard loud cheers from my family and ___*his*___.

6. My friend's family and ___*he*___ have run several races together.

7. That seasoned runner is training ___*him*___ and some of our friends for a half marathon.

8. Here is the training plan for my friend and ___*me*___.

9. It was ___*he*___ and his friend that got me interested in running races.

10. Now my friend Kim and ___*I*___ have joined them in recruiting others to join the world of runners.

Teaching Help 9: Modifiers

Write the correct answer in the blank. Then use your answers to complete the crossword puzzle.

ACROSS

_____best_____ 1. The superlative form of *good* is _?_.

_____positive_____ 4. At the _?_ level of comparison, no comparison is made at all.

_____dangling_____ 5. A _?_ modifier attempts to modify a word that is not actually in the sentence.

_____more_____ 9. The word _?_ is added in front of an adjective or an adverb consisting of two or more syllables in order to make such a modifier comparative.

_____superlative_____ 10. At the _?_ level of comparison, three or more things or groups are compared.

_____well_____ 12. "You did very (*well, good*) on the test."

DOWN

_____two-way_____ 2. A _?_ modifier makes a sentence unclear because it stands between two sentence elements and might modify either one.

_____split_____ 3. When a modifier is positioned between *to* and the verb of an infinitive, the error is called a _?_ infinitive.

_____greater_____ 6. The comparative form of *great* is _?_.

_____good_____ 7. Your car is very (*well, good*) for long trips.

_____comparative_____ 8. At the _?_ level of comparison, two things or groups are compared.

_____est_____ 11. The common suffix for superlative modifiers is _?_.

Teaching Help 11A: Punctuation

Punctuation helps clarify otherwise ambiguous text. Read the following letter and add punctuation to make it understandable. The first words of most sentences have not been capitalized in order to create ambiguity. Correct the capitalization as you add the correct punctuation. *(Answers will vary.)*

dear Serene

the vacation has been great at first I thought all I would see was the airport in Honolulu after spending hours waiting for our luggage we finally got it and headed for the hotel that night we called my grandparents to let them know that we had arrived in the morning we boarded the plane for the big island

a couple of days later a funny thing happened Jason and I spent the day snorkeling and swimming as we returned home I got a little confused so we decided to stop and ask directions to our street the house we stopped at had a high fence around the yard Jason entered first and I was right behind him a large hedge hid half of the yard as we started down the path we heard a loud low growl come from just beyond the hedge I stepped quickly behind the gate but Jason ran across the lawn towards the street in one smooth motion he jumped the fence and quickly stopped panting we turned to see our predator soon a small Chihuahua ran towards us we laughed pretty hard the owner who saw all this knew Granddad and told us how to get back

I'll tell you all about everything when we get home

your friend

Caleb

Dear Serene,

    The vacation has been great. At first I thought all I would see was the airport in Honolulu. After spending hours waiting for our luggage, we finally got it and headed for the hotel. That night we called my grandparents to let them know that we had arrived. In the morning, we boarded the plane for the big island.

    A couple of days later a funny thing happened. Jason and I spent the day snorkeling and swimming. As we returned home, I got a little confused, so we decided to stop and ask directions to our street. The house we stopped at had a high fence around the yard. Jason entered first, and I was right behind him. A large hedge hid half of the yard. As we started down the path, we heard a loud, low growl come from just beyond the hedge. I stepped quickly behind the gate, but Jason ran across the lawn towards the street. In one smooth motion, he jumped the fence and quickly stopped. Panting, we turned to see our predator. Soon a small Chihuahua ran towards us. We laughed pretty hard. The owner, who saw all this, knew Granddad and told us how to get back.

    I'll tell you all about everything when we get home.

Your friend,

Caleb

Teaching Help 11B: Commas

The numbered sentences below are missing commas. Find the rule that will correct the problem and write its corresponding letter in the blank. Each letter may be used more than once. Insert the missing commas into each sentence.

A. Use commas to separate three or more single words in a series or to separate groups of words of the same type that are joined by a conjunction.

B. Use commas to separate coordinate adjectives.

C. Insert a comma before a coordinating conjunction joining two independent clauses.

D. Place a comma after introductory elements.

E. A noun of direct address should be set off by commas.

F. Use commas to set off parenthetical information.

G. Use commas to set off modifying adjectives after a noun.

H. Use a comma to separate a tag question from the rest of the sentence.

____**E**____ 1. Addison,have you ever seen a kangaroo?

____**H**____ 2. Kangaroos are unique animals,aren't they?

____**A**____ 3. Kangaroos can be found in Australia,Tasmania,and New Guinea.

____**F**____ 4. The kangaroo is part of an animal group known as *macropod*,a word meaning "large foot."

____**D**____ 5. Built similarly,most macropods have large hind legs and feet but small front legs.

____**B**____ 6. The strong,powerful legs of the kangaroo can propel it up to thirty miles per hour for a short distance.

____**C**____ 7. Kangaroos usually feed on grass and small plants,and they will sometimes gather at feeding sites in large groups called mobs.

____**D**____ 8. After carrying her baby for one month,the mother gives birth to a baby kangaroo that is one inch long.

____**G**____ 9. The joey,small and undeveloped,lives in his mother's pouch for six to eight months.

____**D**____ 10. Hunted for its hide and meat,the kangaroo's primary enemy is man.

Teaching Help 11C: Commas, Semicolons, and Colons

Insert any missing commas, semicolons, and colons in the sentences below.

1. Alexander Pope, an English poet living from 1688 to 1744, is known for the following kinds of literary works:poetry, essay, satire, and translation.

2. Pope suffered from severe illnesses as a child,and his growth was stunted, a misfortune that caused his height to be a mere 4'6" even as an adult.

3. Pope was almost entirely self-educated;nevertheless, he was admitted into London literary society when he was only seventeen.

4. Pope made many friends who saw his potential and encouraged him;even the satirist Jonathan Swift took an interest in Pope.

5. Pope, self-educated and physically deformed, earned a remarkable title:the greatest English critic and verse satirist of the eighteenth century.

Teaching Help 12: More Punctuation

Key punctuation has been left out of the following paragraph. Find the five punctuation omissions and insert the necessary punctuation. (Punctuation marks used in pairs count as one unit.)

In Charles Dickens's famous tale <u>Great Expectations</u>, the protagonist (or central character) is named Pip. Actually, his real name is Philip Pirrip, but since, as he explains it, "my infant tongue could make of both names nothing longer or more explicit than Pip," that is what he was called. His story is told from the point of view of an older Pip looking back on his life and its mistakes. Pip's father and mother had both died, and he was forced to live with his sister and her husband, Joe, the village blacksmith. The story reveals Pip's growing up to disdain his rustic beginnings and to develop into a gentleman. He grows to hate his common roots partly through his infatuation with the beautiful Estella, who treats him badly. In the end, however, he realizes that true gentility—actually exemplified by Joe and Pip's childhood friend, Biddy—comes not from position, money, and power but from a considerate and compassionate heart.

Teaching Help 13: Revising for Correctness

Rewrite the paragraph, correcting the ten errors in sentence structure, usage, spelling, punctuation, and capitalization.

Lightning produces a sound that we hear as thunder. People in ancient civilizations thought that thunder was the sound of angry Gods, however, scientists today know that thunder is the sound produced by hot air, heated by lightning, colliding with cooler air. The different "parts" of a bolt of lightning causes different sounds of thunder. The main trunk causes the loudest crash; whereas the branches produce the sharp crackling sound. Thunder has different sounds the deep, rumbling roar of thunder is caused by lightning that is furthest away from we observers. We see the lightning before we hear their thunder because light travels faster (186,282 miles per second) than sound does (1,116 feet per second). If we want to calculate how far away lightning is, we count the number of seconds between the lightning and the thunder, and then we divide by five. The resultting distance in miles is the approximate location of the storm. Whenever we see lightning, we know that the sound of thunder is imminent.

Lightning produces a sound that we hear as thunder. People in ancient civilizations thought that thunder was the sound of angry gods; however, scientists today know that thunder is the sound produced by hot air, heated by lightning, colliding with cooler air. The different "parts" of a bolt of lightning cause different sounds of thunder. The main trunk causes the loudest crash whereas the branches produce the sharp, crackling sound. Thunder has different sounds; the deep, rumbling roar of thunder is caused by lightning that is farthest away from us observers. We see the lightning before we hear its thunder because light travels faster (186,282 miles per second) than sound does (1,116 feet per second). If we want to calculate how far away lightning is, we count the number of seconds between the lightning and the thunder, and then we divide by five. The resulting distance in miles is the approximate location of the storm. Whenever we see lightning, we know that the sound of thunder is imminent.

Teaching Help 14A: Sentence Variety

Revise the following paragraph to improve sentence variety and emphasis. *(Answers will vary.)*

Ann Judson kept a journal during the years that the Judsons were in Burma. Her journal records the joys and trials of being a missionary. In the beginning stages of the Judsons' ministry, until prominent men were converted to Christianity, the government of Burma did not pay much attention to the ministry. The unspoken policy of the Burmese government was to allow foreigners to believe what they wished, but the government wanted Burmese people to remain true to the religion of Buddhism. Later in the Judsons' ministry, war with Britain broke out. Adoniram was arrested by the Burmese government as a supposed spy. He was kept in a hot, crowded jail. He had little to eat or drink. He was a prisoner until the end of the war. After Adoniram's release, Ann became ill. She died. Adoniram was away on a trip. Ann had seen some Burmese come to Christ, but only as she followed her Savior in the fellowship of His sufferings.

During the years that she and her husband were in Burma, Ann Judson kept a journal recording the joys and trials of a missionary's life. In her journal, she records that Burma ignored the ministry until prominent men were converted to Christianity. The unspoken policy of the Burmese government was to allow foreigners to believe what they wished, but the government wanted Burmese people to remain true to the religion of Buddhism. Later in the Judsons' ministry, when war with Britain broke out, Adoniram was arrested by the Burmese government as a supposed spy. He was kept in a hot, crowded jail with little to eat or drink. Adoniram remained a prisoner until the end of the war. After Adoniram's release, Ann became ill and died while Adoniram was away on a trip. Ann did see some Burmese come to Christ, but only as she followed her Savior in the fellowship of His sufferings.

Teaching Help 14B: Coordination and Subordination

Correctly combine the following sentences according to the instructions in parentheses. *(Answers may vary.)*

1. Short-term missionaries often go to the field to teach missionary children. The missionaries do not have to send the children away to school. *(Subordinate one sentence to the other.)*

   Short-term missionaries often go to the field to teach missionary children so that the missionaries do not have to send the children away to school.

2. The mother may have been teaching the children. The mother is able to participate more fully in other aspects of the mission work. *(Coordinate the sentences.)*

   The mother may have been teaching the children, but now she is able to participate more fully in other aspects of the mission work.

3. A missionary family may have several children. All the children would probably be in different grades. *(Coordinate the sentences.)*

   A missionary family may have several children, and all the children would probably be in different grades.

4. The missionary family usually has more than one school-age child. The short-term missionary must teach several children. *(Subordinate one sentence to the other.)*

   Because the missionary family usually has more than one school-age child, the short-term missionary must teach several children.

5. The short-term missionary may have to create several different lesson plans each evening. He may have to grade several different assignments each evening. *(Coordinate the sentences.)*

   The short-term missionary may have to create several different lesson plans and grade several different assignments each evening.

6. One child may do well at mathematics. Science might be another child's best subject. The easiest subject for another child might be language. *(Coordinate the three sentences into one.)*

   One child may do well at mathematics, another at science, and another at language.

Teaching Help 14B: Coordination and Subordination (continued)

7. The missionary children may know multiple languages. The short-term missionary may know only one language. The children could communicate in the language the short-term missionary does not know. (*Coordinate two sentences and then subordinate the two sentences to the remaining sentence.*)

   If the missionary children know multiple languages and the short-term missionary knows only one

   language, the children could communicate in the language the short-term missionary does not know.

8. Short-term missionaries are usually exposed to a new language. They have the opportunity to learn a new language. (*Subordinate one sentence to another to show cause.*)

   Because short-term missionaries are usually exposed to a new language, they have the opportunity to

   learn a new language.

9. The short-term missionary teacher must adapt his teaching to each student's needs. The students must adapt to their teacher's teaching style. (*Subordinate one sentence to the other.*)

   While the short-term missionary teacher must adapt his teaching to each student's needs, the

   students must adapt to their teacher's teaching style.

10. Future short-term teachers might major in education or humanities. An education major gives future teachers experience teaching in the classroom. A humanities major exposes future teachers to a variety of subjects. (*Subordinate two sentences to the other sentence.*)

    Future short-term teachers might major in education or humanities because an education major gives

    them classroom teaching experience while a humanities major exposes them to a variety of subjects.

ESL Help 1A: Positions of Adjectives

Adjectives are usually put in a specific order before a noun, although the order may sometimes vary. The typical order of adjectives as they appear from left to right in a noun phrase can be described as follows:

1. determiner(s)
2. opinion
3. size
4. shape
5. condition
6. age
7. color
8. origin

MAIN NOUN

The following chart illustrates this order.

determiner	opinion	size	shape	condition	age	color	origin	MAIN NOUN
a	pretty	little	round	chipped	old	pink	French	saucer

Exercise in Positions of Adjectives

Rewrite the sentences, placing the adjectives in the correct order to modify the noun that immediately follows the adjectives. Do not forget to capitalize the first word of each sentence. (Some answers may vary, especially the order of condition and color adjectives.)

1. (*the, mountain, short*) man sat on the back porch of his cabin.

   The short mountain man sat on the back porch of his cabin.

2. (*old, brown, his*) porch swing creaked under his weight.

   His old brown porch swing creaked under his weight.

3. He watched (*fluffy, the, white, big*) clouds float by.

   He watched the big fluffy white clouds float by.

4. The clouds cast (*huge, gray, their*) shadows on the mountains.

   The clouds cast their huge gray shadows on the mountains.

5. (*yellow, bright, the*) sun reflected off the cabin's tin roof.

   The bright yellow sun reflected off the cabin's tin roof.

6. (*tiny, the, colorful*) hummingbird landed on the hummingbird feeder.

   The tiny colorful hummingbird landed on the hummingbird feeder.

7. (*northwestern, a, cool*) breeze rattled the chime hanging from the porch.

   A cool northwestern breeze rattled the chime hanging from the porch.

8. The hummingbird flew back to (*tall, the, strong*) oak tree.

   The hummingbird flew back to the tall strong oak tree.

9. (*bushy, the, green, tall*) trees covered the mountains.

   The tall bushy green trees covered the mountains.

10. The mountain man's dog buried a bone in (*red, the, sandy*) dirt.

    The mountain man's dog buried a bone in the sandy red dirt.

ESL Help 1D: Exercise in Article Usage

Choose the correct article *(a, an,* or *the)* to put in each blank. If no article is needed, put an *X* in the blank. Above each answer list the appropriate rule number from the Article Usage sheet.

(1.2)
__X__ Samuel Adams was __*an*__ American patriot and a signer of the Declaration of In-
(3.1)

(5.2)   *(1.3)*
dependence. __*The*__ history of Samuel Adams's life began when he was born in __*X*__ Boston

(2.3)
in 1722. Samuel Adams was a cousin to John Adams, __*the*__ second president of the United

(1.2)
States. Samuel Adams grew up and attended __*X*__ Harvard, where he received an undergrad-

(3.2)
uate degree in 1740 and later __*X*__ his master's degree in 1743. He was active in Boston

town meetings and served in the Massachusetts legislature from 1765 to 1774. In 1773 the

(3.1)   *(4.1)*
British tried to place __*a*__ monopoly on __*X*__ tea sales in the American colonies. The

(2.1)
colonies resisted the British monopoly. __*The*__ climax of the American resistance occurred on

(3.2)
December 16, 1773, when a group of __*X*__ Boston's citizens dumped a shipment of tea from

(1.3)   *(2.2)*
__*X*__ Britain into Boston's harbor. Samuel Adams probably led __*the*__ resistance, and his in-

volvement in America's early government shows his dedication to his country. In 1774 Adams

(3.1)
served as __*a*__ representative from Massachusetts to the First Continental Congress, and

from 1775 to 1781 he served in the Second Continental Congress. Later, Adams served as the

governor of Massachusetts from 1793 to 1797.

ESL Help 1F: Exercise in Adverb Placement

Decide whether the italicized adverbs are placed correctly. If the placement is correct, write C in the blank to the left. If the placement is incorrect, write I in the blank and then rewrite the sentence correctly. *(Answers will vary.)*

___*I*___ 1. Adrian balanced *accurately* his checkbook.

 Adrian accurately balanced his checkbook.

___*I*___ 2. Bevan *cheerfully* was cleaning his room.

 Bevan was cheerfully cleaning his room.

___*C*___ 3. *Sometimes* Brandon reads books.

 _____

___*I*___ 4. Bethany had gone on a walk in the city with her dog *daily.*

 Bethany had daily gone on a walk in the city with her dog.

___*I*___ 5. *Gratefully* on graduation day Caitlin received a gift from her friend.

 Caitlin gratefully received a gift from her friend on graduation day.

___*C*___ 6. Caris *respectfully* refused the free lunch from her supervisor.

 _____

___*I*___ 7. *Somewhere* Abbot put his tie.

 Abbot put his tie somewhere.

___*I*___ 8. Cassandra was cheerful *always* at work.

 Cassandra was always cheerful at work.

___*I*___ 9. Abner went to the river *down* for the day.

 Abner went down to the river for the day.

___*I*___ 10. Betsey was obedient *usually.*

 Betsey was usually obedient.

ESL Help 1H: Exercise in Making Sentences Negative Using *Not*

Rewrite the following sentences to make them negative. Add *not* to each sentence. Change the form of the verb and add an auxiliary if necessary.

> **EXAMPLE**   Charleen will throw the baseball.
> Charleen will not throw the baseball.

1. The lake will be calm tonight.
   The lake will not be calm tonight.

2. I am elated.
   I am not elated.

3. The bees pollinated the flowers.
   The bees did not pollinate the flowers.

4. You may need your umbrella.
   You may not need your umbrella.

5. Cheryl was a librarian.
   Cheryl was not a librarian.

6. Baxter would like a new hat.
   Baxter would not like a new hat.

7. Shelly caught the butterfly with her butterfly net.
   Shelly did not catch the butterfly with her butterfly net.

8. We were watching for the comet.
   We were not watching for the comet.

9. Cherie caught the chicken pox from Sylvia.
   Cherie did not catch the chicken pox from Sylvia.

10. The strawberries tasted delicious.
    The strawberries did not taste delicious.

ESL Help 1J: Exercise in Using Prepositions

Choose the correct word for each blank from the choices in parentheses. If none of the suggested words is correct or if no preposition is needed, put an X in the blank.

1. Clayton ate popcorn _____**during**_____ the baseball game. (*during, while*)

2. He was cheering for his favorite team _____**while**_____ he was eating. (*during, while*)

3. To get to the baseball stadium, he had to walk from his home _____**X**_____ uptown. (*at, in*)

4. When the game is over, he will have to walk back _____**X**_____ home. (*at, to*)

5. He often receives a lot of business calls when he is _____**at**_____ home. (*at, to*)

6. He goes to the baseball game so that he won't be _____**X**_____ there when people call. (*on, to*)

7. The baseball game ended _____**at**_____ 10:07 P.M. (*in, on, at*)

8. That is earlier than the baseball games _____**on**_____ Friday nights usually end. (*in, on, at*)

9. Clayton stayed at the stadium _____**until**_____ most of the crowd had left. (*through, until*)

10. He had stayed at the game _____**through**_____ all the innings. (*through, until*)

ESL Help 2B: Exercise in Inverted Subject and Predicate

Change each sentence to a *yes/no* question. Remember to look at the verb tense for each sentence. Then use that same tense for the question.

1. Virginia will sing in the contest.
   Will Virginia sing in the contest?

2. Virginia has a lovely soprano voice.
   Does Virginia have a lovely soprano voice?

3. Virginia's voice is well trained.
   Is Virginia's voice well trained?

4. Virginia had been a poor singer at first.
   Had Virginia been a poor singer at first?

5. Virginia was successful in learning about music, though.
   Was Virginia successful in learning about music, though?

Change each sentence to a *wh* question. Use the word in parentheses to form the question. Write the question and its answer in the blank.

6. Virginia will sing in the contest. *(who)*
   Who will sing in the contest?   **_Virginia_**

7. Virginia has a lovely soprano voice. *(what)*
   What does Virginia have?   **_a lovely soprano voice_**

8. Virginia's voice is well trained. *(whose)*
   Whose voice is well trained?   **_Virginia's_**

9. Virginia had been a poor singer because of her speech impediment. *(why)*
   Why had Virginia been a poor singer?   **_because of her speech impediment_**

10. Due to her many hours of practice, Virginia became successful as a singer. *(how)*
    How did Virginia become successful as a singer?   **_due to her many hours of practice_**

ESL Help 4B: Exercise in How to Combine Sentences

The following chart shows meaning similarities among the three main types of connecting words.

Coordinating Conjunctions	Conjunctive Adverbs	Subordinating Conjunctions
and	besides, likewise, moreover, also	—
or	otherwise	—
so	accordingly, consequently, then, therefore, thus	because, since
but, yet	however, nevertheless, still	while, whereas, although, even though

Combine the following sentences using the formulas indicated. Rewrite each sentence, adding a correct connecting word and the correct punctuation. You may leave the words in parentheses out of the sentence. *(Answers may vary.)*

EXAMPLE Joan pulled weeds. (At the same time,) Hadden mowed the lawn.

IC, cc IC. (Formula 1): __Joan pulled weeds, and Hadden mowed the lawn.__

IC; ca, IC. (Formula 5): __Joan pulled weeds; also, Hadden mowed the lawn.__

IC. ca, IC. (Formula 4): __Joan pulled weeds. Also, Hadden mowed the lawn.__

1. Joan likes yellow. (In contrast,) Hadden likes red.

   IC, cc IC. (Formula 1): __*Joan likes yellow, but Hadden likes red.*__

   IC. IC, ca, IC continued. (Formula 6): __*Joan likes yellow. Hadden, however, likes red.*__

   IC (sc DC). (Formula 3): __*Joan likes yellow whereas Hadden likes red.*__

2. Claire's dad owns a blueberry farm. (As a result,) Claire picks blueberries in the summer.

   IC, cc IC. (Formula 1): __*Claire's dad owns a blueberry farm, so Claire picks blueberries in the summer.*__

   (sc DC), IC. (Formula 2): __*Since Claire's dad owns a blueberry farm, Claire picks blueberries in the summer.*__

   IC; ca, IC. (Formula 5): __*Claire's dad owns a blueberry farm; thus, Claire picks blueberries in the summer.*__

ESL Help 5B: Exercise in Using *Some* Correctly

Read the sentences containing the word *some*. Make each sentence negative by using *not* along with *any*, *anybody/anyone*, or *anything*. (Answers may vary.)

1. We saw some snakes during our mountain hike.

   We did not see any snakes during our mountain hike.

2. We told somebody about the snakes.

   We did not tell anybody about the snakes.

3. My Aunt Beatrice found out about the snakes from someone.

   My Aunt Beatrice did not find out about the snakes from anyone.

4. We had something to kill the snakes with.

   We did not have anything to kill the snakes with.

5. Snakes scare some people away from hiking.

   Snakes do not scare any people away from hiking.

Read the sentences containing the word *some*. Make each sentence negative by using *no*, *none*, *nobody/no one*, or *nothing*. (Answers may vary.)

6. Some of the rabbits in the woods eat clover.

   None of the rabbits in the woods eat clover.

7. Somebody found a rabbit in the woods.

   Nobody found a rabbit in the woods.

8. Someone chased the rabbit.

   No one chased the rabbit.

9. The rabbit found something to hide under.

   The rabbit found nothing to hide under.

10. Some bushes provide good shelter for rabbits.

    No bushes provide good shelter for rabbits.

ESL Help 6E: Exercise in Active and Passive

Change one sentence or part of one sentence in each paragraph so that the new portion uses the passive voice instead of active voice. Use the principle in parentheses as a guide to know which sentence to change. Write the new sentence with passive voice in the blank.

In 1811 Samuel F. B. Morse's parents allowed Morse to go to London to study art. While there, Morse worked with Benjamin West, studied at the Royal Academy of the Arts, and won a gold medal for his first and only piece of sculpture, a piece about the dying Hercules. In 1815 he had used up all his funds for study, so he regretfully returned home.

(The writer wants to be tactful about Morse's finances in order to put Morse in a better light.)

In 1815 his funds for study had been used up, so he regretfully returned home.

From 1815 to 1837, Morse tried several projects in art that he hoped would bring him financial success. Although he became a successful portrait painter, he still struggled financially. From 1829 to 1832, he returned to Europe in an attempt to perfect his artistic technique. In 1832 someone gave Morse a job as professor of painting and sculpture at what today is New York University.

(The doer of the action is unknown.)

In 1832 Morse was given a job as professor of painting and sculpture at what today is New York University.

For Samuel F. B. Morse, invention characterized the 1830s. Morse began working on various projects that he hoped would earn him enough money so that he would be financially free to devote himself to his painting. Since his student days at Yale, he had been interested in electricity. About 1832, however, he became interested in the possibilities of transmitting intelligence by electricity. In his diary he mentioned that these transmissions could occur in underground wires; he also improvised possible codes.

(The doer of the action is very general.)

For Samuel F. B. Morse, the 1830s was characterized by invention.

In 1840 Morse sought and gained a patent from the United States government for his new invention—the telegraph. He lacked scientific skills, but he had still been able to invent the telegraph. From 1840 to 1843, Morse proposed that Congress advance funds to construct a telegraph system. Finally, in 1843, Congress granted him thirty thousand dollars to build a test line between Baltimore and Washington, D.C. On May 24, 1844, Morse demonstrated the telegraph system by tapping out the message "What hath God wrought!"

(The doer of the action is redundant or easy to supply.)

Finally, in 1843, he was granted thirty thousand dollars to build a test line between Baltimore and Washington, D.C.

ESL Help 6E: Exercise in Active and Passive (continued)

Make one sentence or part of one sentence in each group passive, retaining the doer of the action in a *by* phrase. Use the principle in parentheses as a guide to know which sentence to change. Write the new sentence with passive voice in the blank. *(Answers will vary.)*

Samuel F. B. Morse invented the telegraph, but his career in art was not as successful as he would have liked. His career was hindered by his family's lack of support for him and by his inability to support himself from his paintings. Sometime after 1837, frustrated by not being able to devote himself to painting, Morse stopped painting completely.

(The doer of the action is a well-known person.)

The telegraph was invented by Samuel F. B. Morse, but his career in art was not as successful as he

would have liked.

When Samuel F. B. Morse invented the telegraph, he also invented Morse code. Morse code was used to send messages over the telegraph wires. Today it is usually only amateur and maritime radio operators who use Morse code.

(The doer of the action is new information.)

Today Morse code is usually used only by amateur and maritime radio operators.

Morse code consists of long and short sounds. The telegraph machine transmits the long and short sounds. A dash represents a long sound, which is called a *dah*. A dot represents a short sound, which is known as a *dit*.

(The doer of the action is nonhuman.)

Long and short sounds are transmitted by the telegraph machine.

ESL Help 11C: Exercise in Cumulative and Coordinate Adjectives

Look at the adjectives in italics. If the adjectives are from the same meaning category, write *coordinate* in the blank and add a comma between the adjectives. If the adjectives are from different meaning categories, write *cumulative* in the blank.

_____*cumulative*_____	1.	The *talented black* Labrador retriever could do many tricks.
_____*coordinate*_____	2.	His *diligent, hard-working* owner had trained him well.
_____*cumulative*_____	3.	The owner threw the dog's *bouncy rubber* ball.
_____*cumulative*_____	4.	The ball hit the *yellow brick* wall.
_____*coordinate*_____	5.	The *swift, speedy* dog ran after the ball.
_____*coordinate*_____	6.	The dog barked at the ball with a *loud, noisy* bark.
_____*cumulative*_____	7.	The dog ran around the *big dirty* puddle
_____*cumulative*_____	8.	The dog caught the ball in his *large sharp* teeth.
_____*coordinate*_____	9.	The ball popped with a *sharp, piercing* sound.
_____*cumulative*_____	10.	The dog wagged his *long black* tail.

Chapter 1: Using Nouns and Pronouns

Practice A
Identify each italicized noun as common (C) or proper (P) and as concrete (Ct) or abstract (Ab). Remember to place two answers in each blank.

P, Ct   1. My brothers, *Phillip* and Kerry, love to play roller hockey.

C, Ab   2. Having just moved into town, they asked for *guidance* on where they could play hockey.

C, Ct   3. They found a great roller hockey rink—of course, it's made of concrete, not *ice*—near our house.

C, Ab   4. It is nearly always open for the public, and we lace up our in-line skates with *excitement* every afternoon after school.

P, Ct   5. One afternoon, our principal, *Mr. McClusky*, came out to watch us play.

Practice B
Identify each italicized pronoun as personal (P), demonstrative (Dem), interrogative (Inter), indefinite (Ind), reflexive (Ref), intensive (Int), relative (Rel), or reciprocal (Rec).

P   6. Wallace decided to play with *us* today.

Inter   7. *Who* will play for our team when Craig is not here?

Rec   8. It is important in a team sport to assist *one another*.

Rel   9. Perhaps if enough people are interested, we will start a league *that* plays roller hockey in the summer.

Int   10. Will we have to buy uniforms *ourselves*?

Practice C
Write an appropriate noun or pronoun (following the instructions in parentheses) to complete each sentence. (Answers will vary.)

that   11. Kevin told me _?_ he knows a good screen printer. (*relative pronoun*)

each other   12. Perhaps we could help _?_ by allowing him to advertise his printing services on our uniforms. (*reciprocal pronoun*)

uniforms   13. Do we want our _?_ to be the same as those the Pittsburgh Penguins wear? (*plural count noun*)

dedication   14. All of us play roller hockey with a lot of _?_, so we do not often have time to play other sports. (*abstract noun*)

Avalanche   15. We have decided to call our team the _?_. (*proper noun*)

Chapter 2: *S-TrV-DO-OC* and *S*-be-*Advl*

Practice A

Label the sentence patterns *S-InV*, *S-TrV-DO*, *S-TrV-IO-DO*, or *S-TrV-DO-OC*.

        S   **InV**
1. The water in the Bay of Fundy fluctuates tremendously between high and low tides.

  S **TrV**   **DO**
2. It separates the Canadian province of New Brunswick from its sister province, Nova Scotia.

     S   **TrV**   **DO**   **OC**
3. Laura, a member of our mission team, thought the tidal bore amazing.

        S **TrV**   **DO**   **OC**
4. The tidal bore renders the river running into the bay powerless by turning the river back in on itself

   and filling up the riverbed again.

        S   **InV**
5. Soon, a wave of water rushes from one end of the river towards the other.

Practice B

Label the sentence patterns *S-InV*, *S-LV-PN*, *S-LV-PA*, or *S*-be-*Advl*. If the adverbial is a prepositional phrase, underline it.

    S   **LV** **PA**
6. Mr. Grove, the bus driver, was clear about the dangers of walking onto the riverbed at low tide.

    S   **be**   **Advl**
7. Mr. Grove, a constant joker, is also <u>in the business of protecting students</u>.

           S **LV**   **PA**
8. Notwithstanding, we were not brave enough to venture onto the muddy riverbed before the tidal bore.

      S   **LV**   **PN**
9. Owen was the first to see the footprints below the rocks.

      S   **be**   **Advl**
10. Mr. Grove was soon <u>into his tale again</u>, trying to scare anyone listening.

Practice C

Rewrite the sentences to make them *S-TrV-DO-OC* or *S*-be-*Advl*, according to the instructions. (Answers will vary.)

11. This company offers rafting trips on the bore during the summertime. (*S*-be-*Advl*)

    This company's rafting trips are on the bore during the summertime.

12. The quickly moving water causes the ride to be quite fun. (*S-TrV-DO-OC*)

    The quickly moving water makes the ride quite fun.

13. No one in our group had ever rafted the bore before. (*S*-be-*Advl*)

    No one in our group had been on the bore before.

14. First, we climbed into two large rafts. (*S-TrV-DO-OC*)

    First, we made ourselves passengers of two large rafts.

15. Soon we found ourselves in life jackets, whirling on a wave from the Bay of Fundy. (*S*-be-*Advl*)

    Soon we were in life jackets, whirling on a wave from the Bay of Fundy.

Chapter 3: Prepositional Phrases

Practice A
Place parentheses around each prepositional phrase. Identify the phrase as either adjectival (Adj) or adverbial (Adv).

Adv 1. Malawi is located (on Lake Nyasa's western coast.)

Adj 2. Malawi has no access (to an ocean.)

Adv 3. This African country is (beside Lake Nyasa, Tanzania, Zambia, and Mozambique.)

Adv 4. Malawi's previous name was Nyasaland, which the British gave it (during their domination.)

Adj 5. Although it gained independence (from Britain,) Malawi initially struggled to govern itself.

Practice B
Place parentheses around each prepositional phrase. Underline the word that each prepositional phrase modifies. Then identify the phrase as either adjectival (Adj) or adverbial (Adv).

Adj 6. Malawi, "the warm <u>heart</u> (of Africa,") is still a largely undeveloped country.

Adv 7. However, it <u>has</u> many scenic vistas, especially (along Lake Nyasa's beautiful shore.)

Adv 8. Tourists can <u>dive</u>, <u>swim</u>, and <u>snorkel</u> (in the beautiful lake.)

Adj 9. Malawi does have a border <u>dispute</u> (with neighboring Mozambique.)

Adv 10. Interestingly, Malawi <u>celebrates</u> Independence Day (on July 6.)

Practice C
Underline the word the italicized prepositional phrase modifies. Draw a caret (∧) to show where the prepositional phrase should be in order to make it closer to the word it modifies. If the sentence is already correct, write C in the blank.

_____ 11. *By a popular vote,* Malawi's president <u>is elected</u>∧ every five years.

_____ 12. The first presidential <u>elections</u>∧ were won by Dr. Hastings Banda *in the new country.*

C 13. Dr. Banda had been the <u>leader</u> *of the independence movement.*

_____ 14. *In rural areas* most of Malawi's citizens <u>live</u>.
∧

_____ 15. *In state-operated game reserves,* Malawi is also a land of exotic <u>wildlife</u>.
∧

Chapter 3: Gerunds

Practice A
Underline the gerunds. Identify the function of each gerund as subject (S), direct object (DO), indirect object (IO), predicate noun (PN), or object of the preposition (OP).

_**S**_ 1. Hitting was a subject Ted Williams certainly mastered.

_**DO**_ 2. He often greeted pitching rudely.

_**OP**_ 3. One year he joined an elite group by maintaining a great record at bat of over .400.

_**PN**_ 4. His game was also hitting for power, which he did as well as anyone in either league.

_**IO**_ 5. Even from his rookie year, scouts gave his batting tremendous credit.

Practice B
Underline the entire gerund phrase. Underline any gerund complements twice. In the blank identify the function of each gerund as subject (S), direct object (DO), indirect object (IO), predicate noun (PN), object of the preposition (OP), or appositive (App).

_**S**_ 6. Pitching the baseball was also a desire the young Williams had.

_**OP**_ 7. He dreamed of throwing for the Red Sox as he had done for his high-school team.

_**PN**_ 8. In high school, his best performance was striking out twenty-three batters in one game.

**App** 9. The task, hitting his pitches, was one he thought that few could do.

_**IO**_ 10. However, Williams soon gave pitching little thought and concentrated again on his strengths as a hitter.

Practice C
Underline the gerunds. In the blank identify the function of each gerund as subject (S), direct object (DO), indirect object (IO), predicate noun (PN), object of the preposition (OP), or appositive (App). If there is no gerund in the sentence, write *none* in the blank. Do not underline participles.

_**DO**_ 11. A blossoming talent named Ted Williams began playing for the San Diego Padres.

**none** 12. Banking on his continuing success, the Boston Red Sox traded for Williams.

_**S**_ 13. Building on his solid hitting performances won him two Triple Crowns for Boston.

**App** 14. The continuing activity of his bat, a graceful, yet powerful swinging for the fences, resulted in 521 towering round-trippers.

**none** 15. Wanting to be remembered as the greatest hitter that ever lived, he built a living legend for himself by the awe-inspiring exploits of his game.

Chapter 3: Participles

Practice A
Underline the present participles once and the past participles twice. Place parentheses around the entire participial phrase.

1. In 1939 when the Red Sox first obtained Williams, (much <u>needed</u> for his tremendous bat,) he hit .327 and led the league with an (<u>astounding</u>) 145 RBIs.

2. (<u>Amazing</u> every expert two years later,) Ted Williams hit over .400 for the first time.

3. That (<u>famed</u>) average handed him the (<u>batting</u>) title for 1941.

4. He once noted that the only pitch he ever had (<u>continuing</u>) trouble with was the knuckle ball, (<u>fluttering</u> and <u>dipping</u> like a butterfly.)

5. Also in his (<u>storied</u>) 1941 season, he hit thirty-seven (<u>high-flying</u>) home runs.

Practice B
Underline the participles once and the nouns they modify twice. Do not underline passive or progressive verbs.

6. Whenever he was beaten by an <u>opposing</u> <u>pitcher</u>, Williams eagerly anticipated the challenge.

7. Part of the reason he was so successful at the plate was his <u>sharpened</u> <u>eyesight</u>.

8. He could see the <u>spinning</u> <u>stitches</u> on a fastball even at ninety-five miles per hour.

9. Once, when Williams played at another ballpark, he noticed that the closely <u>measured</u> <u>angle</u> at first base was just a few degrees more than it should have been.

10. The officials measured the <u>questioned</u> <u>base</u> and found that it was off by only two inches.

Practice C
Insert a logical participle or participial phrase. Underline each noun modified by a participle. *(Answers will vary.)*

11. Sadly, Williams's _____*famed*_____ <u>career</u> was interrupted by war.

12. _____*Unnerving many of his fans*_____, Williams's <u>draft board</u> classified him as 1-A.

13. The Red Sox's _____*saddened*_____ <u>manager</u>, Joe Cronin, said that if Uncle Sam wanted him, Williams would make a mighty fine soldier.

14. _____*Not respecting any person's career*_____, <u>Uncle Sam</u> did want him, and Williams spent five years out of his baseball career in military service.

15. _____*Being amazingly high in several areas of the game*_____, the <u>marks</u> he left warranted his _____*undisputed*_____ <u>induction</u> into the Hall of Fame in 1966.

Chapter 3: Infinitives

Practice A
Underline each infinitive phrase and identify it as an adjective (Adj), an adverb (Adv), or a noun (N).

___N___ 1. Many biologists wish <u>to see the unclassified wildlife of the Amazon rain forest</u>.

___N___ 2. In fact, <u>to classify the unknown wildlife</u> is what brings many to the region.

___Adv___ 3. In the nearby marketplace, fish that are brought <u>to be sold</u> often remain unidentified.

___Adv___ 4. <u>To see piranhas, jaguars, sloths, armadillos, spider monkeys, and river dolphins</u> one would probably travel to the Amazon.

___Adj___ 5. Another fact <u>to know</u> is that over eighteen hundred species of butterflies are there.

Practice B
A. Underline each infinitive phrase once.
B. Underline each complement of an infinitive twice.
C. Circle any words that split an infinitive.
D. Identify each infinitive phrase as an adjective (Adj), an adverb (Adv), or a noun (N).

___Adj___ 6. The city of Manaus is a good starting place <u>to begin a <u>trip</u> to the Amazon</u>.

___Adv___ 7. Manaus is located beside the Rio Negro, which proceeds <u>to (promptly) join the <u>Solimões River</u> and become the <u>Amazon</u></u>.

___Adj___ 8. Another biological wonderland <u>to (definitely) see</u> is the Pantanal.

___N___ 9. <u>To find the <u>Pantanal</u></u> would not take a long time; it is nearly half the size of France.

___N___ 10. It is a large marshland, and <u>to see <u>everything in it</u></u> would be impossible.

Practice C
Underline each infinitive phrase and identify it as passive (P) or active (A).

___A___ 11. Because there are no towns <u>to stay in comfortably</u>, trips to the Pantanal are usually not long.

___P___ 12. The Pantanal is <u>to be found to the south of the Amazon</u>.

___P___ 13. Giant river otters, anacondas, iguanas, jaguars, cougars, deer and anteaters—these are some of the animals <u>to be watched</u>.

___P___ 14. However, it would be an altogether different experience <u>to be attacked by them</u>.

___A___ 15. The giant river otter has been known <u>to be seven feet long in some cases</u>!

Chapter 4: Adjective and Adverb Clauses

Practice A
Identify each italicized clause as adjectival (Adj) or adverbial (Adv).

_Adj___ 1. The giant sloth *that roamed many years ago* is presumed to be extinct today.

_Adv___ 2. Remains of the giant sloth, *when they were found in both North and South America,* revealed that the animal had existed on a very large scale.

_Adv___ 3. *If you want to see a giant sloth,* its remains are on display at the National Museum of History.

_Adv___ 4. *Although many scientists oppose the view,* some scientists believe that the sloth has been extinct for only about five hundred years.

_Adj___ 5. Others *who have seen large, unusual, and unidentified creatures with characteristics of the giant sloth* believe that the animal may still exist today.

Practice B
Place parentheses around each dependent clause and identify it as adjectival (Adj) or adverbial (Adv).

_Adj___ 6. It was a large creature(that in some instances measured eighteen to twenty feet long.)

_Adv___ 7. (While it usually walked on four legs,)it sometimes walked upright.

_Adv___ 8. Its large tail was used(so it could stand and eat from tree branches.)

_Adj___ 9. The giant sloth,(whose four feet had long claws,)was a fierce, frightening opponent.

_Adv___ 10. (Though it had long, sharp claws,)it was not a carnivorous animal.

Practice C
A. Underline each relative pronoun once and each relative adverb twice. Circle each subordinating conjunction.
B. Place parentheses around each dependent clause.
C. Identify each clause as adjectival (Adj) or adverbial (Adv).

_Adv___ 11. (Although the modern tree sloth is relatively small,)the giant sloth was similar in size and weight to an elephant.

_Adj___ 12. Some sources(that ignore the significant findings in the North American continent)call South America the only home of the giant sloth.

_Adj___ 13. The time of the 1890s, (when a hunting party sighted a large sloth-like creature in Argentina,)generated new interest in finding the creature alive today.

_Adj___ 14. The hunters stopped at the place(where they were)to try to capture the animal.

_Adj___ 15. Soon scientists(who were investigating)found skin from a supposed giant sloth.

Chapter 4: Noun Clauses

Practice A

Identify the function of each italicized noun clause as subject (S), predicate noun (PN), direct object (DO), indirect object (IO), object of the preposition (OP), or appositive (App).

___IO___ 1. Scientists give *what many people call the giant armadillo* a classification closely related to the giant sloth's classification.

___PN___ 2. One interesting fact is *that the giant armadillo has more teeth than any other mammal.*

___App___ 3. It grows to be very large in a few instances, *when it is almost four feet long and weighs over one hundred pounds.*

___S___ 4. *That it stands on its hind feet at times* is perhaps what makes the giant armadillo most like the ancient giant sloth.

___DO___ 5. The giant armadillo, in its armored back, still has *what all armadillos have in common.*

Practice B

Place parentheses around each noun clause and identify its function as subject (S), predicate noun (PN), direct object (DO), indirect object (IO), object of the preposition (OP), or appositive (App).

___IO___ 6. Many Texans can tell (whoever visits their state) stories about armadillos.

___PN___ 7. Armadillos' nine-band armor is (what protects the animals from their enemies.)

___OP___ 8. Some can even ball up into (whatever position they need to protect themselves.)

___DO___ 9. Although armadillos eat insects, they can also eat (whatever plant material they can find.)

___S___ 10. (What dining they do) is done nocturnally since they hide in burrows during the day.

Practice C

A. Place parentheses around each noun clause.
B. Underline each subordinating conjunction once and each indefinite relative pronoun twice.
C. Identify the function of each noun clause as subject (S), predicate noun (PN), direct object (DO), indirect object (IO), object of the preposition (OP), or appositive (App).

___DO___ 11. Scientists consider (<u>whether</u> the armadillo is in one category or another) by looking at its size, appearance, and habits.

___PN___ 12. In Texas, armadillos are (<u>what</u> homeowners want to avoid to maintain their lawns.)

___OP___ 13. However, armadillos' armored bodies protect them from (<u>whoever</u> would hurt them.)

___DO___ 14. Typically slow armadillos can quickly escape (<u>whatever</u> predator would harm them.)

___S___ 15. (<u>That</u> armadillos love to burrow into the ground for shelter and to find grubs for food) is obvious to most Texas homeowners.

Chapter 4: Using Clauses

Practice A
Identify each italicized clause as an independent clause (IC) or a dependent clause (DC).

___DC___ 1. Parasailing is an activity *that George did at the beach.*

___IC___ 2. *He looked like a tiny dot in the sky from the room* where we watched.

___IC___ 3. Once, we saw him swing nearly upside down, and *we began to worry for his safety.*

___DC___ 4. *When his feet touched the boat's deck again,* he encouraged everyone else to try it.

___IC___ 5. *His fifteen-minute ride was well worth the money.*

Practice B
Identify each sentence as simple (S), compound (Cd), complex (Cx), or compound-complex (Cd-Cx).

___Cd___ 6. Wesley decided to parasail also, and he quickly climbed into the harness.

___Cx___ 7. As the boat picked up speed, the large parachute filled up with air.

___S___ 8. Slowly, with one hand over the other, the workers let out the parachute with Wesley into the air.

___S___ 9. Wesley floated higher and higher into the bright blue sky.

___Cd-Cx___ 10. Although he was afraid of falling, he reassured himself that all he would hit was water, and he began to admire the beautiful view of the coastline.

Practice C
Identify each group of words as a sentence (S), a fragment (F), a comma splice (CS), or a fused sentence (FS).

___F___ 11. Wesley, the rider of the skies.

___S___ 12. Thankfully, the ride ended safely.

___CS___ 13. After fifteen minutes, the workers pulled the parachute in, Wesley set his feet solidly within the boat.

___F___ 14. But since Maryann was only two years old at the time.

___FS___ 15. Dad refused to let her parasail that year he said that she could when she was older.

Chapter 5: Subject-Verb Agreement

Practice A

Underline the subjects in the following sentences. Then write the correct form of the verb in parentheses.

__are__ 1. Both <u>Japan</u> and <u>England</u> (*is, are*) known for their beautiful golf courses.

__are__ 2. <u>Hole one</u> and <u>hole four</u> (*is, are*) over five hundred yards.

__is__ 3. Either your <u>driver</u> or another <u>wood</u> (*is, are*) acceptable for this par four.

__are__ 4. There (*is, are*) either <u>trees</u> or <u>sandpits</u> or water <u>hazards</u> to avoid on every hole.

__attract__ 5. <u>Sandpits</u> and <u>lakes</u> always (*attracts, attract*) even my best golf balls.

Practice B

Underline the subject in the following sentences. Place parentheses around any intervening phrases. Then write the correct form of the verb in parentheses.

__is__ 6. Here (*is, are*) a really wide <u>fairway</u>.

__are__ 7. Down the sides of this fairway (*is, are*) <u>groves</u> of trees.

__costs__ 8. A <u>shot</u> (into those trees) invariably (*costs, cost*) a penalty.

__approaches__ 9. A <u>five iron</u> (from here,) not (from the trees,) easily (*approaches, approach*) the green.

__are__ 10. There, (from the tee) of the ninth hole,) (*is, are*) the most beautiful <u>views</u> of the entire course.

Practice C

Underline the subject in the following sentences. Then write the correct form of an appropriate verb. (*Answers will vary.*)

__has__ 11. The <u>United States</u> also _?_ many beautiful golf courses.

__are__ 12. <u>Riches</u> _?_ not required to play on all of them.

__is__ 13. <u>Forty dollars</u> _?_ required to play this course.

__plays__ 14. Nearly <u>every one</u> of my friends _?_ on that public course.

__meets__ 15. My golfing <u>club</u> _?_ every Tuesday afternoon.

Chapter 5: Pronoun-Antecedent Agreement

Practice A
Underline the correct form of the pronoun from the choices in parentheses.

1. Lamentations follows Jeremiah; like the Psalms, (<u>it</u>, they) is a book of Hebrew poetry.

2. Either the Psalms or Lamentations refers to the fall of Jerusalem as (<u>its</u>, their) subject.

3. The sins of God's people or the hope of God's grace is a major theme in each chapter, and (<u>it</u>, they) can be found in nearly every verse.

4. Even the priests and the prophets were found guilty, and the ugliness of (his, <u>their</u>) sins was revealed.

5. The grace of God is emphasized in both verse 22 and in verses 55-57, and (it, <u>they</u>) remind the reader that repentance can still bring mercy.

Practice B
Write the correct form of the pronoun in parentheses. If none of the pronouns in parentheses is correct, write *NA* (no answer) in the blank.

_____**they**_____ 6. The students in the class read Lamentations chapter 5, but (*it, they*) did not understand the parallelism in the Hebrew verse.

_____**NA**_____ 7. While Jeremiah is traditionally considered the author of Lamentations, either of the views about authorship has (*his, their*) own degree of validity.

_____**his**_____ 8. After reading Lamentations, nobody could assert (*his, their*) doubt about whether the mercies of God are beyond what man deserves.

_____**they**_____ 9. Several of the poems speak of the effects of Israel's sins; (*it, they*) lament about the city of Jerusalem or the country of Judah.

_____**its**_____ 10. One of the chapters tells (*its, their*) story about the effects of the judgment upon the speaker personally.

Practice C
Underline any pronoun that disagrees with its antecedent. Then write the correct pronoun in the blank. If the sentence is already correct, write *C* in the blank.

_____**them**_____ 11. The readers of Lamentations have the results of sin impressed upon <u>him</u>.

_____**C**_____ 12. When they read Lamentations, many see the ugly side of sin hidden by Satan.

_____**C**_____ 13. All of the church has people who can identify with the devastating effects of Israel's rebellion against God because of an awareness of their own sin.

_____**its**_____ 14. Each of the books of the Bible, including Lamentations, contains <u>their</u> own version of the theme of God's undying love towards fallen men.

_____**their**_____ 15. Little of Lamentations or few of the Psalms speak <u>its</u> words of comfort as powerfully as the phrase in Lamentations 3 does: "His compassions fail not."

Chapter 6: Auxiliaries and Principal Parts of Verbs

Practice A
Underline each complete verb.

1. <u>Have</u> you ever <u>seen</u> a comet?

2. Comets <u>do travel</u> in a definite pattern throughout the solar system.

3. Some comets <u>can be seen</u> near the sun.

4. By the sun, some comets <u>will develop</u> bright tails.

5. These tails <u>may extend</u> as far as one hundred million miles.

Practice B
Underline each complete verb. Then write Aux above each auxiliary.

6. Edmond Halley, an English astronomer, <u>*Aux*
did increase</u> scientific knowledge about comets.

7. He <u>*Aux*
had calculated</u> the orbit of the comet observed in 1682.

8. He <u>*Aux*
could</u> correctly <u>predict</u> the next appearance of the comet.

9. Halley's comet <u>*Aux Aux*
has been recorded</u> as early as 240 B.C.

10. The comet <u>*Aux*
should appear</u> again around the year 2061.

Practice C
Write the correct present, past, or past participle form of the verb in parentheses.

__*has surrounded*__ 11. Since ancient times, superstition (*surround*) the sighting of comets.

__*believed*__ 12. People once (*believe*) that comets foretold plagues, wars, and death.

__*appear*__ 13. Comets (*appear*) to have "hairy" tails.

__*is*__ 14. The name *comet* (*be*) from the Greek word *kometes*, which means "hairy one."

__*began*__ 15. In the seventeenth century, scientists (*begin*) to understand comets better.

Chapter 6: Tense

Practice A

Identify the tense of each italicized verb as *present, past, future, present perfect, past perfect, future perfect, present progressive, past progressive, future progressive, present perfect progressive, past perfect progressive,* or *future perfect progressive.*

present perfect progressive   1. Our class *has been studying* comets.

past perfect   2. Mr. Littlejohn, our teacher, *had planned* many interesting activities.

future progressive   3. We *will be visiting* a planetarium in a few weeks.

present   4. A comet *differs* from an asteroid in its orbit and chemical makeup.

future   5. Many comets *will* not *develop* tails.

Practice B

Write the progressive form of each italicized verb. Do not change the tense of the verb.

are moving   6. Most comets *move* in elliptical, oval-shaped orbits.

may be traveling   7. Other comets *may travel* in parabolic or hyperbolic orbits.

is taking   8. The time it *takes* a comet to orbit the sun is called a period.

are taking   9. Some comets *take* less than seven years to complete an orbit.

will be traveling   10. Other comets *will travel* hundreds of years before completing an orbit.

Practice C

Write an appropriate form of the verb in parentheses. (Answers will vary.)

had suggested   11. In the fourth century B.C., Aristotle (*suggest*) that comets were bits of Earth sent out into space.

proved   12. In the sixteenth century, Tycho Brahe (*prove*) that comets indeed were heavenly bodies.

disproved   13. Sir Isaac Newton (*disprove*) the theory that comets traveled in a straight line, a false theory earlier developed by Kepler.

used   14. Halley (*use*) Newton's calculations to discover the orbit of the comet that now bears his name.

have been discovered   15. Many more comets (*discover*); each one gives testimony to the magnificence of God's creation.

Chapter 6: Voice and Mood

Practice A
Underline each complete verb. Then identify it as *active* or *passive*.

_____*active*_____ 1. Planetariums <u>strive</u> to create a realistic picture of space.

_____*passive*_____ 2. Many differently sized projectors <u>are employed</u> by planetariums to simulate space.

_____*passive*_____ 3. Planetariums <u>are used</u> to teach descriptive astronomy and celestial navigation.

_____*active*_____ 4. The planetariums <u>offer</u> regular demonstrations, or sky shows, to the public.

_____*passive*_____ 5. The first planetarium <u>was opened</u> in Deutsches Museum in Munich in 1923.

Practice B
Identify the mood of each italicized verb as *indicative*, *imperative*, or *subjunctive*.

_____*indicative*_____ 6. John T. Desaguliers, a friend of Newton, *invented* the planetarium.

_____*subjunctive*_____ 7. If Desaguliers were alive today, he *would be amazed* at how modern technology has enhanced his invention.

_____*indicative*_____ 8. Originally, the term "planetarium" *described* devices used to portray the orbit of the planets.

_____*indicative*_____ 9. Now computers *are able* to create realistic, accurate projections of space.

_____*imperative*_____ 10. *Visit* a planetarium to see and learn about the heavens.

Practice C
Underline each complete verb. If the sentence is passive, rewrite it to change the verb to active voice.

11. The Hayden Planetarium in New York City <u>uses</u> a high-tech virtual reality system to produce the most realistic star show available today.

_____

_____

12. Visits to local planetariums <u>are used</u> by teachers to inspire students toward a deeper interest in science.

   <u>*Teachers use visits to local planetariums to inspire students toward a deeper interest in science.*</u>

_____

13. <u>See</u> the beauty and splendor of God's creation!

   _____

   _____

14. The order of the universe <u>is sustained</u> by God.

   God sustains the order of the universe.

   _____

15. By looking at the heavens, you <u>will be</u> in awe of God's handiwork.

   _____

   _____

Chapter 7: Pronoun Reference

Practice A

Underline each personal pronoun. Identify the pronoun reference in each sentence as *clear* or *unclear.*

_____*clear*_____ 1. A national cemetery is a burial place for men and women of the armed forces of the United States unless <u>they</u> were dishonorably discharged from the military.

_____*unclear*_____ 2. The United States government has 119 national cemeteries in the United States and Puerto Rico, and about 50 of these cemeteries have no more space for additional gravesites. <u>They</u> are maintained by government agencies.

_____*clear*_____ 3. In addition, the Department of Veterans Affairs provides headstones for all graves in national cemeteries without <u>them</u>.

_____*unclear*_____ 4. The government cares for the graves and the headstones; <u>it</u> is an enormous job.

_____*unclear*_____ 5. In 1862, during the Civil War, Congress established the National Cemetery System by granting to Abraham Lincoln permission to establish <u>them</u> for Union army veterans.

Practice B

Questions 6-10: Rewrite the following paragraph, correcting the five pronoun reference errors.
(Answers will vary.)

The Gettysburg National Cemetery was dedicated on the battlefield of Gettysburg on November 19, 1863, by him when he gave the Gettysburg Address. The dedication ceremony set part of it aside to be used as a national cemetery. More than seven thousand men are buried in it. Today, Gettysburg National Military Park contains the battlefield and it as well as numerous monuments to the battle. It was set up in 1895.

The Gettysburg National Cemetery was dedicated on the battlefield of Gettysburg on November 19, 1863, by Abraham Lincoln when he gave the Gettysburg Address. The dedication ceremony set part of the battlefield aside to be used as a national cemetery. More than seven thousand men are buried in Gettysburg National Cemetery. Today, Gettysburg National Military Park contains the battlefield and the cemetery as well as numerous monuments to the battle. The park was set up in 1895.

Practice C
Rewrite each problem sentence to correct any unclear pronoun reference. *(Answers will vary.)*

11. The Arlington National Cemetery is one of the largest and most famous of them in the United States.

   The Arlington National Cemetery is one of the largest and most famous of the national cemeteries

   in the United States.

12. The cemetery was created from the estate of Robert E. Lee's wife, Mary Custis Lee; and before 1864, the estate was where he lived.

   The cemetery was created from the estate of Robert E. Lee's wife, Mary Custis Lee; and before 1864,

   the estate was where General Robert E. Lee lived.

13. Robert E. Lee's wife was the daughter of George Washington Parke Custis; he was the commander of the Confederate army.

   Robert E. Lee's wife was the daughter of George Washington Parke Custis; Robert E. Lee was the

   commander of the Confederate army.

14. George Washington Parke Custis was the grandson of Martha Washington, not of George Washington. He was related to him only by marriage.

   George Washington Parke Custis was related to him only by marriage.

15. Before Martha was married to George Washington, she had been married to Daniel Parke Custis. After he died, Martha married him.

   After he died, Martha married George.

Chapter 7: Pronoun Reference II

Practice A

Underline each personal pronoun. Identify the pronoun reference in each sentence as _clear_ or _unclear._

_____unclear_____ 1. George and Martha Washington adopted George Washington Parke Custis after his father died; <u>it</u> was very sad.

_____unclear_____ 2. Robert E. Lee and Mary Custis Lee lived in Arlington House, which had been built by her father, George Washington Parke Custis. <u>They</u> left the house when the Civil War broke out in 1861.

_____unclear_____ 3. <u>They</u> say that the Union government claimed the property and the house in 1864.

_____unclear_____ 4. The Union government set apart part of the property for Arlington National Cemetery in 1864; <u>it</u> was a relatively new idea.

_____clear_____ 5. <u>It</u> was eighteen years before the government bought the house and property from the owner.

Practice B

Underline each personal pronoun and write its antecedent in the blank. If the antecedent is unclear, write _unclear_ in the blank.

**George Washington Custis Lee** 6. George Washington Custis Lee was declared the owner after the war and received $150,000 from the government for the house and property; <u>he</u> was the son of Robert E. Lee.

_____unclear_____ 7. <u>They</u> say the Arlington House is also known as the Robert E. Lee Memorial.

_____unclear_____ 8. <u>They</u> will bury only certain people in the Arlington National Cemetery.

**men and women** 9. Arlington National Cemetery is a burial place for Americans who served our country; our country honors these men and women by burying <u>them</u> there.

**cemetery** 10. Although the cemetery was originally for Union soldiers, today only members of certain categories within the armed forces and only officials elected to an office of the federal government, given an appointed cabinet-level position, or appointed to the Supreme Court may be buried in <u>it</u>.

Practice C

Correct any unclear pronoun reference by rewriting the unclear sentence. If the sentence is already clear, write *C* in the blank. *(Answers will vary.)*

11. President John F. Kennedy and President William Howard Taft are buried in Arlington National Cemetery; he was the thirty-fifth president of the United States.

    President John F. Kennedy and President William Howard Taft are buried in Arlington National

    Cemetery; President John F. Kennedy was the thirty-fifth president of the United States.

12. The Tomb of the Unknowns is located in Arlington National Cemetery; this has meaning for many people.

    The Tomb of the Unknowns is located in Arlington National Cemetery; the Tomb of the Unknowns has

    meaning for many people.

13. After World War I, officials of the Allied countries discovered that many bodies of the soldiers could not be identified, so they did not know where to bury the soldiers. This created problems.

    This lack of identification created problems.

14. On Armistice Day, 1921, an Unknown Soldier from World War I was buried in Arlington National Cemetery. His white marble tomb and inscription were completed in 1931, and it reads, "Here rests in honored glory an American soldier known only to God."

    C

15. On Memorial Day, 1958, unknown soldiers from both World War II and the Korean War were buried in marble-capped crypts at the head of the larger marble tomb. On Memorial Day, 1984, an unknown soldier from the Vietnam War was buried with these others, but his remains were later identified through advances in DNA testing and then removed from the Tomb of the Unknowns. This is amazing.

    This scientific advancement is amazing.

Chapter 8: Correct Use of Pronoun Case

Practice A
Underline the correct pronoun from the choices in parentheses.

1. Francis Thompson, an English poet of the late seventeenth century and early eighteenth century, is best known for (*his*, *him*) poem "The Hound of Heaven."

2. His own personal experience drove (*his*, *him*) to write the poem.

3. The poem can apply to you and (*I*, *me*) today.

4. (*It*, *Its*) deals with God's pursuing man.

5. The Holy Spirit is pictured as an unrelenting hound that pursues (*we*, *us*) to salvation.

Practice B
Underline each personal pronoun and identify it as subjective (S), objective (O), possessive (P), or as an independent possessive (IP).

__P__ 6. Francis Thompson had tried to become a doctor for his career.

__S__ 7. When he failed at that, Thompson went to London.

__O__ 8. In London, sickness, addiction, and poverty plagued him.

__IP__ 9. Some of Thompson's problems may be similar to ours.

__P__ 10. Thompson found the answer to his problems in God.

Practice C
Insert an appropriate pronoun as indicated in parentheses.

____they____ 11. Wilfrid and Alice Meynell found Thompson in London, and _?_ helped him with his problems. (*subjective*)

____his____ 12. When God helped Thompson overcome his problems, Thompson wrote _?_ poem "The Hound of Heaven." (*possessive*)

____he____ 13. The poem describes Thompson in his search to find peace, security, and happiness outside of God; finally _?_ realized that these things could be found only in God. (*subjective*)

____him____ 14. Thompson saw how God had used all life's circumstances to find _?_. (*objective*)

____yours____ 15. Thompson's search for happiness may not be much different from _?_ or mine. (*independent possessive*)

Chapter 8: Compound Constructions, Appositives, and Comparisons Using *Than* or *As*

Practice A
Identify each sentence as correct (C) or incorrect (I).

__C__ 1. In comparing Gerard Manley Hopkins with Francis Thompson, most people would say that Hopkins was a better poet than he.

__I__ 2. For one thing, Thompson did not write as many poems as him.

__C__ 3. Thompson and he lived at the same time.

__C__ 4. However, Hopkins was about fifteen years older than he.

__I__ 5. Religious poems were written by both Hopkins and he.

Practice B
Underline the correct pronoun from the choices in parentheses.

6. Hopkins used more innovative poetic structures than (*he*, *him*).

7. (*We*, *us*) readers can learn a lot about different poetic techniques through reading Hopkins's poems.

8. (*They*, *them*), the poets, both include nature images in their poems.

9. In "Pied Beauty," Hopkins describes the beauty of God's creation for you and (*I*, *me*) to read.

10. People can be pointed to God through the poems of Hopkins and (*he*, *him*).

Practice C
Choose the letter corresponding to the correct pronoun.

__A__ 11. Like Hopkins and Thompson, George Herbert was a British poet; however, Herbert lived during an earlier time than _?_.
A. they
B. them

__A__ 12. All of these poets—Hopkins, Thompson, and _?_—wrote religious poetry.
A. he
B. him

__B__ 13. Most of the poems written by Hopkins and _?_ were published posthumously.
A. he
B. him

__A__ 14. Hopkins and Thompson were not as active politically as _?_.
A. he
B. him

__A__ 15. You and _?_ should learn more about Herbert's shape poems.
A. I
B. me

Chapter 8: *Who* and *Whom*, Courtesy Order, and Reflexive and Intensive Pronouns

Practice A
Identify each sentence as correct (C) or incorrect (I).

___I___ 1. Whom wrote the shaped poem "Easter Wings"?

___C___ 2. George Herbert wrote the poem himself in the shape of two wings.

___C___ 3. The words in the poem itself form the shape of the wings.

___I___ 4. How many poets do you know of whom try to write shaped poems?

___C___ 5. You and your friends should try to write a shaped poem.

Practice B
Underline the correct pronoun from the choices in parentheses.

6. (<u>Who</u>, *Whom*) frequently used sprung meter in his poetry?

7. Hopkins (*he*, <u>*himself*</u>) wrote poems with sprung meter.

8. Hopkins came up with the term *sprung meter* (*hisself*, <u>*himself*</u>).

9. Hopkins gives you and (*I*, <u>*me*</u>) a variety of different rhythms in his poetry.

10. His poems (*them*, <u>*themselves*</u>) use sprung meter to imitate the strong accents of the way people actually speak.

Practice C
Choose the letter that corresponds to the correct pronoun.

___A___ 11. Hopkins, _?_ did not publish his own poetry, was a major influence on early-twentieth-century poets.
   A. who
   B. whom

___A___ 12. Of the three poets discussed, _?_ do you think is the best poet?
   A. who
   B. whom

___B___ 13. In their poems, these poets did not seek to exalt _?_.
   A. theirselves
   B. themselves

___B___ 14. _?_ did these men write their poetry for?
   A. Who
   B. Whom

___A___ 15. You and _?_ should learn from these men.
   A. I
   B. me

Chapter 9: Showing Comparison with Modifiers

Practice A
Identify each sentence as correct (C) or incorrect (I).

___I___ 1. A lighthouse is a tower with a strongest light that serves as a navigational tool.

___C___ 2. Lighthouses help sailors determine their position in relation to the land and help warn them of dangerous rocks and shorelines.

___C___ 3. Some lighthouses are still in operation today, although they are usually operated by automated electronic and computer navigational equipment.

___C___ 4. Today, many sailors use satellites to help them navigate.

___I___ 5. Before modern technology, sailors had to proceed most cautiously in dangerous waters.

Practice B
Underline the correct adjective or adverb from the choices in parentheses.

6. The Pharos, built in Alexandria, Egypt, was the (*taller, tallest*) lighthouse ever built.

7. Before an earthquake toppled the Pharos, it was (*more, most*) than 440 feet high.

8. One of the (*more, most*) famous lighthouses in the United States is the Boston lighthouse.

9. The (*older, oldest*) lighthouse in the United States, the Boston lighthouse, was built in 1716.

10. The Boston lighthouse is one of the (*better-preserved, best-preserved*) lighthouses in America.

Practice C
Write the correct form of the modifier in parentheses.

___carefully___ 11. In 1993, the Block Island Lighthouse of Rhode Island was (*careful*) moved back from shore approximately 300 feet.

___more___ 12. The move was actually (*some*) complicated than building the lighthouse.

___more___ 13. The move probably made the lighthouse (*some*) widely known than it had been before.

___highest___ 14. Sitting over 258 feet above sea level, the lighthouse is the (*high*) lighthouse in New England.

___better___ 15. In most peoples' opinions, moving the lighthouse back was (*good*) than leaving the lighthouse in a dangerous place.

Chapter 9: Problems with Modifiers

Practice A
Identify each sentence as correct (C) or incorrect (I).

___I___ 1. When lighthouses were first used in the United States, the lighthouses didn't have no modern technology, so people were hired to run the lighthouses.

___I___ 2. Sometimes the lighthouse keepers didn't have some way to get from the land to the lighthouse except by boat.

___C___ 3. Many lighthouse keepers didn't have anywhere they could live except the lighthouse and its island.

___C___ 4. Sometimes, because of inclement weather, keepers would remain stranded at the lighthouse for months.

___I___ 5. All lighthouse keepers know that sometimes the sea looks calmly before a storm.

Practice B
Identify each sentence as correct (C) or incorrect (I). If the sentence is incorrect, write the correction in the blank.

__I; a braver lighthouse keeper__ 6. Idawalley Zorada Lewis was a more braver lighthouse keeper than some lighthouse keepers were.

_____C_____ 7. She was famous because there wasn't a rescue that she didn't try, and she completed many hard rescues successfully.

_____C_____ 8. Her father had been the original lighthouse keeper, but after he had a stroke, he couldn't do the work anymore.

_____C_____ 9. She probably worked harder than other lighthouse keepers did.

____I; much farther____ 10. Because the lighthouse was much more farther than fifty yards from the mainland, Ida had to row her brother and sister to and from school each day, sometimes in very bad weather.

Practice C
Rewrite each sentence, making the modifier clear or correct.

11. We are supposed to begin studying some types of light signals today, but we have not covered none of them yet.

   __We are supposed to begin studying some types of light signals today, but we have not covered__

   __any of them yet.__

12. A fixed light is a much more steadier beam than other signals.

   __A fixed light is a much steadier beam than other signals.__

13. A flashing light is one in which the periods of darkness are more longer than the periods of light.

    A flashing light is one in which the periods of darkness are longer than the periods of light.

14. One of the most greatest practical reasons that lighthouses use different light patterns is so that sailors can distinguish the lighthouses by their light patterns.

    One of the greatest practical reasons that lighthouses use different light patterns is so that sailors

    can distinguish the lighthouses by their light patterns.

15. When the weather grows coldly and foggy, sailors need to be able to distinguish lighthouses by their lights.

    When the weather grows cold and foggy, sailors need to be able to distinguish lighthouses by

    their lights.

Chapter 9: Placement of Modifiers

Practice A
Identify each sentence as correct (C) or incorrect (I).

___I___ 1. Involved in some Revolutionary War battles, many people today know about the Boston lighthouse.

___I___ 2. When the British blockaded Boston Harbor, the minutemen attempted to swiftly blow up the Boston lighthouse to break the blockade.

___C___ 3. However, the minutemen only damaged the lighthouse.

___C___ 4. The British had the lighthouse almost entirely repaired when the Americans attacked the lighthouse again.

___C___ 5. The Americans skillfully drove the British away and started to burn the lighthouse.

Practice B
Write the letter of the sentence in which the modifier is clear and correct.

___A___ 6. A. The British who had come back to the lighthouse attacked the Americans quickly.
　　　　 B. The British who had come back to the lighthouse quickly attacked the Americans.

___B___ 7. A. In the skirmish, one American soldier only died.
　　　　 B. In the skirmish, only one American soldier died.

___B___ 8. A. A key navigational tool, the British also used the lighthouse as part of their blockade of Boston Harbor.
　　　　 B. A key navigational tool, the lighthouse was also part of the British blockade of Boston Harbor.

___A___ 9. A. Eventually the British managed to regain control of the lighthouse completely.
　　　　 B. Eventually the British managed to completely regain control of the lighthouse.

___B___ 10. A. The Americans again attacked the lighthouse, and they drove almost the British away.
　　　　 B. The Americans again attacked the lighthouse, and they almost drove the British away.

Practice C
Rewrite each sentence, making the modifiers clear and correct. (Answers will vary.)

11. So the Americans wouldn't have the lighthouse, the British blew up the lighthouse merely with gunpowder as they were retreating.

    So the Americans wouldn't have the lighthouse, the British merely blew up the lighthouse with

    gunpowder as they were retreating.

12. Most people are aware that the rebuilt lighthouse that know history is over two hundred years old.

    Most people that know history are aware that the rebuilt lighthouse is over two hundred years old.

13. Located on Little Brewster Island, the official name of the lighthouse is the Boston Light.

     The official name of the lighthouse located on Little Brewster Island is the Boston Light.

14. A battle was fought near the lighthouse of the War of 1812, but not for possession of the lighthouse.

     A battle of the War of 1812 was fought near the lighthouse, but not for possession of the lighthouse.

15. Instead of fighting over the lighthouse, the naval battle was between an American and an English ship—the USS *Chesapeake* and the HMS *Shannon*.

     Instead of fighting over the lighthouse, the American and English sailors fought a naval battle

     ***between two ships—the USS* Chesapeake *and the HMS* Shannon.**

Chapter 10: People, Places, Constructions, Organizations, and Businesses

Practice A
Underline each word that contains a capitalization error.

1. Edward Brooke was born in <u>washington</u>, D.C. and graduated from <u>howard</u> <u>university</u>.

2. Brooke served in the United States <u>army</u> in <u>italy</u> in World War II and won the Bronze Star for bravery.

3. After the war, <u>brooke</u> earned a law degree from <u>boston</u> <u>university</u>.

4. In 1962 and 1964, he was elected attorney general of <u>massachusetts</u>.

5. From 1967 to 1979, he served as a <u>massachusetts</u> representative to the <u>u.s.</u> <u>senate</u>; he was the first black ever elected to the <u>senate</u> by popular vote.

Practice B
Underline each word that contains a capitalization error and write the correction in the blank. If the sentence is already correct, write C in the blank.

6. Patricia Roberts Harris graduated from Howard University in 1945 and earned a law degree from George Washington University in 1960.

   _____ *C* _____

7. In 1965 <u>president</u> Lyndon B. Johnson appointed her an ambassador to <u>luxembourg</u>; she was the nation's first black female ambassador.

   _____ *President; Luxembourg* _____

8. In 1971 <u>ibm</u> appointed her as a director; she was the first black woman to serve as a director of a major <u>u.s.</u> company.

   _____ *IBM; U.S.* _____

9. From 1977 to 1979, she served as secretary of the Department of Housing and Urban Development.

   _____ *C* _____

10. In 1979 Harris's department became the <u>department of health and human services</u>; she was the first black woman to hold a post in the U.S. cabinet.

    _____ *Department of Health and Human Services* _____

Practice C

Rewrite the following paragraph, correcting the five errors in capitalization. (Proper nouns consisting of multiple words count as one error.)

Thurgood Marshall graduated from lincoln university and studied law at Howard University; he began practicing law in 1933. From 1938 to 1950, he was chief counsel for the NAACP (national association for the advancement of colored people). In 1954 he presented the legal argument that resulted in the supreme court decision that declared segregation in public schools unconstitutional. In 1965 Marshall was appointed solicitor general of the United States. In 1967 president Lyndon B. Johnson appointed Marshall associate justice; he was the first black justice of the u.s. Supreme Court.

Thurgood Marshall graduated from Lincoln University and studied law at Howard University; he began practicing law in 1933. From 1938 to 1950, he was chief counsel for the NAACP (National Association for the Advancement of Colored People). In 1954 he presented the legal argument that resulted in the Supreme Court decision that declared segregation in public schools unconstitutional. In 1965 Marshall was appointed solicitor general of the United States. In 1967 President Lyndon B. Johnson appointed Marshall associate justice; he was the first black justice of the U.S. Supreme Court.

Chapter 10: Religious, Cultural, and Historical Terms; Titles and First Words; Proper Adjectives and Other Words

Practice A
Identify each sentence as correctly capitalized (C) or incorrectly capitalized (I).

_C_ 1. Hinduism is the main religion of the country of India.

_I_ 2. The main book of Hinduism is called the vedas.

_C_ 3. Brahman, an impersonal world soul, is the Hindu god.

_I_ 4. Hindus believe that all the gods of every religion are part of brahman.

_I_ 5. Unlike Hinduism, Christianity is not an all-inclusive religion; Christianity believes in only one God and creator of all.

Practice B
Underline each word that contains a capitalization error.

6. The <u>augsburg</u> <u>confession</u> was written by Philipp Melanchthon, a friend of Martin Luther.

7. This historic document outlines the beliefs of the denomination now known as <u>lutheran</u>.

8. This document was written during the period in history known as the <u>reformation</u>.

9. A former <u>german</u> priest, Luther was a key figure in the <u>reformation</u>.

10. This document summarized what Luther believed the <u>bible</u> taught.

Practice C
Underline each word that contains a capitalization error and write the correction in the blank. If the sentence is already correct, write C in the blank.

Shorter Catechism 11. Luther had already written his <u>shorter</u> <u>catechism</u>, which presented Scripture doctrines to children.

Roman 12. Luther had tried to reform the <u>roman</u> Catholic Church.

_C_ 13. But the church did not want to listen to Luther's arguments, so the church excommunicated Luther in June of 1520.

Is Our 14. Today, many Christians know of Martin Luther because of his hymn "A Mighty Fortress <u>is</u> <u>our</u> God."

_C_ 15. I think it would be interesting to learn more about the life of Martin Luther.

Chapter 11: End Marks and Other Uses of the Period

Practice A
Identify each sentence as correctly punctuated *(C)* or incorrectly punctuated *(I)*.

__C__ 1. The residence and office of the president of the United States became officially known as the White House when that name was put on President Theodore Roosevelt's stationery.

__I__ 2. I wonder if the White House has any other names?

__I__ 3. You should study about the history of the White House!

__C__ 4. Where is the White House located?

__C__ 5. The street address for the White House is 1600 Pennsylvania Avenue.

Practice B
Write the letter of the sentence that is punctuated correctly.

__A__ 6. A. Wow, the White House has 132 rooms!
      B. Wow, the White House has 132 rooms.

__B__ 7. A. Don't you think it would be nice to have a house with that many rooms to live in.
      B. Don't you think it would be nice to have a house with that many rooms to live in?

__B__ 8. A. The president and his family don't actually live in all those rooms, do they!
      B. The president and his family don't actually live in all those rooms, do they?

__A__ 9. A. No, their living quarters are on the second floor of the White House.
      B. No, their living quarters are on the second floor of the White House!

__B__ 10. A. The dimensions for the main building of the White House are 52 m. × 26 m. or 170 ft. × 85 ft.
       B. The dimensions for the main building of the White House are 52 m × 26 m or 170 ft. × 85 ft.

Practice C
Insert the correct end marks for each sentence.

11. The first president to live in the White House was John Adams and his family.

12. Why didn't George Washington live in the White House?

13. Washington commissioned the building of the White House, but it wasn't completed during his presidency.

14. It's awful that the first president didn't get to live in the White House! or .

15. I wonder whether Washington really minded; he lived in a beautiful three-story home in Mount Vernon, Virginia.

Chapter 11: Commas and Semicolons

Practice A
Identify each sentence as correctly punctuated (C) or incorrectly punctuated (I).

___I___ 1. The third floor of the White House has the guest rooms, and rooms for the staff.

___I___ 2. The Library, China Room, Vermeil Room and Map Room are all located on the ground floor while the Blue Room, Red Room, and State Dining Room are located on the first floor.

___I___ 3. The formal rooms of state on the first floor are where the president and his wife receive guests aren't they?

___C___ 4. While the first lady's guests usually meet the first lady in the Red Room, the president's dinner guests usually meet the president in the Blue Room.

___C___ 5. The president and his wife host the most formal dinners in the elaborate, elegant State Dining Room.

Practice B
Write the letter of the sentence that is punctuated correctly.

___B___ 6. A. The four main additions to the original White House are the South Portico, a porch with access to the ground floor, the North Portico, another porch on the north side of the house, the West Terrace, a patio with an entrance to the Executive Wing, and the East Terrace, a walkway with access to the East Wing.

  B. The four main additions to the original White House are the South Portico, a porch with access to the ground floor; the North Portico, another porch on the north side of the house; the West Terrace, a patio with an entrance to the Executive Wing; and the East Terrace, a walkway with access to the East Wing.

___A___ 7. A. James Hoban, an architect born in Ireland, won a competition sponsored by the federal government for his design for the White House.

  B. James Hoban an architect born in Ireland won a competition sponsored by the federal government for his design for the White House.

___A___ 8. A. During the War of 1812 when the British attacked Washington, D.C., on August 24, 1814, they burned the interior of the White House.

  B. During the War of 1812 when the British attacked Washington, D.C., on August 24, 1814 they burned the interior of the White House.

___B___ 9. A. James Hoban was in charge of the reconstruction of the White House, which was completed by 1817, and Hoban also helped with the design for the U.S. Capitol building, which is also in Washington, D.C.

  B. James Hoban was in charge of the reconstruction of the White House, which was completed by 1817; and Hoban also helped with the design for the U.S. Capitol building, which is also in Washington, D.C.

___A___ 10. A. All of the presidents since John Adams have lived in the White House. The Trumans, however, moved out of the White House from 1948 to 1952 so that the White House structure could be reinforced with concrete and steel.

B. All of the presidents since John Adams have lived in the White House. The Trumans however, moved out of the White House from 1948 to 1952 so that the White House structure could be reinforced with concrete and steel.

Practice C

Insert any missing commas into the following sentences. If the sentence is already correct, write C in the blank.

_____ 11. When the Trumans left the White House so that it could be renovated, the family moved into Blair House, not far from the White House.

_____ 12. Blair House, still stately and majestic, is a historic mansion built in 1824 by the United States Army's first surgeon general, Joseph Lovell.

___C___ 13. In 1836 Blair House was purchased by Francis Preston Blair Sr., a member of President Andrew Jackson's Kitchen Cabinet.

___C___ 14. Jackson had called Blair to Washington, D.C., to edit the party newspaper, the *Washington Globe*.

_____ 15. Blair House, a four-story yellow stucco building, was at one time the official residence of the vice president; and today it is used as a guesthouse for important foreign visitors.

Chapter 11: Commas, Semicolons, and Colons

Practice A
Identify each sentence as correctly punctuated (C) or incorrectly punctuated (I).

___C___ 1. Patrick Henry was born in Virginia; he attended school for only a short time because his father—a very well-educated man—tutored Patrick at home.

___C___ 2. In 1760 Henry received his license to practice law; then, in 1763, the Parson's Cause, a famous lawsuit, won him recognition in Virginia as a great orator.

___I___ 3. In 1764 he was elected to the Virginia House of Burgesses; where, in 1775, he made his famous speech on March 23 before the Virginia Provincial Convention.

___I___ 4. The purpose of his speech was: to urge Virginia to arm its militia for defense against England; this speech may very well be one of the most famous speeches in American history.

___C___ 5. This speech is famous for the following line: "I know not what course others may take, but as for me, give me liberty or give me death!"

Practice B
Write the letter of the sentence that is punctuated correctly.

___A___ 6. A. Earlier, in 1765, Patrick Henry made a speech against the Stamp Act.
   B. Earlier; in 1765, Patrick Henry made a speech against the Stamp Act.

___B___ 7. A. In that speech appear some other often quoted words, "Caesar had his Brutus; Charles the First his Cromwell; and George the Third—*may profit by their example. If this* be treason, make the most of it."
   B. In that speech appear some other often quoted words: "Caesar had his Brutus; Charles the First his Cromwell; and George the Third—*may profit by their example. If this* be treason, make the most of it."

___A___ 8. A. In 1776 Henry began the first of five terms as the governor of the new commonwealth of Virginia: 1776, 1777, 1778, 1784, and 1785.
   B. In 1776 Henry began the first of five terms as the governor of the new commonwealth of Virginia; 1776, 1777, 1778, 1784, and 1785.

___A___ 9. A. In 1796 Henry was elected governor of Virginia for the sixth time; however, he refused the office.
   B. In 1796 Henry was elected governor of Virginia for the sixth time, however, he refused the office.

___B___ 10. A. Before Henry was governor the colony of Virginia elected him as a delegate to the First Continental Congress in 1774.
   B. Before Henry was governor, the colony of Virginia elected him as a delegate to the First Continental Congress in 1774.

Practice C
Identify the punctuation missing from each selection. In the blank write the letter that corresponds to the correct answer.

A. comma
B. semicolon
C. colon

___B___ 11. In 1775 Henry was a member of the Second Continental Congress for a short time then, he became commander in chief of Virginia's military forces.

___A___ 12. Henry recruited the state's quota of six thousand men for the Continental army; in addition he recruited five thousand soldiers for the state's militia.

___A___ 13. Henry himself had initially opposed the ratification of the Constitution because he believed it gave too much control of the states and individuals to the federal government. When the Constitution was ratified, however he accepted it and worked hard to defend it.

___B___ 14. In 1788 Henry retired from public service and returned to practicing law in 1794 he retired to his Red Hill estate near Appomattox, Virginia.

___C___ 15. The title of Henry Mayer's biography about Patrick Henry seems to capture the great orator's spirit—*A Son of Thunder Patrick Henry and the American Republic.*

Chapter 12: Quotation Marks, Ellipses, and Underlining for Italics

Practice A
Identify each sentence as correctly punctuated (C) or incorrectly punctuated (I).

___C___ 1. Mrs. Woodard asked the class, "Does anyone know who Edward Taylor was?"

___I___ 2. Devin raised his hand and said that "Edward Taylor was a Puritan preacher and poet of the late seventeenth and early eighteenth centuries."

___C___ 3. Edward Taylor wrote many poems including "Upon a Spider Catching a Fly" and "Huswifery."

___I___ 4. Edward Taylor begins "Upon a Spider Catching a Fly" by identifying the spider as ". . . Thou sorrow, venom Elfe."

___I___ 5. Taylor addresses the spider directly in lines 2 and 4 when he says, "Is this thy play, . . . To catch a fly"?

Practice B
Insert any missing quotation marks.

6. Although Taylor wrote some poems about personal experiences, he also wrote many poems about religion, including "Meditation 1."

7. Other poems in his meditation series include "Meditation 8: John 6:51" and "Meditation 56: John 15:24."

8. Victoria asked, "What was Taylor meditating about?"

9. "Good question, Victoria," Mrs. Woodard said. "Does anyone know the answer?"

10. Emma answered, "Taylor wrote these poems when he prepared his heart for Communion by meditating on Christ's death."

Practice C
Insert any missing quotation marks or underlining for italics.

11. The collection of Taylor's meditation poems is entitled <u>Preparatory Meditations</u>.

12. Please notice that the vowels in the word <u>preparatory</u> are two <u>a</u>'s, one <u>e</u>, and one <u>o</u>.

13. Taylor's poems were not published until after his death, but Anne Bradstreet's poems were published during her lifetime in a book called <u>The Tenth Muse Lately Sprung Up in America</u>.

14. The poem "The Author to Her Book" records Anne Bradstreet's response to seeing her poems in print.

15. Anne Bradstreet took the ship <u>Arabella</u> from England to Boston in 1630.

Chapter 12: Apostrophes

Practice A
Identify each sentence as correctly punctuated (C) or incorrectly punctuated (I).

C 1. William Howard Taft, the twenty-seventh president of the United States, didn't really want to run for president.

I 2. In 1901, before he was president, Taft had served as the governor of the Philippines' to help the Filipinos become independent.

I 3. After his presidency, Taft was appointed as a chief justice of the Supreme Court at the beginning of the 1920's.

I 4. He enjoyed serving as one of the justices' on the Supreme Court.

C 5. Taft is the first man in the United States' history to be both a president and a Supreme Court justice.

Practice B
Underline the word that is punctuated correctly from the choices in parentheses.

6. William Taft ran for president so he (wouldnt, <u>wouldn't</u>) disappoint his wife, who wanted him to be president.

7. (<u>It's</u>, Its) very unusual for a president not to want to be president.

8. It probably (<u>won't</u>, willn't) surprise you to hear Mrs. Taft described as an ambitious woman.

9. At Mrs. (Tafts', <u>Taft's</u>) request, the mayor of Tokyo gave about three thousand cherry trees to the American people.

10. These trees were planted along the banks of (<u>Washington's</u>, Washingtons') Potomac River.

Practice C
Insert any missing apostrophes.

11. Taft's name *William* has two i's and two l's, and his wife's name *Nellie* has two e's and two l's.

12. Mrs. Taft suffered a stroke in 1909 and couldn't be the White House hostess anymore.

13. One of the Tafts' children, Helen, helped serve as official White House hostess after her mother's stroke.

14. It's amazing that Mrs. Taft actually outlived her husband. He died in '30; she died in '43.

15. William Taft's and John F. Kennedy's graves are in Arlington National Cemetery; no other U.S. presidents are buried there.

Chapter 12: Hyphens, Dashes, and Parentheses

Practice A
Identify each sentence as correctly punctuated (C) or incorrectly punctuated (I).

_I_ 1. Calvin Coolidge—the thirtieth president of the United States—became president when Warren G. Harding died.

_C_ 2. Coolidge was vacationing on his father's farm in Vermont when Harding died. Coolidge was the only president to be sworn into office by his own father (his father was a notary public).

_I_ 3. Coolidge was then elected as president in 1924, an event making him president for most of the preGreat Depression prosperity era of the 1920s.

_C_ 4. Coolidge's wife, Grace, (a former teacher at Clarke School for the Deaf) was a talkative, vivacious woman, quite the opposite of her husband who was known as Silent Cal.

_C_ 5. In 1924 the Coolidges' sixteen-year-old son, Calvin Jr., died of blood poisoning from a toe blister that had developed as he was playing tennis.

Practice B
Identify the punctuation missing from each sentence. In the blank write the letter that corresponds to the correct answer. _(Answers may vary.)_

A. hyphen
B. dash
C. parentheses

_A_ 6. Iowa born Herbert Hoover was the first president born west of the Mississippi River.

_B or C_ 7. Hoover an orphan by the time he was eight became the thirty-first president of the United States.

_B_ 8. Coin laundry operator, secretary, and typist these were the three jobs that Hoover had to pay his way through college.

_B or C_ 9. Mrs. Hoover who spoke several languages was known as a gracious hostess.

_A_ 10. The Great Depression struck during Hoover's first term and probably led to his failure to be reelected as president.

Practice C

Proofread the following paragraph to find the five omissions of hyphens, dashes, and parentheses. Then insert the missing punctuation.

Eighty-two days after Franklin D. Roosevelt was elected to his fourth term as president, he died, and Vice President Harry S. Truman became president. Truman was elected to a second term in 1948. In his first term as president of the United States, Truman had to make the most crucial decision that had ever faced a U.S. president, but that decision—to drop the new atomic bomb on Japan—probably brought a speedy end to World War II. During Truman's second term, the Trumans moved to Blair House late in 1948(the White House was in need of extensive structural repairs)and remained there until March of 1952. On November 1, 1950, two would-be assassins tried to invade Blair House. One gunman and one Secret Service man were killed—Truman was not!

TAPE SHUT—<u>DO NOT STAPLE</u>

BUSINESS REPLY MAIL
FIRST-CLASS MAIL   PERMIT NO. 344   GREENVILLE, SC

POSTAGE WILL BE PAID BY ADDRESSEE

BJU PRESS
TEXTBOOK DIVISION
1700 WADE HAMPTON BLVD.
GREENVILLE, SC 29609-9971

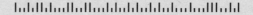

- - - - - - Fold here -

- - - - - - Fold here -

Working Together

Whether you have been teaching for many years or are just getting started, your comments are vital in helping us maintain our standard of excellence. In fact, most of the improvements in our materials started with good advice from consumers. So after you have put our products to the test, please give us your thoughtful comments and honest assessment.

And thanks for your valuable help!

Book Title _____ Grade level _____

Material was ☐ used in classroom. ☐ used in home school. ☐ examined only.

How did you hear about us?
_____
_____
_____

I liked
_____
_____
_____

I'd like it better if
_____
_____
_____

How did our material compare with other publishers' materials?
_____
_____
_____

Other comments?
_____
_____
_____

(OPTIONAL)
☐ Dr. ☐ Miss ☐ Mrs. ☐ Mr. _____

School_____

Street_____

Fold and tape. DO NOT STAPLE.
Mailing address on the other side.

City_____State_____ ZIP_____

BJU PRESS

Greenville, SC 29614

Phone(___)_____

E-mail _____